Detective Lee's heart was beating out of his chest. He had a feeling Mailhot was just about to spill his guts. Lee could hardly breathe. His heart had never pounded so fast in his life. He had a lot of adrenaline rushes on the job, but nothing like that, because Ed Lee knew Jeffrey Mailhot had murdered the three women—and he was just about to confess.

"Do you want to tell me something?" Lee asked, trying like hell to stay calm. "Jeff, your life will be over—over—unless you get this off of your chest. Okay? I know what happened. I know what happened. I know you're not a bad man. I know you just took it too far. What happened? You pushed it too far one night, right? Things got out of hand, huh?"

"Yes," Mailhot said finally, burying his head in his hands and crying.

"All of them?"

"Hm-hmm."

"All three?" Lee asked, just to be sure.

"All three," Mailhot responded.

"All right. Good job. Where are they? Where are they, Jeff?"

"Dead."

Lee was so caught off guard by Mailhot's confession that he could hardly even think. His head was spinning and his heart was racing. For a split second he thought maybe some of the other cops were playing a joke on *him* and put Mailhot up to confessing serial murder.

Then Mailhot started to choke up a little and Lee had to keep the pressure on to find out what he had done with the women's bodies.

"Where are they?" Lee asked, in no way prepared for Mailhot's response.

"They're—they're in garbage bags."

Also by Linda Rosencrance:

AN ACT OF MURDER

MURDER AT MORSES POND

RIPPER

LINDA ROSENCRANCE
WITH CAPT. EDWARD LEE, JR.

PINNACLE BOOKS
Kensington Publishing Corp.
http://www.kensingtonbooks.com

PINNACLE BOOKS are published by

Kensington Publishing Corp.
850 Third Avenue
New York, NY 10022

All Kensington Titles, Imprints, and Distributed Lines are available at special quantity discounts for bulk purchases for sales promotions, premiums, fund-raising, and educational or institutional use. Special book excerpts or customized printings can also be created to fit specific needs. For details, write or phone the office of the Kensington special sales manager: Kensington Publishing Corp., 850 Third Avenue, New York, NY 10022, attn: Special Sales Department, Phone: 1-800-221-2647.

Pinnacle and the P logo Reg. U.S. Pat. & TM Off.

ISBN-13: 978-0-7860-1745-4
ISBN-10: 0-7860-1745-7

First Printing: November 2008

10 9 8 7 6 5 4 3 2 1

Printed in the United States of America

For my friends Craig, Libby, Matthew and Alec Costanza.
—LR

*I would like to dedicate this book to my father, the late
Chief Edward J. Lee, Sr., my inspiration to go into law
enforcement and my greatest teacher.*
—EL

Truth will come to light; murder cannot be hid long.
—*The Merchant of Venice*, Act ii, Sc. 2

Acknowledgments

Many thanks to everyone who helped me with this project, especially my coauthor, Captain Edward Lee, Jr., Lieutenant Steven Nowak, Detective Gerard Durand and all the members of the Woonsocket Police Department. I would also like to thank the families of Audrey Harris, Christine Dumont and Stacie Goulet for their help.

Last, but not least, special thanks to my agent, Janet Benrey, of the Benrey Literary Agency, and my editor at Kensington, Michaela Hamilton.

—LR

I would like to recognize the hardworking men and women at the Woonsocket Police Department. Without their dedication and professionalism this case would not have been possible.

—EL

Prologue

Woonsocket, Rhode Island, was formed in 1888 from six mill villages that sprouted up along the Blackstone River. The villages were Bernon, Globe, Hamlet, Jenckesville, Social and the largest, Woonsocket Falls Village, which occupied what is now the downtown area of Woonsocket.

For a number of years the economic life of the city revolved around its textile and rubber mills. As the city increased in size, more independent stores, including grocery, hardware and furniture stores, opened up. In 1914, McCarthy Dry Goods Company, founded in 1889, opened a new six-floor department store on the corner of Main and Court Streets, the site of what is now City Hall Park.

Until the 1960s, Main Street was Woonsocket's retail district. But soon it could no longer compete with suburban shopping malls, and many shops, like W. T. Grant, F. W. Woolworth Co. and even McCarthy's, relocated to the Walnut Hill Plaza in East Woonsocket. In 1989, city leaders began taking steps to improve the appearance, business and general image of Main Street, and those efforts to attract new retail, housing and businesses to the area continue to this day. Main Street's two anchors are the Museum of Work and Culture and the restored historic Stadium Theatre.

But despite the emphasis on the downtown area, Woonsocket remains a working-class city. The area where Jeffrey Mailhot lived is known as the Cato Hill Historic District. Cato Hill, which sits above Main Street, was typical of Woonsocket's working-class neighborhoods in the mid-1800s. It was home to mill workers from Ireland, Canada and Ukraine.[1]

Around the corner from Mailhot's house on Cato Street is an area known for its dives, drug users and pushers, drunks, prostitutes and johns. That neighborhood is the last place Audrey Harris, Christine Dumont and Stacie Goulet were ever seen alive.

---

[1]www.woonsocket.org

Chapter 1

It was just before midnight on a cold February night in 2003 in Woonsocket, Rhode Island, a working-class city of about forty-four thousand people right on the Massachusetts border. Calling no attention to himself, a clean-cut thirty-two-year-old machinist was driving home from the K2U, a strip club on Front Street.

Audrey Harris, thirty-three, an African-American prostitute who regularly plied her trade outside the neighborhood's seedy bars and tenement houses, was walking down Arnold Street. She was intent on hooking up with a lonely guy to get the money for her next fix. Selling herself on the streets to feed her habit was a way of life for Audrey—try as she might to kick it.

When the man saw Audrey, he pulled his car up close to her and asked if she wanted to go to his place. She agreed and got in his car. The fact that he wasn't bad-looking didn't hurt. Most of the johns that came around were a little on the creepy side, so getting in a car with someone who looked like this would probably have made Audrey feel safe.

On the way to the man's apartment, the pair agreed on $30 for straight sex, and the man told Audrey he'd pay her when they got to his house. Once he got Audrey inside, he slammed the door shut and threw the three dead bolt locks. After giving Audrey a brief tour of his apartment, they went into the bedroom. Audrey took off all her clothes, while her client stripped down to his undershorts.

Audrey then asked the man for the $30 they had agreed on. He got the money from his dresser and was about to give it to her when she turned around and faced away from him. Suddenly hit with an uncontrollable urge, the john went up to Audrey from behind and started choking her. Terrified, Audrey kicked and scratched at her attacker, fueling his rage even more. It wasn't hard to subdue the five-one, one-hundred-pound woman, so he wrestled her to the ground and, lying next to her on the floor, continued choking her.

Although she was still fighting for her life, Audrey was getting weaker and having a hard time breathing. About twenty to thirty seconds after her attacker got her on the floor, Audrey stopped struggling and he loosened his grip around her neck. He stood up and looked down at the dying woman. Audrey's eyes were just staring up, but she didn't seem to be really looking at anything. She was gagging, and blood bubbles were coming out of her mouth. Figuring she was still alive, the man got a pillow from his bed, put it over Audrey's face, pushed down hard and finished her off. After he removed the pillow, the man just looked at Audrey's dead body, then sat back on the floor for a few minutes in a state of disbelief.

Realizing that he had just murdered Audrey, the man paced around his bedroom, trying to figure out what to do next. He checked on Audrey again after a couple minutes just to make sure she was dead. About ten minutes later he dragged Audrey's lifeless body into his bathroom, put her in the bathtub, then put her clothes in a trash bag in the kitchen. Unlike some serial killers who keep souvenirs, he didn't keep any of Audrey's possessions. He threw them all away. Then he went to bed and either fell asleep or passed out.

The next morning the man woke up with no memory of what had happened the previous night. But when he went into the bathroom and saw Audrey's body in his bathtub, it all came flooding back to him. Realizing he needed time to figure out what to do, he called his boss and said he was taking a sick day.

He left Audrey in his bathtub and drove to Wal-Mart, where he bought a roll of heavy-duty plastic wrap and a roll of carpet. He brought the plastic wrap and carpet home, rolled Audrey's body in the plastic and then in the carpet. Then he put her in his GMC Jimmy and drove around town trying to find a place to dump her.

Scared that someone was going to see him, he went back home, carried the carpet into the house and dropped it on the kitchen floor. He left Audrey in the carpet in the kitchen while he came up with a plan to get rid of her so that no one would find out.

Some hours later the man remembered an episode of the television show *The Sopranos* he had seen a few months earlier. In that episode Tony Soprano strangled Ralphie Cifaretto in his kitchen, then got rid of the body by hacking it up in the bathtub.

So the murderer unwrapped Audrey and placed her back into his bathtub. Then he went to the basement to get a saw—not an electric saw—just a regular handsaw. He got some latex gloves from the kitchen, then went into his bedroom and changed into a black T-shirt with *Kid Rock* written on it in red, white and blue letters, and a pair of shorts. He took off his shoes and socks and walked back into the bathroom barefoot.

Standing over the bathtub, he draped Audrey's head over the side of the tub and sawed it off. The he cut off her hands and feet and arms and legs, draping each body part over the tub as he sawed it off. Finally he cut her torso in half. He wanted to make sure her body parts were small enough to fit in his trash bags.

The killer put Audrey's hands, feet and head into one bag and each half of her torso into a separate bag. Her legs and arms went into another bag. Then he wrapped each trash bag up in some heavy black plastic wrap, tied those "packages" up with duct tape and put each package in a couple more trash bags and tied them at the top.

When he was done wrapping up Audrey's mutilated body, he washed out the tub, wiped up any residue and flushed it down the toilet. He cleaned up the blood on the floor, which had seeped out of Audrey while he was cutting her up. Then he threw the bags into his truck and deposited them in a number of area Dumpsters. He also tossed out Audrey's clothes and disposed of the saw.

Chapter 2

On April 3, 2003, Detective Paul Sevigny was assigned to investigate the disappearance of Audrey Harris. That day Audrey's mother, Claudette, had filed a missing person's report on Audrey. Claudette said she last spoke to her daughter on February 9, 2003, when she called to tell her mother she would be by for a visit. But she never made it.

Claudette explained to police that even though Audrey, a mother of three who had a fondness for teddy bears, was a drug user and didn't have a permanent address, it wasn't like her not to call home occasionally to let her family know she was okay.

Claudette told police she had gone to talk to people at some of the local bars that Audrey used to frequent, but no one had seen her around for a while. Claudette hung her daughter's picture on utility poles around the city, and a civic group even offered a small reward for information about her. Still, nothing. That's when Claudette knew something was wrong and went to the police.

After catching the case, Sevigny soon learned that

Audrey hadn't reported to her parole officer since she was released from prison on January 25, 2003. Audrey had been on probation for a simple assault and battery, as well as for resisting arrest. So Sevigny contacted some of the vice squad cops about Audrey, but they told him they hadn't seen her either. The detective then checked with nearby police departments on the off chance that they had her in custody. Another dead end.

Knowing Audrey was a well-known street person and substance abuser, Sevigny made frequent trips to the corner of High and Arnold Streets and Blackstone Street, near Railroad Street, to try and locate her. The other women in the area said she hadn't been around recently.

One of the women said she had last seen Audrey at the end of January. The woman said she let Audrey take a shower at her house and gave her some clothes to wear. She told the police Audrey was seeing a corrections officer named Kerry from the Adult Correctional Institutions (ACI), who had given her a new winter jacket and some money.

The police tracked the guy down, and they discovered he didn't work at the prison, but had been a substance abuse counselor for the state. His name was Kerry Garner, and until his retirement in March 2002, he had been the chief of Treatment Services for the substance abuse division of the Rhode Island Department of Mental Health.

Garner, who had worked for the mental-health department for twenty-eight years, had known Audrey for about ten years. Garner said he got to know her a little better when she went to him for a referral for substance abuse treatment, sometime around 2000. Garner said at that time he referred her to the Talbot House in Providence, Rhode Island, for treatment.

He told police he last saw Audrey on January 25, 2003, when he picked her up in front of the public defender's office in Providence. Audrey had called Garner because she needed a ride home. Garner dropped Audrey off at the top of West Park Place in Woonsocket and went on his way.

A few days later, Audrey called Garner to ask him for a ride to the Adult Correctional Institutions in Cranston so she could pick up some money she had left in an account during her last incarceration. Audrey also wanted to pick up some clothes she had left in Garner's truck. But Garner could tell Audrey was high and he didn't want to get involved with her problems. He told her he'd leave her clothes inside the door in the downstairs hallway of his house.

When Audrey showed up to collect her belongings, she rang Garner's bell, but he didn't want to see her so he didn't answer the door. He could hear Audrey talking out loud and cursing as she picked up her stuff and left. That was the last time Garner heard from her.

Garner said he had no idea where she was, but he did know some of the people she hung around with and some of the places she'd stayed at in the past. Garner said Audrey used to stay with some guy named Pete on Park Avenue and another guy named Dave who lived on Fifth Avenue.

Garner also admitted that sometimes Audrey used to stay at his house when she had no place else to go. She'd stay a couple nights and then take off. That happened a few times. While Audrey stayed at Garner's house, she also had sex with him, but apparently she wasn't good enough to share his bed—Garner made Audrey sleep on his living-room floor in his sleeping bag.

For some reason, Garner refused to let police search his apartment for any of Audrey's belongings. Police checked and determined that Audrey did withdraw $42.30 from her inmate account at the Adult Correctional Institutions on January 30.

Audrey's friend Dave Parker said he hadn't seen Audrey since the end of January or the beginning of February. Parker, who had also known Audrey for ten years, said although the pair initially had a sexual relationship, they ended up being just friends.

In fact, in September 2002, Parker said he had to take out a restraining order on Audrey because she was so high on drugs she became really violent with him. Just before he applied for the restraining order, Parker said he and Audrey were in his car and she started assaulting him while he was driving. So he drove straight to the Woonsocket Police Department (WPD), where she was arrested for assault.

When asked what he thought had happened to Audrey, Parker said, "I guess she got in with the wrong person and someone killed her."

Police interviewed Tim Harris, Audrey's brother, some months later. Like the rest of Audrey's friends and acquaintances, Tim had last seen Audrey at the end of January. Tim said he and a friend were driving down Park Avenue when he saw Audrey in a gray pickup truck near Dunkin' Donuts. Tim stopped, and when Audrey saw him, she got out of the truck and got into his car. Tim's friend left and Tim and Audrey went to a party at a nearby house.

They did some crack and then they talked. Tim said Audrey called their mom and told her she was going into rehab. Hungry, Tim asked Audrey if she wanted to go to McDonald's to get something to eat. She said no, so Tim left her there and went out. It was about 8:00 P.M. when he got back to the party.

When he walked into the kitchen, Tim saw Audrey sitting on a chair, leaning over with her head on her lap, sleeping. But Tim was worried because she was sitting so close to the stove and the oven door was open for heat. He asked the others why Audrey was sitting like that, but no one answered. He woke Audrey up and told her to go lie down on the couch in the living room. He asked her if she was going to spend the night there and she said yes. He offered to take her shoes off, but she said no.

Tim left the house and went to see some friends. When he got back to the party an hour or two later, Audrey was gone. He asked his friends where his sister was, but no one said anything.

"They were just real quiet," Tim said. "They never told me what happened to my sister."

About six months after Detective Sevigny was assigned the case, Woonsocket police sergeant Robert Moreau was assigned to investigate Audrey's disappearance because Sevigny was retiring. He was asked to look into the case to see if he could develop any new leads. Moreau knew Audrey from seeing her on the streets. He often stopped and talked to her to make sure she was okay. Everyone was always worried that something was going to happen to her because she was such a tiny woman and most likely wouldn't be able to handle herself if she got into trouble.

The first thing Moreau did was meet with Claudette to go over the facts of the case and to let her know that the police were still trying to find her daughter. Claudette told the seasoned detective that Audrey was a good person, but she was mixed up with drugs. She kept telling her mother she was going to quit—she swore every time was her last time—but somehow she'd just fall back into the drug scene. The last time Audrey called Claudette, she said, "Ma, I'm going to come over and see you. I'm all done with these drugs," but Claudette never heard from her again.

Claudette told Moreau about the house party Audrey had been at with her brother the night she disappeared, so Moreau talked to Tim Harris about it. Tim told Moreau the same story he had told Sevigny. He said he had to physically pick Audrey up from the chair in the kitchen because she had passed out. The way Tim described her state of mind and her physical condition at the party, Moreau and the other cops figured someone at the party had found her on that couch dead. The cops figured those partygoers didn't know what to do with her, so they just dumped her body.

"I met with the people who were at the party and told them that if it was an accident and they just didn't know what to do, they should come clean so Audrey's mother should get closure one way or the other," Moreau said later. "But, of course, it turned out to be fruitless, but that's why we went down that road for a long time. It's kind of a spooky thing, but right near that house is an Indian burial ground—it's not marked anymore, but we had cadaver dogs go in and search that wooded area, but we didn't find her there, although for some reason that's where Timmy thought she was. We found a woman's black shoe there, but it wasn't hers."

Moreau next got a list of people Audrey knew from Claudette and reinterviewed them. He talked to Dave

Parker again, but he didn't learn anything new about Audrey's whereabouts. Moreau also talked to Pete Gagne, another one of Audrey's boyfriends, who pointed him in the direction of Kerry Garner. When Moreau first took over the case, he thought Garner was good for Audrey's murder. He figured Garner was lying about when he last saw her because he was trying to save his job. He was her counselor and he was supposed to be helping her, but instead he preyed on her just like all the other johns.

In the end none of the leads Moreau followed up on panned out. It would take another nine months before he found out what really happened to Audrey Harris.

Chapter 3

The last time anyone saw forty-two-year-old Christine Dumont was Friday, April 23, 2004. Like Audrey Harris, Christine was walking down Arnold Street when she disappeared. And like Audrey, Christine also had a history of drug abuse and prostitution.

It didn't take long for Madeline Desrochers, Christine's older sister, to figure out something was wrong. For one thing, Christine hadn't picked up her disability check at the post office; for another, she hadn't called her two sons in a couple days. Despite her lifestyle, Christine loved her kids and she called them every night. So when Madeline learned that Christine's oldest son hadn't heard from his mother in two days, she called another relative, who was caring for her sister's youngest son, Derrick, and asked if she had called him recently. The answer was the same—not for two days.

So on April 30, a week after Christine was last seen alive, Madeline went to the Woonsocket police station to report her missing. Unfortunately, the officer on duty refused to take her statement. He told her to return on Monday.

"The police officer who told me that was a smart little guy," Madeline said. "I told him I wanted to file a missing person's report and he told me I couldn't, because he had just seen her the night before. What could I do, I went back Monday."

Maybe it wouldn't have mattered because Christine was already dead.

"Then I go back Monday and it's the same guy and he throws the form at me and he asks me for her name and her description, then he said, 'Oh, never mind, we have all that on record,'" Madeline said. "The guy just stabbed my heart and then he threw the paper at me, and I said, 'Thank you, I'm going to the media.' So I filed a report and I went to the local newspaper and television station and I told them about my sister being missing, just like Audrey, but none of them wanted to talk to me."

To the local media, Christine may have been just another missing drug-addicted prostitute, but to her family, she was so much more.

Christine was the third youngest in a family of eight children born to Roland and Auroe Dumont. Madeline was ten when Christine was born on December 12, 1961. Christine's father, Roland, was a very hardworking man. He worked over forty years in a dye house to support his eight children. The Dumont family may not have been rich, but they lived a comfortable life, and Christine and her siblings had everything they ever needed. "You get what you want second. You get what you need first" was the motto that Roland Dumont lived by.

"Christine was the youngest for a long time growing up and everybody babied her like she was a little doll,"

Madeline said. "She was spoiled. She always wanted her own way. Going to school, she was always well dressed. Her socks matched her clothes and her fingernails matched her outfits. She was a very particular girl. But then the teenage years set in. I was already married and out of the house. My dad tried so hard to be an upstanding citizen, even though he had some rotten kids—two of my brothers were stealing, and then here comes Christine, with problems that didn't help."

Christine didn't have an easy life. In fact, she almost didn't have any life at all. When she was fifteen, she was hit by a train on Hamlet Avenue. According to newspaper reports at the time, Christine and a fifteen-year-old girlfriend had gotten out of a car on Manville Road, near the Hamlet Avenue railroad crossing. Christine, who was walking on the sidewalk a couple of steps in front of her friend, apparently did not see or hear the train coming. According to police the red warning lights were flashing and the warning bell was ringing at the crossing at the time.

Christine was hit by the left front shield of the fifty-two-car train, which was traveling between twenty and twenty-five miles per hour. The shield, which was used to push aside objects that vandals threw on the tracks, prevented Christine from being dragged beneath the wheels of the train. She was hurled about forty feet into the air and landed in a gutter at the crossing. The train finally came to a stop before it crossed Hamlet Avenue. The Woonsocket Fire Department (WFD) rescue squad responded to the accident, administered first aid at the scene, then transported Christine to Woonsocket Hospital. She was then transferred to Roger Williams Hospital in Providence.

That was the official version of the story. Madeline tells it a bit differently. She said Christine and her friend were smoking pot and playing chicken with the train. Christine lost.

As a result of the accident, all the skin on Christine's right side—on her face, as well as her arms and legs—was completely ripped off, and she was already in a coma when the rescue squad arrived. When Christine was first brought to the hospital, the doctor tried to take X-rays of her head to see how much damage there was, but the blood was so thick he couldn't even see her brain.

Christine stayed in a coma for three months, and each day Madeline would go to the hospital to braid her sister's hair because Christine always wanted her hair to look great. Then, on Easter Sunday, Christine started speaking again. Although she wasn't speaking very well, Madeline said it was a miracle. When Christine's injuries started healing, her face looked like one big thick scab. In fact, her whole body was one thick pink scab. Christine was so traumatized by the accident that when she came out of the hospital, she had to go through therapy for two years to help her deal with what had happened to her.

Christine should have learned her lesson about living dangerously—but she didn't, unfortunately. And it didn't help that after the accident Christine's mother let her do whatever she wanted to do, as if to make up for what she had gone through. However, Mrs. Dumont's approach to handling Christine didn't sit well with her siblings, and her sister Denise left home at fifteen because she couldn't deal with Christine's behavior.

After the accident Christine never went back to school. When she was eighteen, she met Joe, who was thirty-one at the time, and she thought she was in love. Christine and Joe moved in together and she seemed to be getting her life back on track. She was clean, sober and very happy. Then when she was around twenty-two, she got pregnant. Her first son, Jason, was born in 1985.

When Jason was twelve, Christine got pregnant again, but by this time she was using cocaine, although Joe was still clean. She got hooked on coke when a friend enticed her to try the powerful drug. Regrettably, she wasn't strong enough to fight it and she continued doing cocaine while she was pregnant with her second son, Derrick. Christine was so addicted to the drug that she even took a hit right before she had the baby. But God was looking out for Derrick because he was born normal, healthy and beautiful.

It's not that Christine didn't want to conquer her addiction. She did. She even voluntarily checked herself into rehab—five times.

"I didn't want to deal with my sister because of these problems," Madeline said. "I pushed her away for ten years. My whole family really did. We didn't want to deal with that. We all had kids and we didn't want them to see her do that, so we pushed her away. Not one of us is better than the other."

Although Madeline didn't want Christine around her family, she finally had no choice but to take her in.

"But I had to take her because within months both my parents got very, very sick," Madeline said. "Christine used to go to my mother and father's house and tell them stories to get money from them and she'd really make them nervous. They were eighty-five and seventy-five. She used to go over there and harass them all the time. So I told my brothers and sisters that out of the kindness of my heart I would take her in. I didn't want to, but I did it for my parents."

So Christine stayed with Madeline for six months.

"My sister was a rip-off artist and I didn't appreciate it," Madeline said. "She would take money from people, tell them she was going to buy them drugs and then take off with the money. I had a front door and a back door and she would rip off somebody outside, run in the front door and run out the back door. She did it to so many people."

Although prostitution was never really her thing— she preferred ripping people off—she sold herself occasionally to get money to buy drugs. Madeline said Christine was once caught soliciting a john for sex, but she was never charged.

In December 2003, their mother passed away and their dad died in March 2004. When their dad passed away, two Woonsocket detectives, Edward "Ed" Lee, Jr. and Kyle Stone, picked Christine up in front of Madeline's house, because she was acting erratically, and brought her to rehab. After that, Madeline told Christine she couldn't live with her anymore. Madeline was planning to move to a new apartment and wanted to make a clean break with her sister.

"My job was done," Madeline said. "I kept her away from my parents for six months and gave them a break. She was really sick. I tried my best to keep her away from the drugs. I had her placed in a rehab facility, but two weeks after I moved, she was knocking on my door. I was so angry, but I wasn't taking her back. I had a fifteen-year-old daughter, who had to watch her go through this for six months. When she tried to come back, she was still doing drugs, and I didn't appreciate it."

After Madeline reported Christine missing, police figured she was dead. And they "liked" a guy named Timothy Scanlon for her murder.

About a year before she disappeared, Christine Dumont had been attacked by a guy who offered to give her a ride. It was 1:05 A.M. on April 11, 2003. Christine was walking down Arnold Street when a guy in a white car stopped and asked her if she wanted a ride. She told him he could drive her to the Fairmount Project and got in his car. The man drove down Arnold Street, turned right at the old Weiner Palace and then turned right again, onto River Street. As the couple drove down River Street, Christine looked at the guy's arms and commented on all the tattoos he had. When they got to the Fairmount Project, the man just kept driving down River Street past the Double J Tavern.

Christine told the man to stop the car because she wanted to get out, but he kept driving. So she opened the door, but he yelled at her to close it. Christine didn't listen; instead, she put her feet outside the car door and thought about jumping out. The guy kept driving down River Street, then made a hard right, trying to force the passenger side door to close. At that point Christine's feet were dragging on the ground. After they crossed a nearby bridge, she jumped out of the car in an attempt to get away from the guy.

But as soon as Christine jumped out, the guy stopped the car, got out and walked toward her. Then he grabbed her like a sack of potatoes, threw her in the trunk of the car and slammed it shut. The guy got back into his car and started driving to a nearby parking lot. Although it was dark in the trunk, Christine felt a soft bristled brush and a tire iron. She started banging and banging on the

trunk, then pierced a hole in it, using the tire iron. She
tried using the tire iron to pry the trunk open, but she
just couldn't do it.

The driver stopped the car, got out and went to the
back of the car. He began to open the trunk slightly,
then closed it again. Each time he opened the trunk, he
said, "Drop it, bitch." The last time the guy opened the
trunk, Christine hit him in the stomach with the tire
iron. Furious, the guy grabbed her, pulled her out of the
trunk and threw her on the ground. Then he started
beating her with a pipe he had in his hands. He smashed
her head again and again with the pipe. Christine was
so weak she couldn't even cover her head with her
hands to protect herself. Finally the guy ran back to his
car and got in. Christine thought he was going to turn
around and run her over, but, instead, he just sped away
out of the parking lot toward the road.

Scared and bleeding, Christine stayed where she was
until she couldn't see his car anymore; then she started
to crawl through the parking lot. She tried to get up, but
she just kept falling down. She managed to walk down
River Street in the middle of the road, trying to flag
someone down to help her. Three cars passed by, but
none of the drivers stopped. When she got to High
Street, she called the police from a pay phone. She was
hysterical, screaming that she had been abducted.

Patrolman Kevin Greenough was dispatched to the
scene a little after 2:00 A.M. When he arrived, he found
Christine bleeding from the head. He noticed that she
had blood on her hands and a number of lacerations on
the top of her head. He called for an ambulance and
then tried to find out what happened. Still hysterical,
Christine just kept yelling that someone had hit her over

the head with something metal. Then she clammed up and refused to say anything else about what happened. She figured the cops weren't going to help her anyway. When paramedics arrived, they began treating her, then took her to Landmark Medical Center.

Greenough then called in the suspect's description and all officers were instructed to be on the lookout for him. Soon another officer, David Antaya, met Greenough at the scene and told him there had been a similar assault about a month earlier. Antaya said as soon as he had heard the broadcast regarding the suspect, he went to the dirt parking lot on Singleton Street, where the previous assault had occurred. While there, Antaya discovered fresh drops of blood on the ground, near what appeared to be tire tracks in the dirt lot. Greenough and Antaya then went back to the parking lot, where Antaya pointed out the tire tracks and the blood drops.

Greenough went to the Landmark Medical Center to talk to Christine again. This time she told him everything that happened. She described her assailant as a white male with short reddish brown hair and a goatee, between thirty and thirty-five years old, about five feet six inches to five feet nine inches tall. She said he was wearing a cream-colored button-down short-sleeved shirt with pinstripes, black khaki pants and a cheap gold watch on his left wrist. She also described the guy's car for Greenough. She said she had never seen him before and had no idea who he was.

While Greenough was talking to Christine, Antaya had called the station to request an officer from the Bureau of Criminal Identification to process the scene. Detective Gerard "Gerry" Durand arrived around 3:15 A.M. and met up with Antaya, who directed him to the crime scene in the rear of an old mill building on Singleton Street. Although the area was hidden from the roadway by brush, the river and the building itself, it was illuminated by several outside security lights attached to the building.

Antaya told Durand he had already checked out the scene and discovered several pieces of evidence. Antaya then pointed out a beer can that had been used to mark off an area on the ground where officers had found blood. He also showed Durand fresh bloodstains on the ground in another area of the parking lot and some tire tracks in the dirt and grass around the corner of the building. Unfortunately, the tracks indicated that there was very little tread on the tires, which meant they couldn't be used as evidence.

After viewing the area, Durand went back to his car to get his camera and other equipment so he could process the scene. The first thing he did was photograph an area in the parking lot where it appeared there had been a struggle. While he was taking pictures, he noticed two open condom wrappers on the ground in the same area; so he photographed them, then picked them up to take back to the crime lab.

When he finished in the parking lot, Durand went to the bridge on Singleton Street, where Christine said the suspect had slammed on his brakes. Examining the ground, Durand noticed a skid mark, which he photographed. Once finished, Durand headed to the Landmark Medical Center to talk to Christine. On the way he got a call from Patrolman Greenough, who said he thought he had uncovered another piece of evidence. Durand immediately went back to the scene, where Greenough gave him a large metal pipe he had found in a Dumpster on the mill property. As Durand photographed the pipe, he noticed bloodstains on it.

After processing the pipe, Durand went to the Landmark Medical Center to talk to Christine, who showed Durand where the man had beaten her. Durand photographed her injuries, then went back to the police station to process the evidence. He tested the pipe for blood and fingerprints, but he came up empty.

During their investigation police learned that another woman had suffered a similar assault several weeks before Christine. On March 2, Antaya and Patrolman George McCann responded to a call to go to Singleton Street, where they found a naked woman lying in the street bleeding. When police arrived, she sat up, told them her name and said her shoulder hurt very bad. The police immediately called for an ambulance. As they waited, the woman explained that she had left Buddy's Café on Arnold Street around 12:30 A.M. She said an acquaintance offered to give her a ride home and she agreed. However, rather than drive her home, the man took her to Singleton Street, where he raped and beat her.

Officer Antaya went to the place the woman described, to see if he could find her clothes, while McCann waited for the ambulance to arrive. When it did, McCann went to help Antaya with the investigation. The officers discovered fresh tire tracks in the parking lot, just northeast of the bridge on Singleton Street. It appeared as if the vehicle drove into the parking lot, then backed up four hundred to five hundred feet to the rear of the building. Antaya found blood in the snow, but he did not find any of the woman's clothes. While Antaya photographed the scene, McCann went to interview the woman, who had been taken to the Landmark Medical Center.

Although the woman told McCann she wanted to file a complaint against the person who raped and beat her, she was reluctant to tell McCann what he looked like. Finally she said he had blond hair and glasses and drove a gray truck. When Officer Antaya arrived, he told the woman that the man may have assaulted other women. Antaya asked her if David Porter was the name of the man who picked her up. She said it was, adding that she wanted to kill him for what he had done to her.

She said that Porter had picked her up near Buddy's Café and she agreed to give him a blow job for $40. Porter drove to the parking lot of Singleton Street and started to assault her, calling her a "fucking whore." Porter made the woman empty her pockets and then strip naked. He said she was going to get what was coming to her. Then he held a screwdriver to her face, neck and throat and started forcibly inserting his fingers into her vagina and calling her a whore. He yelled at her to get out of the truck and he got out as well. He threw her against a wall of the building and kicked her in the stomach. He told her he was going to kill her, but first he demanded oral sex.

As the woman begged him not to kill her, the man took her arm and twisted it behind her back, breaking her shoulder. He forced her to kneel next to the passenger side of the truck while he sat on the edge of the seat and forced her to perform oral sex. While she was doing it, he pulled her hair and called her a "bitch" and a "whore." He told her if she used too much teeth, he'd slap her and make her do it right. When Porter was finished, he shoved the woman and kicked her in the stomach. He told her he was going to leave, and if she looked at his truck while he drove away, he'd come back and kill her. Then he left.

The woman tried to look at the license plate on the truck, but she couldn't see the number. So she ran to Singleton Street to try and flag down a car to get some help. The first person who drove by her kept on going, but the second person stopped and told her he'd call the police.

McCann filed a complaint for her, took photographs of her injuries and called her nephew to tell him she had been assaulted and was in the Landmark Medical Center.

The next day police went back to the hospital to talk with the woman about the incident. She described the suspect to police. She said he was driving an older gray SUV. She told police she remembered the truck from the last time she went with the man, but she said it was red at that time.

Because police thought David Porter, who lived in Massachusetts, was the man who attacked the woman, they started looking for him and asked for his photo from the Massachusetts Registry of Motor Vehicles so they could present it to Dumont and the woman as part of a photo lineup. But when they got the photo, they realized it didn't look anything like the man the woman described, nor did he have a truck that matched the description of her attacker's truck.

So they created a photo lineup, which included Porter's picture, and showed it to the victim, who did not recognize any of the men in the photos as the man who attacked her. She said the man who assaulted her was younger and heavier than the men in the photographs. Police had her go to the station so she could look at photos of men in their system—so they could get a better description of the suspect and figure out who he was. Although the woman was able to describe the man in more detail, she wasn't able to identify him from the photos police showed her.

At the end of the interview the woman told police she forgot to mention that while she was in the guy's truck, he stopped to use an ATM at the Sovereign Bank on Social Street. When he got back into the truck, he told the woman that he had taken out $100 so they could party. She said it was about 1:00 A.M. When she asked the guy to take her home because she didn't want to party, he started stabbing her and assaulting her. He said he was going to party—even if she didn't want to—and then drove her behind the mill building, holding her head down as he drove.

During their investigation the police went to Sovereign Bank and viewed the tape of the ATM transactions from the morning the woman was assaulted. They observed a man who fit the description the woman and Christine Dumont had given them using the ATM at about 12:55 A.M. on March 2, 2003. Police then learned the ATM card the man used was from UniBank. Police went to the Uni-Bank branch in Blackstone, Massachusetts, and provided the manager with the account number of the ATM card, which she identified as belonging to Timothy Scanlon, of Woonsocket.

When the police got back to the station, they entered Scanlon's name into their database and discovered that he had been arrested a month earlier. They checked his booking photo against the photo taken at the ATM and found they matched. They then created a photo lineup and took it to Christine Dumont, who was in Landmark Medical Center. Christine immediately picked Scanlon's photo out of the lineup. When she saw his face, she became emotional and told police, "That's the motherfucker."

After trying unsuccessfully to find the other woman who had been attacked by Scanlon, so she could view the photo lineup, police went to the suspect's home looking for his car. When they didn't find it, they went to his father's auto body shop on Valley Street in Blackstone, Massachusetts, and found it there. They ran the license plate and discovered it was registered to his mother. Police kept the car under surveillance while they obtained a warrant to arrest Scanlon for kidnapping and assault with a deadly weapon. When Scanlon didn't show up at the garage to get the car, police went to his girlfriend's house, where they arrested him.

After Scanlon was taken to the police station, Sergeant Todd Fernandes and Sergeant Luke Simard spoke with his girlfriend. She explained that while Scanlon was her boyfriend, he didn't live with her, although he stayed over on occasion. After she talked with police, the girlfriend gave them permission to search her apartment. During their search police found some of Scanlon's clothes in the bedroom and took them back to the station.

Scanlon's girlfriend told police that Scanlon usually drove the Mercury Marquis, but it was in his father's shop because it needed new ball joints. She said his father hadn't given him the car back because he hadn't paid for the work. She also told police he used to drive a gray GMC Jimmy, but he recently brought it to the Privilege Street junkyard because it was a piece of junk.

Fernandes and Simard went back to the police station to talk to Scanlon, who opted to give up his right to remain silent and talked to the cops about the attacks on Christine Dumont and the other woman. He denied he was the person who assaulted the women. The cops, however, asked how one of the women would know that he had stopped at the Sovereign Bank ATM to get some cash if she hadn't been with him. Shortly after that, Scanlon told police he wanted a lawyer and the interview stopped. While police were booking Scanlon, he voluntarily told them that he had a drug problem and recently had ripped off several dealers, who had probably put the women up to implicating him in the attacks.

After Fernandes and Simard finished processing Scanlon, they went to find the other woman to show her the photo lineup. She immediately pointed to Scanlon and said he was the person who attacked her. She said she was 100 percent positive because she could never forget his face.

When the officers got back to the station, they charged Scanlon with kidnapping and assault with a deadly weapon in Christine's case. They also charged him with first-degree sexual assault and assault to commit rape for the attack on the other woman.

On April 16, police went to talk to Scanlon's mother, who confirmed that although she owned the Mercury Marquis, Timothy drove it. With her permission police searched her apartment, but they didn't find anything that belonged to Scanlon. During their investigation police learned that Scanlon had sold his 1988 GMC Jimmy on April 11, 2003, and they discovered that it had been crushed and was in a pile of crushed vehicles in an auto parts junkyard in Woonsocket. The auto parts company removed the wreck and brought it to the police station to be inspected. Police also had the Mercury towed to a garage at the station so they could also process it for evidence of the alleged attacks.

When police inspected the Mercury, they noticed some damage to the rear quarter of the driver's side, as well as to the top of the lid of the trunk. There was also some other damage to the lid of the trunk. When Detective Durand opened the trunk to check inside, he was able to detect some fresh scratch marks and dents to the inside of the driver's-side wheel well. The dents and scratches matched up with the damage to the outside of the car. As he continued his investigation, Durand also noticed damage to the gray carpeting inside the trunk, and when he examined the black rubber gasket around the opening of the trunk, he saw a reddish stain that looked like blood near the marks on the lid of the trunk. He also noticed red stains that looked liked blood on a driver's-side floor mat that was in the trunk. Durand collected and bagged the evidence.

Police arrested the twenty-four-year-old Scanlon on April 15, 2003, for kidnapping and assaulting Christine and the other woman. A Providence County grand jury indicted him in October 2003. Scanlon was held without bail until his trial on July 22, 2005.

A Providence County Superior Court jury heard five days of testimony from five witnesses, including the Woonsocket woman, before deliberating eight hours over two days and convicting Scanlon of three counts of first-degree sexual assault, one count of first-degree robbery, one count of assault with a dangerous weapon and one count of felony assault.

Although Scanlon had also been charged with assaulting and kidnapping Christine, the Rhode Island attorney general was forced to drop those charges because Christine had been murdered before she had a chance to testify against him.

On November 17, 2005, Rhode Island Superior Court judge Robert Krause sentenced Scanlon to fifty years in prison for beating, raping and robbing the woman he attacked before he assaulted Christine. The judge also sentenced Scanlon to twenty years' probation to be served after his release from prison.

As it turned out, police soon realized that Scanlon had not been involved with Christine's disappearance or her death, even though he had threatened to kill her while he was in prison.

Chapter 4

Stacie Goulet, twenty-four, went missing from the same area as Audrey Harris and Christine Dumont, sometime between the evening of Saturday, July 3, and the early-morning hours of Sunday, July 4, 2004.

On July 7, her boyfriend, James Nelson, went to the Woonsocket police station and spoke with Sergeant Luke Simard and Sergeant Steve Nowak about Stacie's disappearance. He told them he had actually reported her missing for the first time, on July 4.

He explained that on July 3 he and Stacie had done some crack cocaine with a friend in an apartment on Park Avenue and had planned to watch the fireworks at World War II Memorial State Park in Woonsocket at about 9:00 P.M. Instead, at 9:30 P.M., they left the friend's apartment to go to East School Street so Stacie could do a trick and they could get more cocaine.

Around 10:30 P.M., they ran into Stacie's dad, Raymond Boerger, who was driving his green Ford pickup truck, across from the mill on East School Street. Boerger asked Stacie how she was doing and she told him she'd stopped prostituting herself. Boerger then got on Stacie about her bad housekeeping and told her he wanted her to get clean, take care of her kids and stay out of trouble. They ended their conversation on good terms and Stacie hugged her dad good-bye and he drove off. That was the last time he ever saw her.

Stacie and Nelson then walked up East School Street toward Pond Street. Stacie told Nelson she wanted to work that night and began looking for customers near a park in the area. As Stacie kept walking, Nelson stopped a guy he knew on the street to ask for a cigarette, but he didn't have one. When Nelson turned around, Stacie was gone. He looked up and down East School Street, but he couldn't find her. He then walked all the way up to Pond Street, looked up and down that street, but still didn't see her.

Nelson walked back down to the park and hung out there, because that's where they would meet up after Stacie had done a trick. At about 11:15 P.M., a park services worker named Ken passed by and Nelson told him he was waiting for his girlfriend, Stacie. Ken said he knew Stacie and her dad. The two men talked for a bit and then Ken left. A little while later, Nelson was stopped by police, who asked him what he was doing in the park, and then ran his name to see if there were any outstanding warrants on him. There weren't. Nelson asked the cop if Stacie had been arrested, and was told he had to go to the station to get that information. The cop also told him to leave the park.

Nelson walked across East School Street and sat on a hill for a while before deciding to go to the police station. Nelson was getting worried because Stacie was never gone more than an hour when she was turning a trick. He figured she must have been arrested. But when he got to the station, the officer on duty told him Stacie wasn't there. He decided to go back to his friend John's house, where he was living. He got there around 1:00 A.M. and went to bed.

The next day Nelson met up with a friend named Ray, who had a car, and they drove around looking for Stacie in some of the places where she would typically go to turn some tricks, but they couldn't find her. They searched in the Oak Hill Cemetery, a cemetery in nearby Blackstone, Massachusetts, and on the road under the Hamlet Avenue bridge. When they didn't find Stacie there, they went to the Blackstone Police Department (BPD) and the North Smithfield Police Department (NSPD) in Rhode Island to see if she had been arrested. But the police hadn't seen her. So Nelson went back to the Woonsocket police station to file a missing person's report.

Nelson told police that she had been missing one other time for about twenty-four hours. She had been with a guy named Gary, who had a room at the County Squire Motel in North Smithfield. It turned out Gary kept Stacie in the room against her will and forced himself on her. Nelson also told police that Stacie had complained to him in the past about other customers who wouldn't let her leave, including a married guy who drove a blue Oldsmobile and lived on Estes Street. Stacie told Nelson that he had held her for a while against her will, but he eventually let her go unharmed. She never reported those incidents to police.

During the interview with police Nelson was behaving rather strangely. Sometimes he would stare at the cops for long periods of time without blinking. Other times he would become agitated, especially when he didn't like the questions they were asking him.

Nelson also told them he just decided to quit doing drugs and move to Providence. One of the cops, Sergeant Steve Nowak, asked Nelson why he wanted to get clean all of a sudden, especially since his girlfriend hadn't even been missing for twenty-four hours. Nelson explained that he had wanted to do it for a long time, but couldn't do it and just figured it was time to get straightened out. Nowak, who had to continuously prod Nelson for information during the interview, was convinced James had killed Stacie. He would soon learn that wasn't the case.

Like Audrey and Christine, Stacie turned to hooking to earn money to feed her drug habit. But there was more to Stacie than her life as a prostitute.

Stephen Kreig, the father of Stacie's two young children, was twenty-two when he first met Stacie, who was just turning sixteen. At that time in her life she was bouncing back and forth from her mother's house and her father's house in Woonsocket to her aunt's place in Milford, Massachusetts.

Stacie's parents, Ray and Debbie Boerger, split up after she was born, and Debbie married a man named Norman Goulet, who adopted Stacie. But Stacie didn't like living with Norman and she always wanted to live with her real father. Debbie ultimately divorced Goulet, and she and Ray remarried, but they divorced almost immediately after Stacie was murdered.

Stacie and Kreig went out for a couple weeks, and the first time they slept together, she got pregnant with their son Dana. They soon moved in together in Woonsocket.

Stacie was seventeen when Dana was born in 1998. Then a couple years later their daughter, Kimberly, was born.

Although Stacie was a quiet person who usually kept to herself, she and Kreig had the same interests. They liked watching movies, sitting back and listening to their favorite bands and fishing. In fact, the couple would often go out fishing in a little boat Kreig owned. Other times they'd go to the park and walk around or go down to the beach and pick shells; Stacie was always looking for the perfect shell. They'd go out to eat occasionally, but neither one of them really drank all that much. However, they both smoked marijuana, the only drug Kreig ever saw Stacie do. But then she ended up meeting some guy who got her hooked on coke.

When their son was born, Kreig bought Stacie a ring and asked her to marry him. She said no. Then when she got pregnant with their daughter, Kreig again asked Stacie to marry him. He told her that's what people who had children did, but she said she didn't know if that was what she wanted. She felt she was too young to get married. On the other hand, Kreig was getting older and all he wanted to do was settle down, get married and raise his kids.

Kreig tried to get closer to Stacie and kept trying to change her mind, but she pushed him away. Ultimately she pushed him out of love with her. He told Stacie that although he loved the death out of their kids and would do anything for them, he just couldn't stay with her. Stacie begged Kreig not to leave her, but he packed up his stuff and moved out.

Shortly before Kreig left Stacie, he met someone else—his next-door neighbor's sister-in-law, who used to watch his kids some nights when neither he nor Stacie was home. At that time Stacie was going to night school to get her GED because she wanted to go to cosmetology school, and Kreig, a self-employed contractor, was working and attending court-mandated counseling sessions for some trouble he had been in.

Things between Kreig and the babysitter, who was older then he was, started out innocently enough. One night she had dinner waiting for him when he got home from work. Soon she began filling Stacie's role as woman of the house and Kreig started having feelings for her. He found her very interesting and liked the fact that she was a very mature and responsible person.

At the time the babysitter had a husband, who was in jail, but they were in the middle of a divorce. Before Kreig knew it, the two were exchanging kisses and beginning to fall in love. When Kreig moved out of the apartment he shared with Stacie, he moved in with the babysitter for a month until he saved up enough money for them to move into another apartment in Woonsocket. After her divorce was final, Kreig and the babysitter got married.

When Kreig left Stacie, he told her that if she continued to let him see his children, he would pay all her expenses, including her rent, which was $775 per month, as well as her utilities and even her cable bill. And he said he'd buy the kids whatever they needed. Stacie agreed. But then her family got involved, and her parents told her not to let Kreig see the kids if he didn't want to be with her.

"So she didn't let me see the kids. Then she took me to court for child support and I was ordered to pay seventy-four dollars a week, every Friday," Kreig said. "I made my payments every week. And I thought if she wanted to be like that, she could see what seventy-four dollars a week would get her. But she still didn't let me see my kids. So this went on for a month, two, three, eight months, and finally I said, 'I'm not buying your oil. I'm not paying the electric bill.' And since the apartment was in my name, I told her I was telling the landlord to take my name off the lease. I said I wasn't going to do anything extra for the kids if she didn't let me see them. It was like I didn't even have children."

Shortly after that, Stacie called Kreig and his wife and said she needed them to babysit the kids. Kreig found that strange because she hadn't let him see them for 8½ months, even though he was supposed to have court-ordered visits with them.

"So I told my wife to go pick up the kids and we brought them back to our house, but at eleven P.M. we still didn't get a call from her, so we just brought them back to her house," Kreig said.

When he walked into Stacie's apartment, her roommate was there, but Stacie wasn't. It was the middle of winter and the apartment was freezing. Stacie's roommate said they didn't have any heat. Kreig looked around and noticed there was dog shit and piss all over the house. The roommate said Stacie's boyfriend had a dog and he never took the dog out, so it messed wherever it wanted.

"I'm thinking my daughter is crawling around in this," Kreig said. "Next I go to the pantry and open cupboards and there's nothing in the cupboards and there's nothing in the refrigerator. All the baby's clothes and toys are just thrown in piles all over the place. The whole apartment was in shambles. So I called the Department of Children, Youth and Families and I told them what was going on. I told them I wasn't living in the house, but I paid my support and I was ordered to see the children, but she wouldn't let me see my kids and she was going against a court order. I told them she had no food in the house, she had no heat and the kids were living in unsanitary conditions."

The agency sent over a police officer, who went in the house himself so he could document the situation first-hand and note it on file. Then he immediately granted Kreig temporary custody of his children until further notice.

"It made me happy but sad at the same time," Kreig said. "I was hurting her but helping my kids. It was hard to hurt someone you love to help someone else you love. We went back and forth in court about visitation. I wanted full custody because she was still out running around and that guy got her hooked on crack, and that's when she turned to the street. They split up because she couldn't control her habit. She was only on the streets for about a year before she was murdered."

Kreig finally got full custody of his two children two years before Stacie was killed, and the court even stopped her visitations because she tried to remove her daughter from the Kreig household on one of her visits.

During their investigation of Stacie's disappearance a Woonsocket police officer called Kreig and asked him to go down to the police station for questioning. The cop told him he was the number one suspect in her dis-appearance. The officer explained that when someone was missing, they usually looked at the person closest to the missing person.

Kreig was dumbfounded. He told the cop he wasn't all that close to Stacie. In fact, he said, they couldn't stand each other and stayed away from each other.

"If we see each other, she chucks me the bird and I'll

say something stupid to her," Kreig told the officer. "Other than that, we don't see each other."

But the cop said he still needed Kreig to go down to the station. So he told Kreig to go down the next morning, but shortly after, he called Kreig back and told him to forget it. The police had a lead.

"When I heard she had been murdered, I felt real sad. I wanted to cry," Kreig said. "No matter what was going on between us, I always loved her because she was my kids' mother. The kids saw it on the news and I had to be honest with them because I didn't want them to hear it from someone else or from a kid my son was going to school with."

Kreig said Stacie was a good person before she got hooked on drugs.

"She had a good side to her, she was bright and had the most balls I've ever seen on a woman," he said. "She would just stick up for herself if she thought she was right. She was a little spitfire. She was unbelievable. She was one big ball of energy. But she was also very gentle. She liked simple things. She wasn't one of the flashy 'I want, I want' girls. She just wanted the simple things. She just wanted to get by in life and be happy."

But Stacie, like Audrey and Christine, never had that chance.

Chapter 5

As Audrey, Christine and Stacie undoubtedly learned, the life of a prostitute was not an easy one. Many a young woman entered into prostitution because she came from a dysfunctional family: her parents drank, her father probably abused her mother, and both parents probably abused their kids physically and emotionally. Maybe her dad couldn't hold down a job, so there was never enough food to eat and no money for heat. Her mom was probably too afraid to take the kids and leave. And if her mom was brave enough to strike out on her own, living in a broken home was no fun either. Maybe she saw her mother turning tricks to make enough money so they could have a roof over their heads.

Thanksgiving, Christmas and birthdays probably didn't mean anything to her when she was growing up. And she probably got picked on at school because she was on the school lunch program and wore the same clothes three or four days in a row.

Then before she knew what was happening, her new "uncle" or maybe even her own father started sexually abusing her—a touch here, a tickle there and then the re-pulsive acts she tried to forget, but never could. Hoping, praying that someone, anyone, would save her. But no one ever did. She blamed herself. She must have done something to make that man do those horrible things.

School was never easy, but then it became a night-mare. Homework began to suffer and she figured she was just stupid. So the first chance she had, she ran away. A young girl—fourteen or fifteen or sixteen—on the street. Everywhere to go. Nowhere to go. But free.

She had a little money that she'd borrowed from a friend, so she bought a ticket and hopped a bus to a new city—any city. But when she got there, she was scared, so she hooked up with the first guy who talked to her and offered to take her home. At first, she was happy. She had food to eat, nice clothes to wear and, best of all, she wasn't being abused.

But that soon changed. Her friend gave her drugs—pot at first, then cocaine. And when she was high, he demanded sex. Then he told her she had to pay for her upkeep and he turned her out onto the streets. She couldn't run away—she needed him and the drugs. Be-sides, where would she go? So she sold herself for money to give to her guy. At first, she thought it was ex-citing, but then he started telling her she needed to bring in more money.

Soon she got tired of working for him, so she left, headed for a new city and went out on her own. She found a cheap room and worked day and night to sup-port her drug habit. She knew she could go to jail if she was picked up, but she didn't care. She needed to get high. Life on the street wasn't good to her. She was only twenty, but looked forty.

She tried to get out of the life. She found a real boyfriend, not a john. She got clean. They had a couple kids. Everything was going great—for a while. She became too overwhelmed taking care of the kids and a house. And the pull of the drugs was too great, so she left and went back to the only life she could really handle—a life on the street. Not because she was a bad person, but because she needed to feed her habit.

Somewhere in the back of her mind, she knew that getting into a car with a stranger was dangerous, but she knew she could take care of herself.

That's what they all thought—all the women, all the prostitutes, who went missing or were murdered in Woonsocket before Audrey, Christine and Stacie.

There was the Jane Doe who was discovered, nearly naked, floating facedown in the Blackstone River on January 31, 1990. Her arms, torso and left leg were floating freely in the river's strong current, but her right leg appeared to be caught on some rocks. Jane was about seventeen or eighteen years old, five-two and about one hundred pounds. She was wearing red socks with white socks under them on both feet. There was a pair of black sweatpants wrapped around her ankles. She was wearing three rings on the fingers of her left hand. On her index finger was a yellow band with double hearts. On her ring finger was a gold band with what looked like a diamond and on her baby finger was a ring with a turquoise stone.

Jane's body was blotched and disfigured and the medical examiner couldn't tell exactly what her race was or how long she had been in the water. However, he estimated she was probably in the water for four weeks and she appeared to have dark skin. What he did know for sure was that the front of her head had been cracked open. A large portion of the hair from her scalp was missing, but what was left appeared to be curly—similar to the hair of an African-American woman.

Police were never able to identify the woman.

Jane wasn't the only woman to get murdered in Woonsocket that year. On November 9, 1990, police found the body of a white female lying facedown on the ground behind Shaw's Meats on Social Street. The woman was partially dressed—she was still wearing her jeans on her right leg and she still had a sock on her left foot. Her left shoe was on the ground next to her right leg. She was also wearing a red pullover-type shirt with a multicolored sweater over it. Next to her right arm, which was extended to her side, was a blue winter jacket. A man's white handkerchief was lying on the ground next to it. On the middle finger of her left hand was a gray metal ring with a red heart and a blue heart. There was a piece of rope wrapped around her neck.

Her body was surrounded by trash. To the right of her body was an old condom, which was deteriorating. There was an empty Marlboro cigarette box near her right leg, and a few feet from her body toward the building was what appeared to be a recently smoked cigarette. A few feet from the woman's hand was a green plastic cap and several feet from that was a sixteen-ounce bottle of Sunburst Lemon Lime Drink. To the left of the bottle was an unopened package of Bristol Lights Menthol 100 cigarettes. Police noticed a puddle of liquid that was probably urine coming from her body.

When the doctor from the medical examiner's office

arrived to view the body, he noticed a small piece of glass on the woman's right cheek, which he removed, placed in an envelope and gave to police. Examining the scene further, police picked up a similar piece of glass near her body.

After the woman's body was taken to the medical examiner's office, police tried to determine if the killer had left any fingerprints on it. He hadn't. During her autopsy the medical examiner (ME) noted needle marks on the woman's arms, indicating she had been a junkie at some point. The medical examiner said she was strangled to death with some type of ligature. Police identified her as Dianne Irene Goulet (no relation to Stacie).

Dianne's murder remained unsolved for five years. But it wasn't because police didn't actively work the case. Sure, maybe she was just a prostitute to the guy who murdered her, but to the Woonsocket police she was someone's daughter, someone's mother, someone's sister. But as hard as they worked, they still came up empty in the beginning.

They finally caught a break on October 16, 1995, when a guy named Marc Dumas walked into the station and claimed he had information about Dianne's murder. For twelve hours he gave police a detailed account of how she was killed. He said that in the early-morning hours of November 9, 1990, he and another guy left a local bar and saw Dianne, who they knew was a prostitute. He said Dianne agreed to go with them to the back of Shaw's Meats and have sex with them. When they finished, the other guy said he wanted to kill Dianne and started choking her with his hands. Dumas said he tried to stop him, but couldn't. Dumas said after Dianne was dead, the other guy told him he "knew a lot of people" and insinuated that Dumas would be in deep shit if he ever told anyone what had happened. Dumas told police there were some details that he couldn't remember.

During the interview police decided to show Dumas some photos of Dianne's body to try and jog his memory. When he looked at the photos, he told police he was the one who put the rope around Dianne's neck. The minute those words came out of his mouth, police stopped the interview and read him his rights. At some point he used the word "lawyer," a word that would become a bone of contention later in the case.

Despite making a reference to a lawyer, Dumas continued talking and told the police he figured Dianne was already dead, so he put the rope around her neck—he said the other guy told him to do it—and then had sex with her corpse. Again he said the other guy forced him to do it so that he would also be implicated in the crime.

On January 19, 1996, Dumas was indicted and charged with murder. The other guy was also arrested, but was never indicted for Dianne's murder. Dumas was tried and found guilty of second-degree murder in January 1997. He was sentenced to fifty years—thirty in prison and twenty on probation. Dumas appealed his conviction, claiming that his rights were violated because he asked for a lawyer but didn't get one. He won his appeal and got a new trial. Again he was found guilty of second-degree murder, and his appeal of that second conviction was denied.

Then there was Katrina Marie McVeigh, who disappeared sometime in May 1992. She was twenty-seven years old and had three small children. Katrina's mother,

Charlotte Saulnier, who had custody of her grandchildren, reported her missing in June of that year. She called police after receiving a disturbing telephone call from her son-in-law that convinced her something had happened to her daughter. She said her son-in-law told her that Katrina was dead and that she could be found by a riverbank. Charlotte told police she hadn't seen Katrina since April when she delivered an invitation to her for her brother's wedding. Katrina told her mom nothing would make her miss that wedding. The wedding took place May 16; Katrina didn't show up.

Officer Edward Lee just happened to be assigned to Katrina's case. Lee went to Katrina's last known address and talked to Judy, her roommate, who was also her lover. Judy told police she last saw Katrina on May 14 when they left a local pizza joint. Judy said as they were leaving, a white male driving an older-model car pulled over next to them and Katrina got in his car, presumably to turn a trick. Lee talked to some of Katrina's other friends, who said they thought she had gone to drug rehab.

Police also talked to her estranged husband—the man who had called Charlotte—and asked him what he knew about Katrina's disappearance. The man denied telling Charlotte that Katrina's body could be found by a riverbank or making any other statements that could lead her to believe Katrina was dead. He said the last time he saw Katrina was in January and he had no idea where she was at that point.

He told police that Charlotte didn't like him and blamed him for all of Katrina's problems. He said Katrina was a drug addict who was living all over the place. The last he heard, Katrina was a "coke whore."

Police never found Katrina.

Now fifteen years later, Katrina's mother, who lives in Mississippi, wants to know why the case still hasn't been solved.

Katrina's mother, who had been following the case of another missing Woonsocket woman, took police to task for never finding out what happened to her daughter. As far as Charlotte was concerned, police never located her daughter's body, even though the family believed she had been murdered by someone who was close to her and buried on the banks of the Blackstone River. Katrina's family claimed that the person they thought was responsible for her disappearance recently got out of jail and was back in Woonsocket.

Charlotte has always believed that Katrina was murdered after a long and abusive relationship. She has also believed that the Woonsocket Police Department was never really interested in investigating her daughter's disappearance.

"Every time we go up there asking about it, they say, 'Oh, there is nothing new. We're working on it. It's an open case,'" Charlotte told the *Woonsocket Call* in November 2007.

Charlotte said she asked to see the police reports on Katrina's disappearance, but she was told they were not on file in the department's computer records. Charlotte was told Katrina's case wasn't in the system because when she disappeared, the police only kept paper files and those files hadn't yet been put into the computer system.

"I don't think the Woonsocket police could find the end of their noses," Charlotte told the *Woonsocket Call*.

Charlotte and her husband tried to meet with the detective working her daughter's case in May 2007 when they were in Woonsocket for the funeral of Katrina's grandmother. But Charlotte told the newspaper that they were left waiting in the lobby of the police station for over an hour before they were told that the detective wasn't working that day.

Katrina's stepbrother, a police officer in Lake, Mississippi, has also tried unsuccessfully to get information about her case by sending e-mails to the station. However, department officials claimed her case was still active and said they still hoped to solve it.

But after fifteen years, the case was considered a cold case and a new break would be needed to close it, according to police. But police said after recently finding a woman who had been missing for two months, they were again taking a look at all their old cases. The police said even in a case as cold as McVeigh's, there was still the chance that someone would come forward with the information needed to solve it.

But Charlotte is still afraid her daughter will never be found.

"The picture I have in my mind all the time is of my daughter in the landfill with trash all over her," she told the *Woonsocket Call*. "I would like to know where she is. If she is still there by the river, I would like to have her removed. I have a grave for her."

Unfortunately, what happened to all those missing and murdered women wasn't enough to make women like Audrey, Christine and Stacie think twice about their lives as prostitutes. And it wasn't enough for thirty-one-year-old Cindy Roberts either.

Cindy, who had a history of prostitution and substance abuse, was reported missing on July 4, 2001. Cindy's mother, Margaret, called Woonsocket police and told them no one had seen her daughter for about a week. Margaret said she had been having problems with Cindy because of her drug habit. The last time she talked to Cindy was on June 14 just after Cindy had been arrested. Margaret had helped Cindy pay her fines so she could stay out of jail. Margaret also said it wasn't uncommon for her not to talk to Cindy for more than a week.

The police listed Cindy in their computer systems as an "endangered missing person" and launched an investigation. During their investigation they learned that none of the people who usually had contact with her had seen her around.

A woman named Joan told police the last time she saw Cindy was on June 27 when Cindy tried to sell her a bicycle, which she didn't buy. The woman said Cindy told her she was with some Hispanic men, but the woman never saw them. As Cindy was leaving, she told the woman she would call her later because she wanted the woman to do her nails. But the woman never heard from Cindy again.

A man named Kevin told police he had met up with Cindy late Saturday, June 23. He said they got high together, but then went their separate ways. He said he saw Cindy again early Sunday morning when he was sitting on the steps of an Arnold Street dwelling. He said Cindy was with another guy, named Steve. He said the three talked for about twenty minutes when another guy they knew, Joe, came by and Cindy and Steve got in his truck and left. Kevin said he never saw Cindy again.

The police then questioned Steve, who wasn't very cooperative. He said he was with Cindy and Joe that Sunday, but they later split up. He said he had no idea what happened to Cindy after that. When police caught up with Joe, he confirmed that he had given Cindy and Steve a ride on Sunday morning. He said they went to a local coffee shop and later he dropped them off in the area, although he wasn't sure exactly where. Joe said he saw Cindy the next day, Monday, using a pay phone next to the Donut Express on Front Street. He said she was with an African-American male called Boo.

When police tracked Boo down, he said Cindy had stayed with him at one point over that weekend and had left a leather coat and a bag in his apartment. He turned those items over to the police. He said the last time he saw Cindy was probably around lunchtime on Monday, June 25. Boo said she was with a short Hispanic man with a pockmarked face. Boo didn't know who the guy was, but said he had seen him around the city. Boo told Cindy he was on his way to work and he would see her later. But he never did.

Another of Cindy's friends, Ron, told police he had tried to help her and get her off drugs and off the street. He said he didn't do drugs, but he had seen Cindy do drugs in his apartment. Ron admitted to having sex with Cindy on several occasions. He said he picked Cindy up outside of the Heritage Coffee Shop on Main Street on the morning of Saturday, June 23. They went back to his house, where Cindy ate, slept and cleaned up. He said he gave her a pair of white sneakers.

Later that night Cindy wanted to go back out on the street, so he dropped her off on Ascension Street, where she hooked up with an African-American woman, whose name he didn't know. He said he stopped the car for a few minutes and the woman asked him if he wanted a date. He turned her down, but he gave her a cigarette. At that point

Cindy started yelling up at someone in one of the nearby apartments, asking if she could stay over. She took her leather coat and other things out of Ron's car, including two bags of random stuff like soap, shampoo, a hair dryer and food, and left. Ron agreed to let police search his apartment, but they didn't find anything suspicious.

Police also tried to track down the three men who had fathered Cindy's three children—the kids lived with their respective dads—but Cindy's sister was only able to give police the name of one of the men. She didn't know who the other guys were.

In their reports police noted that everyone they talked to was vague about times and events because most of them were drug addicts. That was a problem police always had when they tried to investigate the disappearances of known prostitutes. It wasn't that they didn't try hard, because they did. It was just hard trying to get any information from the people they hung out with.

Woonsocket police continued their investigation into Cindy's disappearance, but they didn't turn up anything. They continued talking to people in the Arnold Street area, where Cindy often went to pick up johns. They worked with a state police K-9 unit, combing the woods next to the Providence-Worcester rail line. They even drained a portion of the Blackstone River, behind the South Main Street Dam. They never stopped searching for her.

Then on October 27, 2002, a year and four months after she disappeared, a man riding a four-wheeler came across a human skull and other bones in a wooded area of Lincoln, Rhode Island. The state medical examiner said it was Cindy. Her bones were found just about four miles from the Arnold Street area of Woonsocket, where she was last seen. The case has never been solved.

Chapter 6

After Stacie disappeared, Edward Lee, Jr., then a sergeant, was called by his superior, who told him there was a case involving a missing prostitute named Stacie Goulet. Lee, who was in charge of detectives that weekend, would ultimately become the lead investigator on the case of the three missing women. Steve Nowak, also a sergeant at the time, would become the second in command on the case. Before Stacie disappeared, Nowak had been investigating Christine Dumont's disappearance.

Lee, who was born in Woonsocket, grew up in nearby Blackstone, Massachusetts. At twenty-four, his father, Edward Lee, Sr., was the youngest chief of police in Massachusetts. His mom, Maryjane Lee, was a housewife who worked in social services. She was a social worker, now retired. His dad passed away at fifty-three of multiple myeloma.

"He was military police and a patrol officer before he became chief," Lee said. "He was considered a real tough guy in Blackstone. Back in the day he used to get in fights behind bars. But he also had a reputation for being a nice guy."

Edward junior's dad would regale him with great stories of his work on the force. As he went through high school, there was no doubt in Ed Lee, Jr.'s mind that he, too, was going to work in law enforcement.

"The apple doesn't fall too far from the tree," he said, recalling the father he still loves so much. "I didn't understand why other people wouldn't want to do it. It's a job filled with excitement and it's lived up to every expectation I thought it would. Of course, it's dangerous as well, but there are certain personalities that are drawn to that life. While other people are running away from trouble, cops are running toward it. I don't know if it's the adrenaline rush or what."

Lee graduated from Blackstone-Millville Regional High School, then enrolled in the law enforcement program at Roger Williams University in Bristol, Rhode Island. About a year later, Lee asked his dad if he had to complete four years of college before he could apply to become a police officer. The answer was no. After his dad talked to a friend, who was the Woonsocket chief of police at the time, Lee applied to join the force, took the requisite test, did well and was called in for an interview.

"And I even sold it to my dad," Lee recalled. "He wanted me to stay in school and get a degree. But I think he was proud of the fact that I wanted to follow in his footsteps, although he was a little hesitant too. But I sold him on the fact that they paid for college. So I figured why not become a police [officer] and have college paid for. And that's what I did. I finished up my associate's degree in criminal justice and now I'm working toward my bachelor's degree."

Lee was only nineteen when he joined the Woonsocket Police Department in 1988. He got married in 1993 and he and his wife, Cheri, had two children, Wyatt, six, and Tatum, five, at press time.

As a patrol officer Lee had a pretty good reputation for making a lot of arrests and being able to physically take down the big guys. However, he always remembered that his father said being physical was good, but a police officer had to use his brains—a piece of advice Lee remembered when he was investigating the disappearances of Audrey, Christine and Stacie.

Lee got his big break when he was able to get into the narcotics division—an assignment he truly loved.

"Before I got on the cases of the missing women, I had a lot of good cases in narcotics," he said. "I was pretty good undercover. You have to be a quick thinker and cover your tracks. You have to sell yourself to people and convince them you're not a police officer and you have to have the gift of gab, and I was pretty good at both those things."

After narcotics Lee made detective and then became a sergeant. Before catching the case of the three missing women, he had been involved in four other homicides, as well as a couple high-profile cases involving the kidnapping and attempted murders of several prostitutes. He said it was too bad that none of those incidents had any effect on the working girls in Woonsocket. If they had had some effect, he said, maybe Audrey, Christine and Stacie would still be alive.

* * *

The first case involved a woman named Gloria, who ultimately escaped her abductor, but never quite got over the trauma of her experience.

As Lee told it, he was driving down Center Street on December 21, 1997. It was just about 2:30 A.M. As he approached the intersection of Sayles and Center Streets, Lee noticed a man driving an older-model gray Dodge. The man was exiting Sayles Street, which was a dead end, and he was speeding.

The guy sped through the intersection, heading east on Sayles Street. Lee followed the driver, caught up with him and pulled him over. Before Lee could get out of his cruiser, the guy got out of his car and started walking toward Lee. For his own safety Lee called for backup, then quickly got out of his vehicle and ordered the guy to put his hands on the back of his car.

As Lee approached the man, he noticed he was sweating profusely, even though it was December. He also noticed that the guy's pants were soaking wet from the knees down, his hair was messed up and there were leaves stuck to his sweater. As Lee got closer, he saw what looked like smeared blood on the guy's jacket and hands.

Lee asked the guy for identification and quizzed him about what he was doing in the area. The man, Ronald Guertin, told Lee that he had once lived at the end of Sayles Street and, feeling nostalgic, decided to visit.

As he was talking to Guertin, another officer, Patrolman David Hopkins, arrived to help. Lee told Hopkins that he was suspicious of Guertin's behavior and his appearance and he wanted to go check out the end of Sayles Street, where Guertin had just come from. As Lee started to head to that location, he heard the police dispatcher send two patrol cars to nearby Oak Street, on a report of a woman screaming.

Lee rushed to the Oak Street address and arrived at the same time as the two other officers. When they got out of their patrol cars, they heard screams coming from a wooded area and raced to the scene. The officers located the woman on Olo Street, near the railroad tracks, which was less than a quarter mile from the end of Sayles Street. She was naked and covered with blood from the waist down. She told police she had been raped, but because she was so distraught, she wasn't able to tell them exactly what had happened. Police tried to calm her down, but she just kept screaming and yelling that she had been raped. The officers immediately called for an ambulance to take her to the Landmark Medical Center and began searching for the woman's clothes, as well as any evidence of an assault.

Because Lee had told the other officers that he had stopped a man driving on Sayles Street who was all wet and had blood on him, they searched along the banks of a small river from Olo Street toward Sayles Street. Lee also told the other officers that the man had a piece of tinsel on his shoe.

One of the officers located a multicolored bra on a branch of a tree and noticed that it had a frozen drop of water mixed with blood on it. Police also found the woman's panties, overalls and shoes on the side of a building at the end of Sayles Street, near the Blackstone River. They also located an old Christmas tree with tinsel on it near the building. And they found some bloodstains on the ground in the same area. They collected the items as evidence and brought them back to the police station, where they were processed. Lee had already arrested Guertin and transported him back to the station, where his clothes were seized and processed for evidence.

Lee said later that day he sent the police to the medical center to talk to the woman, but at that point she was so drunk, she wasn't able to give them much information. Although she didn't remember where she had been attacked or what had happened to her clothes, she was able to tell police that she had been raped vaginally by a man who was choking her while he was raping her. She said she tried to get away but he was too strong.

Several times during the interview, Gloria began having seizures. The doctor who was treating her said it was probably because she was suffering from hypothermia. The detectives then took pictures of her wounds and scratches and took the photos, as well as the rape kit done at the hospital, back to the station. Police tried to get a judge to sign a warrant to search Guertin's car, but the judge refused, saying there wasn't any evidence to link the woman to the car.

So later that day the police went back to the medical center to talk to the woman one more time. When they arrived, they learned she had been admitted to the intensive care unit (ICU) and was heavily medicated. Although they were allowed to speak with her, she still wasn't in any condition to give them much information. The only information they were able to get from her was that she had been at the Hillside Café on Arnold Street—the same area where Audrey, Christine and Stacie met up with their killer.

The detectives went to the bar and talked to Gary, one of the regular bartenders, who told them that the woman, named Gloria, had definitely been at the bar around 12:45 A.M. Gary said Gloria was so drunk that he refused to serve her any drinks. Gary also said he remembered there was a heavyset guy with a beard who tried to get Gloria to leave with him. Gary said he kept watching the guy, who left the bar and came back several times, because he kept bothering Gloria.

Finally Gary told Gloria to stay in the bar and he would give her a ride home, but the other man walked up to Gloria again and started talking to her. That time Gloria left the bar with the guy. Police showed Gary a photo lineup and he was able to pick Guertin out as the person who had been bothering Gloria.

Police talked to a woman who said she saw Gloria and Guertin together at Buddy's Café on Arnold Street at about 12:30 that morning. However, the woman said Gloria, who was very intoxicated, and Guertin left the bar separately.

When police got back to the station, they ran a records check on Guertin and discovered he had been arrested in 1988 in Worcester, Massachusetts, for multiple violent crimes against women.

A couple days later the police went to the hospital to show Gloria the same photo lineup. Like Gary had, Gloria picked out Guertin and said he was the guy who attacked her. Because Gloria was still in a lot of pain and on medication, the detectives gave her a card and asked her to call them when she felt better.

When Gloria was released from the hospital, she contacted the police and they set up a time for her to come in and talk to them about the assault. On January 3, she went to the station and gave the police her statement.

She said that she had gone to Buddy's Café with a friend named Ernie to celebrate her birthday. She said she was also supposed to meet her mother and her aunt at a Christmas party at the Amvets Post next door. Gloria said she was going back and forth from Buddy's to the Post and was first approached by Guertin at Buddy's. After telling him it was her birthday, Guertin offered to buy her a drink. She declined his offer and said she was going down the street to the Hillside Café.

A short time later she left Buddy's and walked down to the Hillside. When she arrived, she noticed that Guertin was in his car outside the bar. She walked into the bar and he walked in after her, asking her if she needed a ride home. At first, Gloria didn't answer him, but the guy kept bugging her. Finally she agreed and left with him.

Gloria said the guy drove down Sayles Street, but when she told him to turn left onto River Street to go to Park Avenue, where she lived, he just kept driving straight across River Street and continued down Sayles Street. Gloria asked the guy where he was going. Instead of answering her, he started hitting her and she said she may have lost consciousness.

The next thing she knew, she was out of the car and on the ground. The guy grabbed her, picked her up and told her to walk and do what she was told and he wouldn't hurt her. When Gloria asked the guy what he wanted with her, he started to hit her again and kick her.

Then she felt the man put something around her neck and pull it tight. All the while he kept yelling, "You're going to die, bitch!"

Gloria tried to pull the ligature off her neck but couldn't; she lost consciousness. When she came to, she was in the water and the man was pushing her head down. Scared for her life, Gloria took a deep breath, then decided to play dead. Finally the man let go of her and left the area. When she didn't see him anymore, she got out of the water and started screaming for help. Gloria told police she didn't remember how she ended up naked.

Guertin ultimately pleaded guilty to assault with intent to murder, and in February 1999, he was sentenced to twenty years in the Adult Correctional Institutions.

Gloria wasn't so lucky.

On March 5, 2005, Woonsocket police were dispatched to a Green Street residence for a possible overdose. When they arrived, they discovered Gloria lying faceup in bed. She was dead. Police also observed a large amount of prescription medication on the kitchen table. The medication was prescribed to a man named Walter Myers, who lived in the house.

Myers told police the dead woman was his fiancée, Gloria, and the two had been living together for two weeks, although they had known each other for a number of years. Myers said he went to bed around twelve-thirty in the morning, but Gloria stayed up for a while. She went to bed about a half hour later, gave Myers a kiss and a hug, then told him she loved him.

When he woke up, he noticed that Gloria wasn't moving. He started to shake her, but she didn't respond. So Myers ran to a nearby nursing home and asked officials there to call police and an ambulance because he didn't have a phone.

Police processed the scene and contacted the medical examiner, who arrived and pronounced Gloria dead and transported her body to the medical examiner's office. The medical examiner also confiscated the medication.

Myers told police that the night before she died, he and Gloria had been drinking wine and she became depressed over memories of the night Guertin raped her.

Myers said he gave Gloria two Valiums to help calm her down. Then they smoked some weed. They finally went to bed, but Myers said Gloria kept getting up and going into the kitchen. He figured she must have been getting more medication. He said he fell asleep, and when he woke up, Gloria was dead.

The ME ruled that Gloria, forty-seven, died from a drug overdose. Most likely, it was an accidental overdose.

Several years before Gloria died—and about ten months after Christine Dumont was reported missing—Lee investigated the kidnapping and assaults of two other prostitutes. Every time there was a report of a missing prostitute, Lee wondered if it was related to the disappearances of the other women. And he wondered if there really was a psychopath on the loose in Woonsocket.

According to Lee, sometime around December 2, 2003, a man walked into the Woonsocket police station and said he had picked up a visibly upset woman and given her a ride to the Landmark Medical Center. The man told the police the woman was crying and very upset. He said she told him another woman was tied up in a nearby house and was being held against her will.

Police went to the medical center to speak with the woman, named Sabrina. She was just nineteen years old. Sabrina told the police she and her friend, Tiffany, twenty, were working at an area strip club when a couple men, Jerome Vance and John Graff, gave her some cocaine. One of the other dancers was jealous and snitched on Sabrina to the manager of the club and the manager fired her. She then left the club with Tiffany and Graff, and they drove to Graff's Woonsocket apartment, where Vance had also been staying. Graff was letting Vance sell drugs out of his house. Vance decided to spend a little more time at the club before heading back to the apartment.

Once at Graff's apartment the trio did cocaine and partied for a while. While they were doing cocaine, Tiffany started to freak out. She kept walking around the house and going into the kitchen. Graff started to get nervous and wanted to get Tiffany out of the house, because one of the rules of the house was that no one went into the kitchen. So they figured out a way to get rid of Tiffany before Vance came home. The plan was that Sabrina would take Tiffany to a local doughnut shop and leave her there.

When Sabrina got back to Graff's apartment, Vance was already there. He asked where Tiffany was and became angry when Sabrina told him she left her down the street. Vance told Sabrina that Tiffany was the sister of his drug connection and wanted her back in the apartment so she wouldn't tell her brother what had happened. Sabrina immediately went back to the doughnut shop, picked up Tiffany and brought her back. The group continued partying.

At about 1:00 A.M., Vance told the group he was missing about thirty-one grams of cocaine. He said he had had about three hundred grams, but thirty-one grams were gone. He began accusing Tiffany and Sabrina of taking his dope. Sabrina told the police she didn't steal it, but she didn't know if Tiffany did. Tiffany and Sabrina started arguing and fighting. Vance grabbed Sabrina and punched her in the face a few times; then he separated the two women and made them take off all their clothes. Next he opened all the windows so it would be cold. He made the women lie down on the floor in the living room and searched them for the drugs. He forced his fingers into their rectums and vaginas. Sabrina tried to fight him off, but he overpowered her. Tiffany just let him do what he wanted.

During the search he hit Sabrina several more times and then went to the kitchen and started to boil water to pour on them. He told the women they had twenty minutes while the water was boiling to tell him where the coke was. While the water was boiling, Vance got a knife from the kitchen, ran it across Sabrina's throat and asked her if that was the way she wanted to die. Sabrina told him to go fuck himself and he grabbed a nearby cane and beat her legs with it.

Vance then went to get the pot of boiling water and put it on the coffee table in the living room. He made them stay down on the floor and tied them up with duct tape. He taped each woman's ankles together and taped their hands behind their backs. He took a facecloth, dipped it in the boiling water and flung it around so the water would splash on the girls—all the while he was screaming that they were going to talk.

Finally Sabrina lied and said she knew where the stuff was so she could get out of the house. She told Vance that she saw Tiffany throw it out at the doughnut shop and she could show him where it was. So Vance untied Sabrina and told her to get dressed. Then she and Graff went to the doughnut shop, where she pretended to look for the drugs. She was really hoping that someone would see her, realize she was in trouble and help her. She even told people she needed help and asked them to call the police, but they ignored her. She thought about running away, but Graff had the car and she was afraid he'd run her over because Vance told him to do whatever he had to do to keep Sabrina from escaping.

When Sabrina didn't find the drugs, Graff brought her back to his house. Vance was so pissed that he beat her with the cane and punched her in the head so many times that she passed out. When she woke up, Vance was still hitting her. Vance said the girls would talk or he was going to sodomize them until they were dead. Then he continued beating Sabrina.

At about 7:00 A.M., Vance sent Graff to a local convenience store to buy more duct tape. When he returned with the tape, Vance tied Tiffany up, even tighter, then took Sabrina back to the doughnut shop to look for the dope. Sabrina again tried to get help, but no one paid attention to her. When he realized Sabrina couldn't find the drugs, he drove her back to the apartment, punching her in the face on the way. Once they got to the apartment, Vance kicked Sabrina out of the car and told her to walk back to the doughnut shop and find the drugs. He said if she didn't come back, he would kill Tiffany.

Sabrina walked down the street and flagged down a car. She told the driver what had happened and he drove her to the Landmark Medical Center and then went to the police.

When Sergeant Ed Lee got the information that a woman was being held against her will, he and some other officers were dispatched to Graff's apartment. Maybe this was the break they were looking for that would help them find out what had happened to Audrey and Christine.

While they surrounded the building, they found Vance outside the side door of the first-floor apartment. Vance told police he was trying to get into the apartment, but no one was answering the door. However, police soon realized that Vance, who was wearing just a T-shirt and pants, had really just left the apartment. So they arrested Vance, put him in a police car and took him to the station.

Lee pushed the buzzer to the first-floor apartment, and when the door opened, he and another officer went inside. Police saw a man they later identified as Graff holding a cane. They also saw a woman sitting on the couch with her hands tied behind her back. She was screaming for help. As police took Graff down, brought him out to a police vehicle and transported him to the police station, Lee went into the kitchen to look for other suspects.

When Lee went back into the living room, he noticed that the woman's legs were also bound with duct tape. He called the department's Bureau of Criminal Identification (BCI) for an officer to come and photograph the scene. Police asked Tiffany if she could tolerate being tied up a bit longer until the photos were taken. She said she could and added that she wanted to press charges against Vance and Graff. One officer kept talking to Tiffany to keep her calm while they waited for the BCI unit to arrive.

As they waited, Tiffany, who was wearing a gray sleeveless top, jeans and only one sneaker, told the detectives that Vance and Graff had been holding her captive in their apartment since the previous night. She said she thought the two men were going to kill her. She told police that Vance had used the cane to beat Sabrina. She then told police that there were drugs all over the apartment. Police had already noticed evidence of narcotics use in plain sight in the living room. As they looked around, they saw white residue on a cedar chest, as well as a glass pipe used to smoke cocaine.

When the BCI officer arrived, he took pictures of Tiffany, and then another officer cut the duct tape off. Once Tiffany was free, she was transported to the Landmark Medical Center to be checked out.

As they continued their investigation, police learned that Graff had signed a consent form so they could search his apartment. As they looked around, they saw a glass coffeepot on the stove in the kitchen with a white residue on the glass; it was consistent with the way powdered cocaine is processed in crack cocaine or rock cocaine. There was also baking powder, a large number of plastic bags and other paraphernalia used to process cocaine. Police also found a large quantity of crack cocaine in a couple plastic bags. In addition to the drugs, police also seized nearly $900 in cash from the apartment.

The two men were charged with a number of narcotics offenses, as well as kidnapping and various assault charges. They were ultimately sentenced to fifteen years in prison.

Despite her brush with death, Tiffany didn't change her ways and ended up in prison for two years for assault and theft. Sabrina seemed to have fared a little better—she was only arrested several times for driving with a suspended license.

Unfortunately, that incident had nothing to do with whatever had happened to Audrey and Christine.

Before taking on the case of the serial killer, Lee said he had also been involved in another, rather strange, well-publicized case of a serial criminal who was dubbed "the serial foot licker."

On June 6, 2002, Lee said he was assigned to investigate two simple assaults that took place in a Shaw's Supermarket on Diamond Hill Road. Lee said two women had reported that they had been assaulted by a black man who licked their feet.

One of the women, who was wearing sandals at the time, said while she was shopping, the man began to follow her. At one point he stopped and told her he liked her feet. Then he bent down pretending to get an item off a bottom shelf, but he instead reached down, grabbed one of her feet and licked it. The woman immediately left the area, but the guy followed her. He only stopped when she went to a cashier for help.

Shortly after that, the guy, who was later identified as Raymond Dublin, approached another woman in the cosmetics department of the same supermarket. Dublin told the woman she had pretty feet, then placed his nose or tongue on one of them. The woman called her husband as Dublin walked out of the store. She noted his license plate number, then called the police, who tracked the car down to a George Dublin.

When Lee contacted the suspect, he said his brother, Raymond, had been driving his car on the day the women were allegedly assaulted. The women then picked Raymond Dublin out of a photo lineup and Lee got a search warrant for Raymond, who lived in Providence, Rhode Island. But before he could execute the warrant, Raymond, who found out that the police were looking for him, called Lee and told him George was lying.

Raymond ultimately had a change of heart and turned himself in. He told Lee that he had never licked the women's feet. He said he had just dropped a can on a woman's foot and the woman misunderstood what had happened. Despite Dublin's explanation, Lee arrested him.

After the local newspapers got wind of the case, several other women called Lee and told them they had been assaulted by a man who licked their feet. One woman told Lee that about three weeks earlier a man had licked her feet in another area store. She said she filed a police report with the Woonsocket police about the incident on May 18.

The woman said she was in the Ocean State Job Lot store on Park Avenue in Woonsocket doing some shopping. While there, she said, she was followed by a black man who approached her while she was looking at lamps. The man told her he liked the lamp she was looking at and wanted to buy one for his fiancée. Not wanting to talk to the man, she put the lamp down and walked away to continue shopping, but the guy approached her at least six more times trying to make small talk.

The last time the man stopped to talk, the woman was bent over looking at an item on the bottom of a display shelf. At that point the man complimented her feet and said her toenail polish was pretty. He then bent down near her and touched her ankle. The woman said she felt something wet on her ankle like a tongue. Frightened, she went directly to the registers to make her purchases. While she was cashing out, she looked up and saw the man standing at the entrance. He was staring at her.

When she walked out of the store, the guy walked directly behind her. She said he was so close she could almost feel his sweatshirt against her back. The woman then made an abrupt turn and went back into the store to ask the manager if the store had any security personnel available. The manager said he didn't. The woman then left the store and drove to the police station to fill out a report on the incident. That woman also picked Raymond Dublin out of a photo lineup.

Another woman said a man had called her at her office at Northern Rhode Island Community Services, saying he wanted to suck her feet. She notified the police and they traced the call to someone other than Dublin. She told the police that several months earlier a black man had gone into the center's offices looking for assistance, but she sent him to another social services agency.

She said she ran into the guy again as she was leaving the center one evening and he asked her directions to the Landmark Medical Center. After giving him the directions, the woman left the area and went to her gym. She said the guy then showed up at the gym and said he wanted to join, although he had previously told her he was homeless and had no money. She said the man never attempted to touch her, but, even so, she felt very uncomfortable. She said after reading the stories in the local newspapers about Dublin, she wanted to find out if he was the same guy who had approached her. Police showed her Dublin's picture and she confirmed that he was the guy who was bothering her. She also said the guy who telephoned her and the guy who asked her for directions both spoke with a lisp.

Police soon discovered that Raymond Dublin had been in trouble with the law in the past. In 1991, he was convicted of first-degree sexual assault and sentenced to serve ten years of a fifteen-year sentence, and in 1998, he was convicted of second-degree sexual assault and sentenced to five years of a fifteen-year sentence.

Police arrested Raymond Dublin and charged him with three counts of simple assault rather than sexual assault for licking the feet of the women at the Shaw's Supermarket and the Ocean State Job Lot.

On July 8, Dublin pleaded no contest to the three charges. He was sentenced to one year at the Adult Correctional Institutions because he had violated his probation on a previous sexual assault conviction.

Like Lee, Steve Nowak, thirty-six at press time, was also born in Woonsocket. He had three brothers and a sister. When his parents divorced, he went to live with his father in nearby Burrillville. He was about ten years old. He graduated from Burrillville High School in 1988. And like Lee, Nowak always wanted to be a cop.

"I always wanted to be a Woonsocket cop," Nowak said. "I thought of going to a bigger city, but my mother lived in Woonsocket and I spent the weekends in Woonsocket and I always respected the police. My grandfather was a World War II vet, who worked for the United States Postal Service for twenty-seven years. He was very civic-minded. He used to always talk to me about being a public servant. He said it wasn't about making a lot of money, it was important to do something worthwhile—it was about doing the service."

After high school Nowak went into the army and was a military policeman overseas for 3½ years. He served in the Sixty-fourth Military Police Company in Bremerhaven, Germany.

"We did law enforcement and we were responsible for transferring ammunition in and out of Europe," he said.

Nowak got married in Denmark to Dolores, an American, who was an emergency room (ER) technician. They have one son, Devin, sixteen in 2008. They left Germany and headed back to the States in 1993.

"The military is probably the reason I got the job here because it sets you up afterward and it helped me on the test," Nowak said. "Police departments like to hire people with military experience—they figure if they went through that . . ."

In his first year on the job in Woonsocket, Nowak got selected to work on the vice squad.

"My first year on the job was in plainclothes and consisted of buying drugs and dealing with prostitutes," Nowak recalled. "We were hanging out in bars and sometimes I'd be wearing shorts, trying to hide the gun somewhere."

From 1995 to 2000, Nowak worked in the uniform division, and in 2000, he got promoted to sergeant— first he was a patrol sergeant on the third shift, then he became a district court prosecutor sergeant, and was soon assigned to the detective squad. In April 2007, he was promoted to lieutenant.

Despite their extensive law enforcement backgrounds, neither Lee nor Nowak was prepared for what was about to happen in the case of the missing prostitutes.

"I was only there probably two months when Stacie went missing," Nowak said later. "When she went missing, I was the union president and I had gone with the chief of police to the mayor's office to explain to her that the disappearances of Audrey Harris, Christine Dumont and Stacie Goulet might be connected. We told the mayor that we needed to start stepping it up. She agreed, but said she wanted to keep things quiet until we had some proof."

When Lee and Nowak started working the Goulet case, they learned that Stacie's boyfriend reported her missing and told police that he had a feeling something was wrong.

"Normally, I wouldn't be called in on missing persons case, but because of Audrey and Christine, my boss thought it was something we should look into—the third one in a short period of time," Lee said later.

Lee handled the case just like any other missing persons investigation. He traced Stacie's last steps and talked with her family members. But he was most interested in her boyfriend at the time—a guy who was pretty much her pimp and kept track of her movements.

"Stacie was out there working to supply their habits," Lee explained. "He was very cooperative and basically said she just walked up East School Street and disappeared. But I was able to speak with Stacie's dad, who happened to see her at the fireworks display and basically gave her boyfriend an alibi. Her dad said that was the last time he spoke to her. Little did he know, her walk up that street would be her last and that would be the last time he saw her."

Lee and Nowak interviewed everyone, including the guy she and her boyfriend were staying with in the Vernon section of the city. They tried to track down what happened to her and whom she was last with. All that took about a week or so.

After talking to all those people, the police determined that Stacie pretty much disappeared.

"Her boyfriend was convinced she went with a

customer, but he said it only took her a certain amount of time to perform a trick and they always had a place where they would meet after she was done," Lee said. "So he kept going back to the park where they were supposed to meet up. But after a couple hours when he didn't see her, he got concerned. He saw a police officer sitting in the park and he even asked if Stacie had been arrested—he figured maybe she got into the car with an undercover cop. But the officer checked the computer and determined she hadn't been arrested."

It appeared that Stacie, like Audrey and Christine, had just vanished off the face of the earth.

But then cops caught a break in the form of an anonymous tip about a woman who had been kidnapped and choked by a john, but had lived to tell about it. That tip led detectives to a woman named Jocilin Martel, who was incarcerated at Rhode Island's Adult Correctional Institutions for violating probation that was related to a drug charge.

On July 12, 2004, Nowak and another officer went to ACI to interview Jocilin about the attack. She told police that sometime during the first week of June 2004, she was walking in the area of High and Arnold Streets. She said it was about 1:30 A.M. when a clean-cut, well-dressed man in a dark-colored SUV pulled up to her and solicited her for sex. Jocilin agreed and got into the man's vehicle. She said the guy was about five-five or five-six, in his late thirties or early forties and wore his brown hair in a brush cut. He was wearing black denim shorts, a V-neck polo shirt and sandals.

The guy took Jocilin back to his apartment, which was in a lime green house with dark green shutters near Arnold Street. She said the house was two or three houses from Arnold Street and on the left side of the street. She told police she didn't remember the name of the street, but Joseph's Restaurant was on the corner of that street and Arnold Street.

After the guy parked his SUV, the pair got out and climbed the stairs to the front door. They went inside, walked down a hallway and entered the guy's apartment, which was on the right side of the hall. Once inside, the guy led Jocilin to the kitchen. As they walked through his apartment, Jocilin couldn't help but notice how neat it was. In fact, there was even a vase with plastic flowers in it on the kitchen table.

Jocilin asked the man if he wanted to go to his room, but he suggested they go into the living room instead. Just then, he walked up behind Jocilin and grabbed her around her throat with his arms. As he started choking her, Jocilin jammed her finger in his eye. As he let go of her to grab his eye, Jocilin ran out of the apartment. She told police she truly believed the guy was going to kill her. She said she told some people about it but didn't go to the police. She said she never saw him again, but she had heard that he had attacked other women.

When detectives got back to the police station, they decided to check department records for similar assaults. They lucked out and found an incident report filed by a Woonsocket woman named Teese Morris. In her report Teese said she had been attacked by a guy in his Cato Street apartment. After doing a little more research, Lee and Nowak discovered that the attacks on Jocilin and Teese had happened sometime between the time Audrey Harris and Christine Dumont disappeared.

Several days later, Lee and another officer interviewed Teese, who told them a horrific story of her struggle for her life.

It was February 15, 2004, her birthday. She was walking on High Street when she was approached by a guy in a truck who asked her if she wanted to go have a drink with him. Teese said she had a couple drinks before she met the guy, but she wasn't bombed and she knew what she was doing when she agreed to get in the guy's car.

"He seemed very nice," she told the police. "He was a clean-cut man—very friendly. He didn't live very far from where he picked me up."

When they got to his place, Teese was impressed by the way the outside of the house looked.

"We got out of the car and I said, 'Wow, this is nice,'" Teese explained. "He said, 'Let's go in and have a drink.'"

Once inside, Teese sat at the kitchen table and the guy asked her if she wanted something to eat and told her to make herself at home.

"So me being me, ballsy, I'm making something to eat, and out of the clear blue sky, he started acting weird, but he didn't seem crazy," Teese told police. "He said his name was Mark and he asked me if I had a pimp, and I said, 'No, why would I want a pimp?' And he said, 'Who you giving your money to? Who's waiting outside?' That's what he kept asking me in the kitchen, 'Who's waiting outside for you? Where's your pimp?' I guess to make sure the coast was clear."

Teese said she was a little taken aback by the way he was acting.

"You know a nutty person when you see a nutty person, but this person was very clean-cut, very well spoken, very well manicured, very clean, so it shocked me because I wasn't expecting it," she said. "It threw me off. I was like, 'Where's this coming from?' It was as if he had a few issues upstairs. So I sat back down at the kitchen table and the food was cooking and he was like, 'You got a nice body' and shit like that and coming on to me and I was being very flirtatious with him."

Then the guy told Teese to go into the refrigerator and get another beer, which she did. Then she grabbed a napkin off the kitchen to hold the beer. At that point the man told her to follow him because he wanted to show her his bedroom.

"It was a very, very small apartment, and it was neat and clean," Teese told police. "The guy didn't appear to be crazy. Everything was clean and in order. I don't know if that's how nuts do it. The man was very neat. That's the kind of person that would attract a lot of women. You don't want to go with some dirty scrub. He was very clean and he had a brand-new truck—a four by four."

But before she had a chance to answer, the guy went up behind her and Teese thought he was going to try something sexual.

"But it wasn't nothing sexual—the man grabbed me and had me [in] a choke hold," she explained. "I dropped my beer because I couldn't breathe. I could not breathe and I couldn't scream. My neck was in his arm and he was squeezing and I was trying to grab him, but he was very clean-cut and there was very little for me to grab onto. So I'm trying to scratch his face, but I have no nails. So I'm thinking, 'Oh, my God, I'm gonna die, I'm gonna die.' I couldn't breathe and I was getting kind of dizzy."

Teese said she thought about kicking the table to make some noise, but it was all the way against the wall and too far for her to reach. But she figured even if she kicked, it wasn't going to make enough noise to draw the kind of attention she needed.

"So when he had me, I was swaying toward the table, and when I pushed myself back up, I went to swing back around and I grabbed his shirt and I pushed him toward the stove," she said. "And he was just looking at me like he didn't even see me—like I wasn't even there. Like he was going to kill me. He didn't say one word to me and I knew at that point that my life was over. And I started crying and I said, 'Please, sir, I have a baby. I'm sorry for getting in your car. My money's in my pocketbook, take whatever you want, please just don't hurt me.'"

But the guy didn't let her go. Instead, he grabbed her shirt and dragged her into his bedroom.

"When I went in, I knocked over his little boom box radio and I went to pick it up, but I couldn't find a handle because he was dragging me," she said. "Everything was happening so fast. He had, like, a queen-sized bed, it could have been smaller, but I wasn't trying to measure no fuckin' bed—I was just trying to get out of there. He grabbed me and threw me toward the bed and I ended up jumping on the bed and there was a double-pane window and I was banging on it. I was banging on it and yelling, 'Help, help,' but I couldn't bust it for some reason. He grabbed me and he just kept choking and choking. And I'm saying, 'Please, no, please, no, please don't kill me.' And I knew I was going to die, I knew this man was going to kill me."

But suddenly the guy just let Teese go.

"I don't know what came over him," she told the police. "I don't know why he let me go. I don't know why he didn't kill me. He just said, 'Get out of here. I don't want to see you around here no more.' And I ran out the door, and ran out the apartment, and I didn't have any shoes, and I remember there was ice and I slid on the ice. But there was a narrow little path to the street and I could see the street."

Teese ran into the middle of the street, flagged down some guy and asked him to please bring her to the police station. At the station Teese told the cops she was attacked and that she had to run for her life and left all her belongings in his apartment. One of the cops offered to drive her back to the guy's apartment.

"When the officer drove me back, I said, 'There's his truck. He's still in there' and the cop said, 'What do you want me to do, bust the door down? There's nothing I can do.' And I was like, 'Why are we here if I can't get my pocketbook and my belongings back?'" she told detectives.

Teese told police that she was furious that the cop wasn't going to help her get her property back. She said she left her purse containing personal papers and photos, a medium-length brown wig, an earring, a blue sweater and some other clothing in the guy's apartment. She asked him why he brought her back to the scene of the crime if he wasn't going to confront her attacker.

Police identified Jeffrey Mailhot as the person who lived in the apartment where Jocilin and Teese had been attacked. Both women ultimately picked Mailhot out of a photo lineup. Lee and Nowak also interviewed three other women who said they had been attacked and choked by a guy who lived on Cato Street. Two of the women couldn't pick Mailhot out of the photo lineup and the other refused to file a complaint against him.

After they got the statements from Jocilin and Teese, the detectives got a warrant to search Mailhot's apartment for any evidence of the attacks against the two women. That evidence they were looking for were Teese's blue sweater, small black pocketbook, brown medium-length wig, personal items in her name and any pictures of her. They were also looking for any physical or trace evidence of the assaults on Jocilin and Teese, including hair, blood or fibers.

Then, on Friday, July 16, 2004, warrants in hand, Lee and Nowak staked out Cato Street, waiting for Jeffrey Mailhot to arrive home from work. When Mailhot showed up at around 7:20 P.M., the two officers pulled their car up behind his tan Chevy Blazer. After they got out of their car, Lee approached the suspect, who was still sitting in his SUV, and asked if his name was Jeffrey Mailhot. When he said yes, Lee asked him to get out and put his hands on the car. Then Lee arrested him for assault with a dangerous weapon—his hands—for allegedly assaulting and trying to choke a prostitute named Teese Morris. Lee also told Mailhot the police had a warrant to search his apartment. Lee cuffed Mailhot and called for another officer to take him to the police station. He also called the department's BCI, the unit responsible for the forensic processing of crime scenes and evidence seized by police officers during criminal investigations.

"When I first saw Jeff Mailhot, I noticed that he was a short guy," Lee said. "He was very polite, but he was confused. He really didn't know what was going on."

While Mailhot was on his way to the station, Lee and Nowak, who had gotten the key to the apartment from

Mailhot, and another officer entered the suspect's house. They did a quick walk-through to make sure no one else was inside.

At about seven that night, Detective Gerard Durand, of the department's BCI, got a call at home telling him to go to Mailhot's apartment. Durand, who was about to go on vacation to Hershey Park, Pennsylvania, wasn't very happy about getting that call. After stopping by the station to pick up his equipment, he went to Cato Street, where he met Lee and Nowak, who told him that Mailhot was under investigation for assaulting several area prostitutes.

Durand began by photographing the apartment; then he helped the detectives look for evidence that would tie Mailhot to the assaults. As he searched the apartment, Durand was struck by how remarkably orderly it was, especially for a guy who lived alone.

"I walked in and surveyed the scene and just started processing the scene," Durand said. "I took photos and looked for anything that had connection to the assaults. I was also looking for possible weapons, and sometimes they collect trophies, so I was looking for anything that belonged to Teese or Jocilin. And I was checking for anything we could get fingerprints off. Then we started searching the basement, the attic and the other empty apartments to see if possibly the assaults happened in the other apartments. The landlord gave us permission to search the common areas and the other apartments."

When Lee looked around Mailhot's apartment, he, too, thought it was a little too neat for a guy who lived alone.

"When we went in the apartment, I wanted to check it out to find something that might help me out in the interview—you're always looking for little things that you can bring up so you can try to get a picture of who you're talking to," Lee said. "So the first thing that stuck out in my mind was how neat the apartment was—it was immaculate. Everything was neat and in order. His remotes were lined up on the table. All his DVDs and videos were lined up in alphabetical order. You opened up his drawers and his underwear and socks were folded. I don't fold underwear, so I thought that was kind of strange. I remember even making the comment to Lieutenant Kyle Stone, the officer in charge that night, that this guy was too obsessive/compulsive. I figured this guy was either a serial killer or a district court prosecutor, because one of my good friends on the job was a district court prosecutor and everything in his office was just perfect—so, obviously, there was a little cop humor about that."

But as neat as some of Mailhot's apartment was, there were other areas that were not quite so tidy. His bed was unmade and the sheets didn't quite fit—he was using twin sheets on a double bed—and there was a lot of sand and dust on the rug in the den. And the bathroom was especially dirty.

As Durand continued his work, Lee and Nowak looked through some photographs Mailhot had lying around and thought one was particularly odd—it was a blurry photograph of Joseph's, a restaurant that had been closed for some time. It was obvious the photo had been taken from a moving vehicle. Another photo showed Mailhot dressed up as a wrestler for a costume party holding a stuffed animal in a choke hold.

"I thought that was strange and something I could use in the interview later because we were investigating him choking two women," Lee said. "From there we searched the rest of the house, but we weren't finding any incriminating evidence—we were looking for items that belonged to Teese, which were labeled in the search warrant, but at first glance there was no obvious blood or anything."

Soon another officer, Sergeant Marc Turcotte, arrived at the scene to help Durand complete the search, and Lee and Nowak went back to police headquarters to interview Mailhot.

Chapter 7

It was a little after eight-thirty on a typical warm summer evening in Woonsocket. Children played in the parks, waiting impatiently to hear the familiar sound of Scott Joplin's "The Entertainer" signaling the approach of the ice-cream man. Adults relaxed at outdoor cafés, sipping iced coffees and chatting about the weather or politics. In a seamier part of the city, prostitutes—mostly junkies and runaways—trolled the streets and bars in search of anyone with money to pay them for sex.

But what was about to happen in a small, sparsely furnished room on the second floor of the Woonsocket Police Department would be anything but typical. In that room Detective Sergeant Edward Lee and Detective Sergeant Steve Nowak were about to question Jeffrey S. Mailhot about the string of assaults on area prostitutes.

When they got back to the station, Lee and Nowak located Mailhot in one of the rooms where police typically write up their reports. Lee asked Mailhot if he would consent to talk with police and he agreed, so Lee removed his handcuffs and brought him up to the detective's interview room on the second floor of the two-story building. Lee set up a video camera so he could tape the interview, then handed Mailhot a card containing his Miranda rights and asked him to read those rights out loud.

"Okay. 'I have the right to remain silent. I do not have to give [a] statement or answer any questions. If I give up my right to remain silent, anything I say can and will be used against me in a court of law. I have the right to the presence of a lawyer and to talk with a lawyer before and during any questioning. If I cannot afford a lawyer and I want a lawyer, a lawyer will be appointed for me at no cost to me before any questioning. If I do talk to the police, I can stop at any time. The police have made no threats or promises to me.'"

"Do you understand your rights?" Lee asked.

"Yes."

Lee then instructed Mailhot to make a check mark in a box next to each right indicating he understood what he was reading. He complied, and Lee, who was sitting across a rectangular table from Mailhot, and Nowak, who was sitting at the end of the table, began the interview.

"All right, Jeff," Lee said after Mailhot had completed the paperwork. "Any idea why you're here?"

"No idea," Mailhot responded.

"At all?" Lee asked.

"No idea. All I know is you—is assault with a dangerous weapon. I have no idea what this is about," Mailhot said.

"Okay, now we've had a few complaints come in recently," Lee said.

"A few complaints?"

"Yeah, I'll get into them in a little bit," Lee said.

Lee and Nowak made sure they treated Mailhot with respect as they interviewed him.

"I feel you can get more flies with honey than with vinegar," Lee said. "You treat people with respect, talk to them in a kind way and offer them a drink, anything like that in order to get information. There are a number of interview techniques, but the most effective way is to be straightforward with them. The whole idea is to gain their trust, make them comfortable and make them want to open up and talk to you. If you're going to be a hard-ass with them and give them a hard time, then they're just going to close up and you're never going to get anything out of them. The days of hitting people with phone books or something like that are over. That just doesn't work."

Lee said as soon as Mailhot sat down at the table, he was very nervous.

"He was probably wondering what the hell we were going to talk to him about—wondering what we had on him and if we were going to ask him about the dead girls," Lee said. "Obviously, that's going through the back of his mind because he's sitting there knowing he's guilty of murdering these three girls."

But Lee didn't ask Mailhot about the three dead girls right away.

"So he's probably going out of his mind—are they going to look at the other things, maybe they aren't, maybe they are," Lee said. "But you could tell there was some apprehension there. And when we started asking him about being with prostitutes, he was going to deny ever having any association with them. So basically we just let him talk, and we explained what we had from Teese Morris and Jocilin Martel."

Lee said the cops told Mailhot about their investigation and how they zeroed in on him.

"We told him the girls weren't conspiring against him. Eventually he did admit to picking up prostitutes and then assaulting these two women—that was a big break," Lee said. "Once he admitted that, we were definitely headed in the right direction because my theory always was if he choked these two girls out—which is a dangerous move outlawed even for police because you can kill someone—then if he just did it to these girls who just happened to come forward, then there was a pretty good chance that he probably did it to someone else who didn't make it."

As they talked, Lee started to explain about the few women who had taken out complaints against him, but decided to change tack and ask Mailhot about himself.

"Are you married?" Lee asked.

"No. I'm single."

"You're single. Girlfriend?" Lee asked.

Mailhot said he and his girlfriend had just broken up a couple weeks earlier and he wasn't seeing anyone else.

"Where is she living now?" Lee asked.

"Um, she's living with her mom. I'm not sure where."

"Okay. So no one's currently living with you?"

"No."

"And the last person to live with you [was your girl-friend]?"

"No, we didn't live together," Mailhot explained.

"You didn't live together?"

"No."

"Okay. Do you see any other type of girls?" Lee asked.

"Nope."

"Any relationship with any other girls?"

"Not right now."

"No one-night stands or anything like that?" Lee asked as he wrote something down on a legal pad.

"Well, yeah, but nothin'—I mean I actually haven't had one in a long time."

"How long would you say?" Lee asked.

"The last one—probably, like, four or five months ago."

"If you don't mind me asking—with who?"

"Um—all I know is her first name. Her name was Dawn. That's it. That's all I know."

"Where did you meet her?"

"At the White Horse saloon in Chepachet."

"Did you take her back to her apartment?"

"Yeah."

"That's it? In the last four months."

"Yeah."

"Okay—that's it. Did you ever pick up a prostitute?" Lee asked.

"I've seen them around, but I haven't picked any up."

Mailhot told Lee he often saw prostitutes on Olive Street in the area where he lived, but he added he never picked any up. But Lee pressed Mailhot on the issue.

"Are you sure about that?"

Clearly nervous, Mailhot changed his story just slightly.

"I'm positive. I mean, I've picked up a girl that I thought I had seen before who was looking for a ride and then she kind of propositioned me, I just let her out," he said.

"Where did you pick her up?" Nowak asked.

"Arnold Street."

"Can you give me her name?" Lee asked.

Mailhot could not.

Lee then explained the seriousness of the situation to Mailhot and how important it was for him to answer the questions truthfully.

"It's important that you search your memory," Lee said.

"Okay."

"If you picked up a prostitute—you picked up a prostitute, okay?"

"Yeah."

"If you're embarrassed about something like that—we really don't care. Okay?"

"Okay."

"We're trying to get to the bottom of something. But if we start off like this, where it appears that you're not telling us the truth . . . it doesn't look good for you," Lee explained.

"It goes downhill from there," Nowak said.

"Okay," Mailhot said.

"Did you ever pick up a prostitute?" Lee asked again.

"Yes."

"Okay. When was the last time you picked one up?"

"Um, probably about, like, four or five weeks ago."

"Okay. Do you remember who it was? Or what she looked like?"

"Um, she was . . . probably about my height, dark hair—that's pretty much all I remember. I don't remember any details."

"What happened? Where did you bring her?" Lee asked.

"We went back to my place . . . and did the sex," Mailhot said, not quite finishing his thought.

"Blow job? Sex?" Lee asked, not mincing words.

"Yeah, blow job," Mailhot said.

"Okay, and everything went well? No problems?"

"Yeah, it was. Um, she, she left right after."

That fact that Mailhot was a little tongue-tied wasn't lost on Lee and Nowak.

"How many times were you with this particular girl?"

"Just once."

"Just once? Do you remember her name?"

"No."

"Was it on the weekend, or during the week?" Nowak asked.

"I think it was Saturday night."

Mailhot told the detectives that she was the only prostitute he had ever picked up.

"How about any other girls," Lee said.

"That's the only one I've been with."

"Are you sure about that?" Lee asked.

Mailhot said he was.

When Lee asked him if he had had a disagreement with the girl about anything, Mailhot immediately said no, but quickly changed his story.

"Nothing went wrong in the apartment?" Lee asked.

"No. Well, she kind of got upset because I didn't have as much money for her as she would have liked."

"How much did she want?" Lee asked.

Mailhot said she wanted $30, but he only gave her $20.

"After?" Lee asked.

"Yeah."

"She took care of you without a down payment?"

"Yeah."

"Wow. Pretty trustworthy hooker, huh?"

"Hm-hmm."

Lee then switched from asking Mailhot about prostitutes to asking him about himself again. What was about to unfold in that small room was a lesson in interrogation techniques that would have made detectives working in big-city police departments proud.

Lee and Nowak wanted to have a friendly conversation with Mailhot so that he'd feel comfortable talking with them. They wanted to create a nonthreatening atmosphere. Then as soon as he started to relax, they'd begin talking about the assaults again. The detectives knew that once Mailhot started opening up to them, it would be hard for him to stop. And once Mailhot started to tell them the truth in response to inconsequential questions, it would be harder for him to lie when they asked him the real nitty-gritty questions. In addition, Lee and Nowak wanted to use his verbal and nonverbal reactions to the mundane questions as a baseline to determine his reactions to the tough questions—Interrogation 101.

"Do you have any problems in your life right now?" Lee asked.

"No."

"No? Everything's good? Mentally, okay?"

"Yup."

"You're a neat guy, huh?" Lee asked, referring to the state of Mailhot's apartment.

"Yup."

"Inside of your house."

"I'm sure you saw."

"Geez . . . you even fold your undies," Lee said.

"What's that?"

"You even fold your underwear," Lee said as they all laughed.

"Huh? Yeah. I get that from my mom."

"Oh yeah?" Lee asked.

"Yeah."

"She taught you well," Nowak said.

"Oh yeah."

"Where does your mom live?" Lee asked.

"My mom's dead."

"She died?"

"Yeah, my mother and father—back when I was a kid. They both died of cancer. My mom died in 1988 and my father in 1993."

"That's terrible," Nowak said.

"Your mom in '88—how old were you?" Lee asked.

"Um, seventeen, and then with my dad, I was twenty-two."

"Whew—same kind of cancer?" Lee asked.

"I believe it was lung cancer," Mailhot said. "They were both fairly regular smokers."

"How old were they?" Lee asked.

"My mom was forty-one. I think my dad was forty-seven."

"You're kidding me," Lee said.

"Nope."

"That must have been hard on you," Lee said, crossing his arms, putting them on the table and leaning in closer to Mailhot. "Who took care of you? You were seventeen."

"They divorced when I was nine and we moved," Mailhot said. "They both remarried and I, you know, I've got a pretty large family."

"You know what month they died in?" Nowak asked.

"What month? My mom was July and my father was September."

"You coped with that pretty well?" Lee asked.

"Yeah, it was rough for, like, the first—I mean, when my mom died, it was like—it was devastating. It was obviously devastating."

"Yeah," Lee said.

"But, you know, after a little while, you know, you get over it."

"Yeah," Lee said.

"And with my father it wasn't such a big surprise, you know, because—at first when my mom died, it was like, 'Oh, my God, I can't'—you don't believe that somebody in your family is going to die like that—that young and stuff," Mailhot said.

Lee then asked Mailhot if he had any problems with drugs or alcohol. Mailhot said he never took drugs, but he did drink beer, although he didn't consider himself an alcoholic.

The detective also asked Mailhot if he had ever picked up a prostitute after he had been drinking.

"No, I was sober," Mailhot answered.

Lee then wanted to know why Mailhot decided to pick up a prostitute.

"I had just been unlucky lately and it just happened."

Lee again changed his approach and asked Mailhot if he had any hobbies or other interests.

"I drive motorcycles. I go on motorcycle runs and things like that," he said.

"Weight lifting or anything like that?" Lee asked.

"Yeah. I don't know if you saw my basement? I have a gym down there and it's—that's all my equipment."

"All right, Jeff, I appreciate you being honest with us as far as telling us about the prostitutes. I know it's embarrassing," Lee said.

"Yeah, I apologize for that," Mailhot said.

But Lee wasn't about to let Mailhot get off that easily.

"But, to be quite honest here, I believe there's a little bit more than that. Maybe a few other hookers at your apartment?" Lee asked.

"Well, not recently."

"How about in the past year?"

"In the past year, probably three."

"What about in the last two years?" Nowak asked.

"Like maybe a couple," Mailhot said.

"Listen, we're guys too," Nowak said, trying to establish a connection with Mailhot.

"Yeah."

"Do you remember what these prostitutes looked like?" Lee asked.

"No, not really."

"What was the earliest date that you picked up a prostitute?" Nowak asked.

"It was probably, like, four or five years ago."

"Four or five years ago—that was the first time ever?"

"Yeah."

"So three in the past two years, you said," Lee said. "And that's about it?"

"Yeah, probably, like, one."

"So . . . there's probably been four prostitutes that came to your house or three?" Lee asked.

Mailhot explained that although he only took one prostitute back to his house, he went to motels with a couple others. He also said the first prostitute he had ever been with about four or five years earlier took him to her place in Providence.

"Is that when you were still living in Woonsocket or were you living on River Road?" Lee asked.

"I was living in Woonsocket. I was still living there."

"How long have you been living in Woonsocket?" Lee asked.

"Ah, seven years, just since January of '97."

"And you were living on River Road before that?" Lee asked.

"Yeah."

"Did you have an apartment out there? Were you staying with somebody?" the detective asked.

"My stepmom. I was living with my stepmom."

"What's her name?"

"Janice."

The questioning again turned to the subject of the prostitutes. Lee asked Mailhot how many prostitutes he had ever been with in his entire life. Mailhot said four—three of them in the previous four years and one about five years ago.

"Let me ask you this again, okay? Have you ever had a problem with a prostitute in your house? Any physical activity other than what you agreed to?" Lee asked.

"No, nope. No real problems, no."

"Any reason why prostitutes are having a problem with you at all?"

"No. A couple of them actually said I looked like a cop."

"Any of them ever get hooked up on that and think you're a cop and freak out or anything like that?" Nowak asked as he leaned back in his chair.

Stumbling over his words, Mailhot told the detectives that the prostitutes didn't really freak out, but just got a little nervous around him.

"Looking, looking around, thinking, like, somebody was going to jump out and arrest them or something like that. Thinking I'm trying to, like, play a sting or something."

"Jeff, did you ever have a problem with a prostitute

in your house?" Lee asked, trying to get Mailhot to talk about the women he was accused of assaulting.

"I've never—I've never had a serious problem with a prostitute in my house. No."

"What do you consider serious?"

"Well, assault with a deadly weapon."

Lee told Mailhot that his hands could also be considered deadly weapons, referring to the fact that he had been charged with choking two prostitutes.

"That's never happened. I've never assaulted anybody. Period. I'm not a vicious person."

"No?" Lee asked.

"No."

"Did you ever get into it with them physically? Pushing, shoving?" Nowak asked.

"No."

But Nowak wasn't about to let up.

"Nothing? Some of these girls—they freaked out or whatever and they just go on like normal? They leave? Do they run out?"

"Yeah, well—they're in a big hurry to leave 'cause they're out to get their next fix," Mailhot said, letting the detectives in on his real feelings about prostitutes for the first time.

"How do you know that?" Lee asked.

"'Cause the last one I was with, she was like, 'I need, I need to go party, and I need, you know, I need to get some shit.'"

"Yeah," Lee said.

"Yeah. That's what she needed the money for—'I need to go find my man. . . . He's got [to] give me my fix.'"

"Did she threaten you because you didn't give her enough money?" Lee asked.

"No, she didn't threaten me. She was just aggravated. She was like, 'Whatever asshole, fuckin' dickhead,' you know. She started swearing at me and shit like that and just left."

"What would you say if I told you several girls told us what your apartment looks like to a T and we could pretty much verify that . . . and one thing that pops out is your neatness and how everything is set up in that apartment. How could that possibly happen unless they'd been there?" Lee asked. "What would you say about that?"

"What would I say about them describing my apartment?" Mailhot asked. "I really don't know."

Lee made it clear to Mailhot that there was no way the women could have described his apartment unless they had been inside.

"And that's why you've got to start being a little more honest with us, okay? Because this can look worse than what it is."

"Yeah."

In an attempt to get Mailhot to bare his soul, Lee and Nowak tried to convince him that it would be in his best interest to talk to them.

"Maybe you just got something going on in your life and you've got problems and you're not this bad guy that . . . you're being portrayed as. Do you understand what I'm saying?" Lee asked.

"Yeah."

"You have no record. You've never been arrested before. You've never had a problem—you're saying you're not a violent man or anything like that," Lee continued.

"Yeah."

"But some fucked-up shit has taken place in your

apartment, okay? And you're going to have to help yourself out with this problem."

"Yup."

"Because you can end up in a big fuckin' pickle, okay?"

"Okay."

"Do you know what I'm talking about?" Lee asked.

"Yeah."

"What happened?"

"What, as far as the prostitutes?"

"Yeah."

After a slight pause Nowak started in on Mailhot, trying to get the suspect to trust him.

"Jeff, we understand what you're going through, man," Nowak said.

"No, I just can't do that. I've had prostitutes in my house, yeah, but I never . . . ," Mailhot said, not finishing his thought.

"Jeff, Jeff, Jeff," Lee said, trying to calm the suspect down.

"I've never . . ."

"You're on the right track, okay? What happened? You've had some problems?" Lee asked.

"I've had misunderstandings. But I've never—I've never touched anybody. I've never physically forced myself on anybody."

"No? I can tell something is eating away at you—it's very obvious. We've been doing this for a long time," Lee told Mailhot.

"Hm-hmm."

"All right? This isn't fucking stories that we're getting—this is serious stuff, okay?"

"Hm-hmm."

"We're hearing about—and you've had some problems in your apartment with these girls. And you know. And I'm thinking it's because you've had some problems in your life, okay? I don't think you're a bad guy," Lee said, once again trying to befriend Mailhot.

"Yup."

"But I think people are going to portray you as this bad guy," Lee said. "Do you understand what I'm saying?"

"Yup."

"I think that's your job—to help us out here. To let us understand what's going on in your head. Okay? So we can help you," Lee said.

"Okay," Maihot said.

"Because it's so clear in your eyes that something is bothering you and I think things happened sometimes—which isn't you," Lee continued.

"No, I'm not. I'm just amazed that this is actually all happening right now—that I'm being accused of, like, being abusive to people. I don't know what else to say."

At this point Nowak decided to hit Mailhot with some other evidence.

"What would you say if we told you that more girls have told us the layout of your apartment and described you physically to a T than you're saying you've seen in five years?"

Lee picked up where Nowak left off.

"Let's get down to this—several girls told us certain things that you've done, okay? Do you know what I'm talking about?"

"Yeah."

"What is it? If you get this off your conscience, it's

going to be like someone lifted a frickin' car off your back. I've seen this a thousand times. What is it?" Lee asked.

"Um, I've . . ."

"You what?" Lee asked.

"I've gotten a little physical," Mailhot confessed.

Now Lee and Nowak knew they were getting to the suspect.

"Yeah. Okay. What do you usually do?" Lee asked, trying to conceal his excitement.

"I—I choked them a little bit."

"Okay. Yeah? That's what I'm trying to get at. Okay, I'm sure you felt better getting that off your chest. . . . I'm looking at you and it doesn't seem like something that you would normally do," Lee said, trying to convince Mailhot that he still thought he was a good guy.

"No, it wasn't."

"What happens? What makes you do this?" Lee asked.

"Well, it was from drinking."

"You think it's from drinking?"

"Yeah."

"How many girls have you choked? Now be honest with me," Lee said.

"I'd say, like—probably five or six."

"Five or six. And how long has this been going on?"

"Maybe, like, the last year or two."

"The same choke every time?"

"Pretty much."

"How's that?" Nowak asked.

"From the back with my arm," Mailhot said, showing them how he would put his left arm in front of his victims' necks.

"Where did you get that from? Like wrestling or _____?" Lee asked.

"Well, maybe."

"Yeah," Lee said.

"It's—" Mailhot said.

"Not normal," Lee said before Mailhot had a chance to finish his thought.

"No."

"Not normal at all," Lee said. "All right, I mean this is something that you're going to have to deal with in your life and you're going to have to get help for. All right?"

"Hm-hmm."

"And that's going to start by you being honest with us like you have. We appreciate that," Lee said, again trying to make Mailhot feel comfortable.

"Okay."

"And you're showing your true colors of you being a man," Lee said. "When was the first time you had a girl in your apartment—when you'd first done it?"

"I can't remember exactly. It was probably in the last year, year and a half."

"Okay, and could you describe, like, the first girl and how it happened?"

"Um, I don't remember what she exactly looked like, but I just came up behind her and choked her. That's pretty much all I remember."

"Did she pass out?" Lee asked.

"Yeah."

"All of them?"

"No. Some of 'em."

"And what happens when they pass out?"

"I just left her there until she woke up and then she left the house."

"All of them?"

"Yes."

"That passed out?"

"Hm-hmm."

"Do you get any sexual gratification when this happens?" Lee asked. "Be honest."

"No, actually, I don't."

"No?"

"It's just when I've been drinking."

"Yeah, you've been drinking every time this happened?" Lee asked.

"Yeah."

"What would you normally drink before you go out?"

"Just a beer."

"Do you feel a little bit of rage there?"

Mailhot admitted that he did feel some rage when he choked the women. He also told police that the women who didn't pass out after he choked them did their best to fight him off. Once they started fighting, Mailhot said, he just let them leave his apartment. He said they "ran out of the house."

Lee then asked Mailhot if he ever worried that the women would tell their stories to the police.

"Each time it happened, do you wait for the . . . police to come knocking on your door?"

"Yeah, I kind of thought it might happen."

"Yeah, and it's probably been eating away at you. Living with that stress when some of this stuff happened."

"Yeah."

As they sat in the small interview room questioning Mailhot, Lee and Nowak had a feeling that something big was about to happen. After all, the suspect was playing right into their hands. He was committing the biggest sin any suspect could commit—he was talking.

Chapter 8

If Mailhot had been smart, he would have asked the cops for an attorney before he ever opened his mouth. But Mailhot had never been in trouble with the law before and most likely didn't even know the first thing about police interrogations.

If he did, he would have realized that Lee and Nowak weren't really his friends and they had no interest in helping him or becoming his friends. All they wanted to do was get Mailhot to confess to murdering Audrey Harris, Christine Dumont and Stacie Goulet. And they would use any legal means at their disposal to get that confession.

So, while the crime scene unit continued to search Mailhot's apartment for any evidence that he had assaulted Teese and Jocilin, Lee and Nowak continued to question Mailhot. Sometimes they acted as if they knew more about what happened in Mailhot's apartment than they actually did. And sometimes they asked him nonthreatening questions—offering him comfort and trying to lull him into a state of complacency so he'd tell them what they wanted to know.

* * *

"When was the last time [you choked anyone]?" Nowak asked.

"Probably—honestly, I don't remember the exact time. It was probably within the last couple of months."

"Last couple of months? So it could be one month or it could be five months—one month or two months?" Nowak asked.

"Probably one month or two."

"Okay, well, why don't we get into each one of them and try to describe these girls," Lee said.

Mailhot agreed and told the police the women he attacked were white. He emphasized that none of them were black. He added that he didn't know their names and said none of them had ever tried to do anything to make him pay for what he did to them.

"Anyone try to retaliate against you and come back?" Lee asked.

"No, they pretty much just tried to get away."

"What's going on in your head when this is happening?" Lee asked.

"I honestly don't know. Like I said, I just think it's due to the alcohol."

"It very well may be," Nowak said. "But what were you thinking? I mean, what's going on in your head? Are you enjoying it? Like he asked you if it's sexual gratification. Was it control?"

"No, it wasn't for gratification."

"Sorrow? Did you cry afterward or anything?" Nowak asked.

"Yeah, I mean, I feel bad afterward, you know, why did I do that? You know?"

"Yeah. . . . Have you tried to seek any professional help on this?" Lee asked.

"No, I haven't."

"Gone online to try to figure out what's going on?"

"No, I haven't done that. I probably should."

"Did you tell anybody about you liking this?"

"Nope."

Lee and Nowak next tried to get Mailhot to be specific about exactly what happened to the women he choked. In response to a number of questions, Mailhot said the longest any of the women had been unconscious was probably a minute or two before they woke up again. He explained that once the women woke up, they didn't say anything to him—they just left his apartment, upset and disoriented. He said they didn't yell or scream; they just looked for a way out. He did admit that one of the women fought him off and then ran out the door.

"So what do you tell them once they wake up?" Lee asked.

"They really don't say anything. They just leave. They just look for the door."

"They don't seem upset then?" Nowak asked.

"Oh yeah, they're upset."

"None of them lashed out at you—hit you back or anything like that?" Nowak asked.

"Ah, one did."

"What happened?"

"She fought me off and got away."

"That was a black girl?" Lee asked.

"Honestly, I think that it might have been. She might have been black."

"All right," Lee said. "I mean, obviously, you understand when you're choking them."

"I'm not sure. I'm not sure."

"A choke hold isn't allowed," Lee continued. "I mean, they're outlawed for officers because they're dangerous. They're dangerous, right?"

"Yes."

"What can happen?" Lee asked.

"You could kill somebody."

"How?" Lee asked.

"Suffocating them."

"Yeah. Did that ever cross your mind?"

"No, I never intended to kill anybody."

A curious statement at best—was Mailhot admitting he had killed someone, but had never intended to; or was he just saying even though he choked the women, he never intended to kill them? Picking up on Mailhot's comments, Lee and Nowak were obviously intrigued.

"And that may very well be the case," Lee said. "But you could have been squeezing them and things went too far and then you'd have a big problem, wouldn't you?"

"Hm-hmm."

Lee then asked Mailhot what he would have done if one of the women he choked never woke up. Mailhot said he probably would have called the police because he wouldn't have been able to live with himself if he had killed someone. He told his interrogators that he wouldn't have been able to hide it and that he probably would have been a wreck.

"How do you know?" Lee asked. "How were you able to live with these other things that you're remembering now?"

"That's something—honestly, it feels good to talk about it right now."

"Yeah, I imagine it does," Lee said.

"You've been hiding it for a while, huh?" Nowak asked.

"Yeah, like two or three years."

Lee asked Mailhot if there was a chance he took his choking game too far. Mailhot said it had never gone too far. Again he said he had never killed anybody.

"I have to be honest—that's another thing we need to talk about to you," Lee said. "Did you push it a little too far with some of them, or one of them? I mean, that's something you've got to relay to us. Do you know what I mean? If you took it too far, if you've got a problem."

"Yup."

"And you've let all these other girls go and stuff like that," Lee continued. "I mean, obviously, you're showing that you're doing this for God knows what reason. And we could delve into a few things and try to figure out why, but there's a very high chance that it could have gone too far."

"It's never gone too far. I'd never—I've never killed anybody."

"You've never choked someone that didn't wake up?" Lee asked.

"Nope."

Lee and Nowak tried to get Mailhot to confess to the murders of Harris, Dumont and Goulet by explaining that if he accidentally killed the women, it would be better for him to confess because he would face a lesser punishment than if he had intentionally killed them— not necessarily a true statement, however.

"Do you understand the difference at what I'm getting at?" Nowak asked.

"Yes, yes."

"And that's what we're trying to get at with you," Nowak continued. "We can't tell you what to say, but we want to let you know what the story is—what we're looking at."

"Right."

"And that's why it's important for you to tell us the one hundred percent truth," Nowak said.

Suddenly Lee threw down the pictures of the three dead prostitutes on the table in front of Mailhot.

"I—I don't know any of these girls," Mailhot said before Lee or Nowak had even asked him a question about them.

"No?" Lee asked.

"Mm-mm. None of these is the ones that I had."

"Are you positive? That was a pretty quick look," Lee said.

"Yeah, well, there's three of them."

"They all kind of look the same?" Lee asked. "I mean, I can think of some of the girls that talked to us about it. I mean, are you sure?"

"Positive."

But Lee wasn't about to let up because he saw something in Mailhot's eyes when the suspect first looked at the photos of the three women—a hint of recognition in Mailhot's otherwise cold, vacant stare.

"Well, you weren't even sure it was a black girl. So how can you look at these three pictures and right away say it wasn't any of these girls?" Lee asked.

"Well, because, you know, I'm looking at their faces."

"Have you seen them before?"

"No," Mailhot said as he looked at the photos.

"You've been out there for two years now," Lee said.

"Yup."

"These girls are all over—you never even seen them before?"

"If I did, I wouldn't recognize them, you know, 'cause it's usually dark out."

"So you're not a hundred percent sure?"

"No, I'm pretty sure."

"But you're pretty sure they've never been in your apartment," Lee said.

"They've never—none of these have ever been in my apartment."

Lee wanted to know how Mailhot could be so sure, considering the fact that he was drunk when he choked the other women.

"You're drunk when these chokings go on, but you're still not drunk enough where you would be able to recognize these girls [with] no problem that you've had in your apartment," Lee said.

But before Mailhot could say anything, Lee hit him with another question.

"So I'm going to be able to show you other girls, and more than likely you're going to be able to point out which ones you had the choke session with?"

"Yes."

"Maybe next time I throw a picture down, I think you're going to be able to pick 'em out like that because you were awfully quick on these three girls."

"Hm-hmm."

"How come?"

Stammering quite a bit, Mailhot said that he would know by looking at pictures of the women if they had ever been in his apartment.

"It's easy to know when I see them like this. I mean, I would remember if I had them in my apartment because if I saw a picture of each girl that I was with, I could probably identify her."

Next it was Nowak's turn to try and get Mailhot to say something to incriminate himself.

"Jeff, you know something, we deal with these girls all the time. Maybe I'm not a very good cop or anything, but I forget their names," Nowak said. "We've been dealing with them for ten or fifteen years and I forget their faces—forget who they are, and yet somehow, you're telling us that you drink so much that you go into doing this thing that you like, but yet you can still clearly, one hundred percent, on the drop of a dime, tell us that none of these are them?"

"No, they're not."

"Can you pick them out?" Lee asked. "Keep looking."

"Don't matter," Mailhot said.

"No? Do you think we're trying to get at something?" Lee asked.

"I don't know."

"No? It's just odd that you answered awfully quick," Lee said.

"Are you sure that these girls were never in your apartment?" Lee asked.

"Do you watch TV?" Nowak asked.

"Yeah."

"What do you watch?"

"I watch comedies, like *Seinfeld, Simpsons,* stuff like that."

"Watch the news?"

"Once in a while."

"National news—local news?"

"Both of them."

"Do you get a newspaper?"

"No, I don't subscribe to a newspaper."

Nowak was trying to point out that because the story

of the missing women was all over the local newspapers and television station, Mailhot should have recognized the women. But the fact that he kept insisting that he had never seen them made him look guilty.

"Are you sure that these girls were never in your apartment?" Lee asked.

"No, I said I'm pretty much positive I've never seen— any of those girls have never been in my apartment. I may have seen them walking down the streets and stuff."

"So our evidence collectors from our BCI division aren't going to find any of their hair anywhere," Lee said.

"Nope."

"And if they do—what? Just mistaken identity? 'They were probably in there, but I don't remember.' They're going to go through that apartment with a fine-tooth comb," Lee said. "Are there going to be any fibers from those girls in there?"

"No."

"And if there are?"

"There's not going to be."

"How do you know there're not going to be? How are you so damn sure that these [girls] aren't coming forward?" Lee asked.

"Because I've never done any—I've never killed any-body. That's what you're getting at."

"Who said these girls were killed, first of all?" Lee asked.

"Because you—you're basically accusing me of, you know, choking, choking this girl, you know, choking her until she didn't wake up," Mailhot said, clearly nervous.

"Right. What does that have to do with whether these girls were in your apartment?" Nowak asked.

"You're just saying . . . 'Are we going to find these

girls somewhere in the apartment?' That's what you guys just asked me," Mailhot said, although that wasn't what Lee had asked him.

"No, I said are we going to find any of their hair in the apartment," Lee said, explaining that Mailhot misinterpreted his comments.

"Oh."

"I think you misunderstood that, although I said it pretty clear. [I said] any traces of their hair, not traces of their bodies. I mean, you come out and tell me—'Because I never killed anybody,' which I never said anybody in these pictures [was] killed, but they are missing," Lee said.

"Okay," Mailhot responded.

"Okay, but you wouldn't know that because you don't read the newspapers or anything like that, right?" Nowak asked.

"No."

"I'm going to say it one more time—we know you have a problem," Nowak said. "You've admitted that."

"Right."

"Mailhot was getting more nervous, especially when I threw down the three pictures of the three missing girls," Lee said later. "And it looked like someone walked over his grave when he saw those three pictures and he immediately said, 'I never saw these girls before.'"

Lee said Mailhot didn't have a reaction to any of the photos of the prostitutes he had been looking at, but the minute he saw the three dead women, he nearly fell off his chair.

"Before that, we were looking through the book

of photos of the other girls, still not accusing him of anything else," Lee said. "He looked at them and said he really didn't recognize any of them. But when he saw the three [dead] girls, he had an immediate reaction, so my questioning intensified a little bit more to make him aware that I knew that he had a reaction. So we then tried different techniques of talking to him. Steve tried talking to him about the guilt weighing on him—that's when we stepped up the questioning a little bit more. We said those three women are all missing, and that's when he blurted out, 'I never killed those girls,' and that's when I came back on him and said, 'Jeff, what are you talking about? I never said anything about anyone killing them.' Then I saw his reaction and it's like he knew he was caught. He even looked over at Steve, like he was asking Steve to get him out of the mess he just made for himself. He was looking for some way to back out of it."

Lee said at that point his goal was to get Mailhot to tell him his side of the story. Lee explained that if any of the dead women had ever been in his apartment, the police were going to be able to find DNA, hair fibers—something that would prove that the women had been in the Cato Street home. Lee told Mailhot he understood that he wasn't a bad guy; he was just a guy who took things too far one day and something bad happened.

"When I'm talking to him about this stuff, tears were welling up in his eyes and he was getting real nervous," Lee said.

Trying to establish a connection with Mailhot, Nowak told him that they were all guys, and as such they probably all had some "weird tendencies" that they didn't share with anyone.

"We already know that you have your own things. You've already told us that you've done this with these girls, okay? You've already agreed that things could go bad with these girls, okay?" Nowak said, referring to Mailhot's statements that he had choked some women. "Now I've already told you that what it looks like is that one of these things could have happened [and it was] an accident. All right? So we're all clear on that?"

"Hm-hmm."

"[It's] like the sergeant told you, these girls are missing. We want to find out what happened to these girls. We want their families to have closure. If you have something to do with it, we want you to have closure if it was accidental."

"I have nothing to do with this."

Lee then played to whatever sense of decency Mailhot had by reminding him that he knew what it was like to lose a loved one because he had lost both his parents. The detective told Mailhot that he would never be able to live with himself if he had something to do with the death of the three women and didn't get it off his chest.

"Jeff, you know what it's like to lose a loved one," Lee said.

"Mm-hmm."

"I mean, God Almighty, especially losing your parents like that."

"Mm-hmm."

"If you took it too far with one of these girls . . ."

"I never did."

"Because, like you say, you'd never be able to live with yourself," Lee told him.

"It'll eat at you forever," Nowak added. "It will never go away."

"You know nothing about these three girls I showed you?" Lee asked.

"No."

"And you know nothing about their disappearance?"

"No, I swear I don't."

"You can understand why we're asking."

"Yes."

"Why?"

"Because of what I just told you."

It was clear Mailhot knew nothing about interrogation techniques. If he had, he would have known that experienced investigators would pick up on his excessive statement of truth: "No, I swear I don't." Making such statements to police was one of the pitfalls of talking to them in the first place.

Lee then asked Mailhot if it was just a coincidence that he'd been choking prostitutes for the past year or two and now three prostitutes were missing.

"It is a coincidence that I've been choking girls and these girls are missing," Mailhot said.

"Since how long?" Lee asked.

"Since what?"

"Coincidence that these girls have been missing," Lee said. "How long have they been missing? Do you know?" Lee asked.

"I have no idea. You just told me they were missing."

"And you told us they were dead," Nowak said, throwing Mailhot's statements back in his face.

"I didn't tell you—I said that you were accusing me of killing people," Mailhot said, not falling into Nowak's trap. Again he told the cops he didn't do anything to the three women who were missing.

"That's what I thought. I mean, I'm sorry if I misunderstood."

"We're looking for you to answer truthfully," Nowak said. "And I think my partner here knows that you want to answer truthfully and we know it's difficult. It's not easy to blurt out these things that you're telling us. You know, it wouldn't be easy for me. It wouldn't be easy for him."

"I already told you what I did," Mailhot said.

"But you gave it to us piecemeal—a little at a time. We want to skip right to the chase and get right to the end," Nowak said.

"Well, as far as I go, there's no end to me and these girls," Mailhot said. "I've never done anything to those girls."

"No, and you're positive about that?" Lee asked.

"Hmm."

Lee looked down at the photos of the dead women and then asked Mailhot if he could pick out the women that he had done something to, and Mailhot replied that he could.

Then Nowak asked the suspect if any of the prostitutes he had been with had ever talked to him about the missing women or told him they were afraid of walking the streets.

"No," Mailhot responded, adding he wasn't even aware of the missing prostitutes.

"No? You knew nothing about this at all?" Nowak asked.

"No."

"The whole community is well aware of what's going on with this, so . . . You know nothing?" Nowak asked.

"They've never said anything to me about it."

"It never came up—when they're drinking?" Nowak asked. "They said, 'Holy shit, we're worried—we're scared'?"

"No, the only thing they're scared of . . . is they actually keep asking me if I'm a cop. That was the thing they were nervous about."

Nowak told Mailhot that at least a hundred people had talked to the police about the missing women, so it was hard to believe that he didn't know anything about them.

"I hope you're telling the truth, because if we find any stuff in your apartment . . . you know all about DNA and all that stuff now, right?" Lee asked.

"Oh yeah."

"Christ, everybody's getting nabbed on that."

"Yup."

"I mean, this is your opportunity to be straightforward, so . . . if it went too far, I mean, obviously, you're showing a pattern that you're letting these girls go. But look, all over the country, I mean, it's happening to police. A suspect's put in a choke hold and they end up dead. I mean, obviously, the police didn't intend to kill people," Lee said.

"Right."

"But it happens, okay? That's what you need to think about yourself. If something happened . . . one of these girls was in your apartment and something took place and you said, 'I can't deal with this,'" Lee said.

"Nope, I never did anything like that. I couldn't. Like I said, I couldn't."

"Jeff, you can't say, 'I'd never,' or 'I could not do it,'" Lee continued.

"Well, no."

"Any of these other girls could well have passed away in your grasp. Okay? You're a rugged, big guy and you put the squeeze on a few of them, okay? To the point of passing out. I mean, are you trained in the choke hold?" Lee asked.

"No."

"Well, don't say, 'I would never do it,' because any one of these other girls that you're talking about could have died. Okay?"

"Yup."

"And while your intent probably wasn't to do that, but your intent was to let them go, but an accident could have happened. And you're fulfilling whatever fantasy and your rage that you get built up when you drink—if it happened, this is the time to tell us, because this is before you're made into this monster or something," Lee explained.

"Yup," Mailhot said, not biting.

"Jeff, do you understand what I'm saying?"

"Yes, I understand. It didn't—it didn't happen. I never—I never killed anybody," Mailhot said nervously. "It never got . . . it never went that far."

Lee asked Mailhot if he'd be willing to prove that he never killed anyone by taking a polygraph test. Mailhot said he would do anything to prove he was telling the truth, including taking a lie detector test.

"Did you think something was up when I showed you those three [women]?" Lee asked as Nowak looked at the pictures of the three dead women still on the table.

"I thought—I thought something was up. I thought you guys was trying to get at something."

"Why? Why did you think that?" Nowak asked.

"Well, you just laid three pictures out in front of me. I thought something was up."

Showing Mailhot pictures of other women, Lee asked if he had ever choked any of them. Mailhot said he didn't know the girl in the first photo Lee showed him. Then Lee handed the photos to Mailhot and told him to flip through them to see if he recognized any of the women. At that point Lee stepped out of the room to talk to the other detectives who were monitoring the interview, and Nowak continued to question Mailhot about the girls in the photos. Mailhot said several of them looked familiar, adding that he had taken one of them to his apartment.

When he was finished looking at the photos, Nowak told him there were about five or six women that Mailhot hadn't recognized, even though he should have.

"Well, what would you say if I told you that . . . there's about five or six more of them that you missed, even though you had such a good memory? What would you say to that?"

"I'd say, 'I didn't—I didn't have that good of a memory of every—of everybody.'"

But Nowak continued to press Mailhot, asking how he could be so sure he never saw the other three women if he couldn't even identify the women he had taken to his house.

"Is that kind of odd to you?" Nowak asked.

"Yeah, that's kind of odd," Mailhot said.

"Well, that's what we're looking at. I'm not trying to be an asshole, really. I mean, what we're trying to do is help you out. We're trying to get your side of what happened. I mean, it's a weekend. We could go home, you know what I mean?" Nowak asked. "We're trying to help you out with what happened. You've got a bigger problem than what you're telling us. It may not be those girls, but you've got a bigger problem than what you're telling us. Do you know what I'm saying?"

"Yeah."

"And eventually, at some point, we're going to get to the end of this, whether it is today, tomorrow, a year from now, five years from now, forty years from now," Nowak said.

Nowak told Mailhot that the story was going to be told one way or another and it would be better for him if he told them the story right then.

"I personally think, as does my partner, that the best time to get this whole story out is right now. Especially for you, especially for you. You're the only one who can benefit by the truth coming out today rather than five years from now, tomorrow, an hour from now, whenever," Nowak said. "You're the only one that can benefit. Us— I've got another fifteen years before my pension. Whether we find out things about you—you deny things, you admit things—it's not going to change that fact that in fifteen years I'm going to get my pension."

"Right."

Nowak told Mailhot that it was clear he wasn't telling them the truth. Nowak said the cops didn't know exactly what Mailhot was holding back, but they were going to find out eventually.

"So it's you that has to live with all this—whether it's something to do with those missing girls, something to do with a bigger scope than what you're telling us, like there are more than five or six girls that this has happened with," Nowak said. "There's something more there, because you're still not being one hundred percent truthful. We don't know what it is yet. We don't know if it's more girls. We don't know if it's more girls from other towns—we don't know anything, but we do know that there's more to come. You know what I'm saying?"

"Yup."

"So we're going to get it eventually," Nowak repeated. "Like I said, either today or tomorrow, five years from now, forty years from now—it's gonna come out. The only guy who benefits by getting it out now is you—and for obvious reasons. You know how much better you felt when you just let that little bit out."

"Right," Mailhot said, still not willing to give anything up.

"The floodgates are going to open, and when we get to it, the floodgates are going to open and you're going to feel a thousand times better. We've seen people . . . thank us afterward," Nowak said. "Do you understand where we're going with this?"

"Yup."

"You're going backward—we're trying to take you forward and you keep running backward," Nowak said. "You've got to walk with us and get to this common goal. Do you understand?"

"Yeah, I understand."

"All right," Nowak said.

"Yeah, it's been more than five or six girls," Mailhot said.

"How many?"

"I honestly don't know."

Mailhot then told the police he had probably been with thirty or so prostitutes over the last ten years—some from Woonsocket, some from other Rhode Island cities, like Providence and Pawtucket. He said most of the time they went back to his place, but sometimes they went to the women's apartments and other times they just stayed in his car. As soon as the words were out of his mouth, the detectives knew they were on the right track.

"How many times has it gotten out of hand?" Nowak asked.

"It's only gotten out of hand a handful of times."

"A handful of times?" Nowak repeated.

"Yeah, like probably five or six times."

"What's the worst it ever got out of hand?"

"When they passed out."

As Nowak started to question Mailhot about exactly how many women passed out after he choked them, Lee walked back into the room and sat back down across from Mailhot. The suspect told the detectives that only two women had passed out and they woke up after a couple minutes. But Nowak pressed Mailhot to tell him the rest of the story.

"There is more in there. Come on, guy," Nowak said.

"This is all because of drinking?" Lee asked.

"This, it all happened, you know, doing the choking, it all happened when I was drinking."

Mailhot told the cops that he had choked about five or six prostitutes, but only two of them had passed out. He said nothing ever happened with the rest of the women he had been with.

"Every time?" Lee asked.

"Yeah."

"How many times?"

"Like six."

"How many passed out?" Nowak asked.

"Two."

"How many times did you choke them?" Nowak asked.

"Choked two, um, five or six of them."

"What happened to the forty you just told us you were with?" Nowak continued hammering away at Mailhot.

"Before that, they got away before anything else happened."

"The one that passed out? It was only two minutes and she got up?" Nowak asked.

"Yup, it was, like, a minute or two and she got up, yeah."

"How many girls did you put the squeeze on?" Lee asked.

"I think five or six."

"And how many have you tried to?"

"That was it."

"How many prostitutes have you picked up and choked?" Nowak asked again, trying to trip Mailhot up.

"About five or six."

"Altogether?"

"Yes."

"You just told me not a minute ago that over the last ten years you picked up forty prostitutes and choked them, but only five or six got out of hand."

"No, I told you I picked up about thirty prostitutes," Mailhot said. "I didn't say I choked them all. I said I only choked, like, five or six."

"And what were the locations?" Lee asked. "Were they all in Woonsocket?"

"Mostly in Woonsocket, a couple in Providence, Pawtucket."

Lee wanted to know how Mailhot could be so sure he

had never seen Harris, Dumont and Goulet, since he had been with so many prostitutes in the past.

"So how the fuck do you know if you've never seen these girls before, or never had anything to do with them since you picked up thirty?" Lee asked.

"I don't know, I just knew."

"Jeff, come on . . . we went through the fucking thing," Nowak said. "Now it's on you—you want to fucking come out. You're backing off on it now. Get it out so we can work from here on—where we're going to go. How we're going to help you, you know. How you're going to help yourself. How everybody in your family is going to help you out. Let us know how we're going to be able to do that. You've got to get it out of your mouth as soon as possible. Okay? You've got to get it all out. I'm not getting mad or anything. I'm getting a little frustrated because I know you want to let it out. I know—I can see it in your eyes. I know you want the whole story out there. You want to know and you want to get it all off your chest."

As soon as Nowak stopped badgering Mailhot, Lee jumped right in.

"'Cause you looked at these pictures and—whammo—there was something that bugged you about these right away," Lee said, adding that Mailhot was too quick to tell police he had never before seen the three women in the photos on the table. "When I put them on the table before, you were telling me that you had never seen them before, and now you're telling me you've been with thirty prostitutes over the last ten years. How the hell are you going to know that you've been with these girls? . . . How do you know I wasn't showing you pictures of three girls that we know you choked out?"

"I don't know."

"Well, then you were saying, 'Well, I didn't kill them.' Who the fuck said anything about killing?" Lee asked.

Mailhot was clearly nervous.

"Because you had asked me if you were gonna find any hairs or any evidence or anything like that."

Lee explained that he just wanted to know if there was any evidence in Mailhot's apartment that would indicate that any of the women had ever been in his apartment. Mailhot thought the police were implying something else.

"All right, hypothetically, Jeff, I'm not saying you did this, okay?" Nowak took up where Lee left off. "You say you didn't kill 'em—we never said they were dead. But for the sake of argument, we'll say one—one or two of them are dead. Okay?"

"Yeah."

"Their bodies are God knows where. All right? Your mother and father died when you were at a young age, right?"

"Yeah."

Nowak tried playing to whatever sense of compassion Mailhot had.

"You don't have any kids, though, right?"

"No."

"So your mother and father were the closest people to you that died?"

"Yeah."

"All right, and you know that they had proper burials and you know that they were put in the ground, the consecrated ground. I don't know, are you a religious guy?" Nowak asked.

"Yeah."

"Do you go to church? Are you Catholic?"

"Catholic," Mailhot answered.

"All right, so you had the final sacrament of burial and all that. Any of these girls that may or may not be dead ain't got that, and their family don't have the ability to go to a wake and kneel down in front of the coffin . . . and say good-bye and will have to live with this for the rest of their lives or until we get to the bottom of this. . . . These people, for however long it takes, are in the worst agony that you've ever imagined. You know, you've lived it. Your parents died at a young age. You shouldn't have been that young when they died. You felt, you know, what these people feel like. Hypothetically, if something happened to these people, don't you think it's awfully horrible that these relatives have to go on like this?"

"Yeah."

"And live that way?"

"If something happened to them, yeah," Mailhot said, still not ready to admit anything.

"If you did something to them, do you think that it's going to eat you up—if you did? I'm not asking you if you did. Would it eat you up for the rest of your life?" Lee asked.

"Yes, it would."

"Where do you think that would leave you?" Lee asked. "Can you ever have a productive life after that? Could you ever have a happy life?"

"If I did that, I wouldn't be able to have a life. I wouldn't be able to—that would just consume me. I wouldn't be able to think or do anything."

"Exactly, exactly," Nowak said. "Are you able to have a life now?"

"Yes."

"After what you've done to these other girls?" Lee asked.

"Yes, I mean, I feel bad about what I did and I—" Mailhot said as Nowak got up and walked out of the room.

"Have you ever tried to reach out and apologize or anything like that to any of these girls," Lee said, having cut Mailhot off in midsentence.

"I didn't. To be honest with you, I didn't think that they would want to come near me at all. You know? Which is understandable."

"Yeah," Lee responded.

"I mean, I am sorry for what I have done."

"Like I said . . . if you did have something to do with these girls, we're gonna know. We're definitely gonna know, okay?"

"Hm-hmm."

"We're going to find out. We're going to get to the bottom of this. Do you understand the importance for you?"

"Hm-hmm."

"What would be important to you? What would be important to tell us if you did it?" Lee asked.

"To just get it out. If I did something like that, I would just want to . . . get it out. 'Cause like I said, I would not be able to live with myself."

"And you've portrayed the reason why—not that you're a horrible monster that kills for the sake of killing . . . [but] there's something wrong, where you go a little too far and you do your squeeze and it was taken too far on some occasions. I mean, that's the thing that would be important for you to relay to us. Okay?"

"Yeah."

"Not a frickin' murderer going to jail for the rest of

your life, but someone who just went a little too far. Do you understand?"

"Hm-hmm."

"You need to relay that to me. You need to get that out, because we're going to find out, and if you want to be looked at as this horrible monster that does this to people, or someone that just went a little too far for emotional reasons, then that's what you have to relay to me. Do you understand that?"

"Hm-hmm."

"And I think you want to tell me that, don't you?"

"I'm not looking to do anything like that," Mailhot said.

"Then why are you getting emotional right now? I can tell there's something bothering you," Lee said.

An obviously shaken Mailhot said it was because the cops believed he had something to do with the murder of the three prostitutes.

"'Cause basically you guys have it in your head that I have something to do with these girls being missing."

"You can understand our point of view and why."

"Yes, I can."

"You're playing a dangerous, dangerous game out there with these girls," Lee said. "Any one of these girls could have ended up dead. You know that."

"Yeah."

"And you roll the dice like that on five girls, like you said, six girls. Let's add a few more into the picture—seven, eight, nine. Chances are someone's not going to get up. Okay?"

"Yeah."

"And I think that happened."

"I know you do."

"I know you said you wouldn't be able to live with yourself or something like that, but I think you're more afraid of the consequences of what's going to happen," Lee said. "Let me tell you something, the consequences of you not telling us what happened are going to be far worse than if we find the evidence, which we will, that they were in your apartment," Lee said. "This is not some rinky-dink operation here. . . . Okay?"

"Hm-hmm."

Lee told Mailhot that the resources of the Woonsocket Police Department, as well as the resources of the Rhode Island State Police (RISP), were going to be put on his case. He said the cops would scour his apartment and his neighborhood and talk to everybody in the area to determine if the three murdered women were ever in his apartment, or if they had ever been in his car. Not talking was only making Mailhot look like a bad, bad person, Lee said.

"And if that's the path you want to go down, that's fine. But you just might as well throw your life right down the toilet. Okay? Because there's no coming back from that if you don't portray the real Jeff. Okay? Do you understand what I'm saying?"

Lee had given it all he had. He held his breath, waiting to see what Mailhot was going to do.

Chapter 9

Lee's heart was beating out of his chest. Lee had a feeling Mailhot was just about to spill his guts. Lee could hardly breathe. His heart had never pounded so fast in his life. He had a lot of adrenaline rushes on the job, but nothing like that, because Ed Lee knew Jeffrey Mailhot had murdered the three women—and he was just about to confess.

Then Lee started telling Mailhot that he knew Jeffrey wasn't a bad person—it was just that something bad had happened and things got out of hand. Mailhot started to nod his head while he was crying, and that's when the whole room got weird. It was the most surreal moment Lee had ever experienced in his life because he knew Mailhot was going to confess. And he did.

"Do you want to tell me something?" Lee asked, trying like hell to stay calm. "Jeff, your life will be over—over—unless you get this off of your chest. Okay? I know what happened. I know what happened. I know you're not a bad man. I know you just took it too far. What happened? What happened, Jeff? What hap-

pened? You pushed it too far one night, right? Things
got out of hand, huh?"

"Yes," Mailhot said finally, burying his head in his
hands and crying.

"All of them?"

"Hm-hmm."

"All three?" Lee asked, just to be sure.

"All three," Mailhot responded.

"All right. Good job. Where are they? Where are they,
Jeff?"

"Dead."

Lee was so caught off guard by Mailhot's confession
that he could hardly even think. His head was spinning
and his heart was racing. For a split second he thought
maybe some of the other cops were playing a joke on
him and put Mailhot up to confessing serial murder.

Then Mailhot started to choke up a little and Lee had
to keep the pressure on to find out what he had done
with the women's bodies.

"Where are they?" Lee asked, in no way prepared for
Mailhot's response.

"They're—they're in garbage bags."

"Garbage bags, where?"

"I just dumped them in trash containers."

"Where?"

"All around Woonsocket," Mailhot said, adding that
the women were probably in the landfill at that point.

"Okay, are you going to show us where you put these
girls?"

"Yeah."

As Mailhot talked, Lee was wondering what was going
on outside the door. He could have sworn that he heard
a celebration in the room where the other cops were

watching the interview. He also knew that phone calls were being made to the chief and to the other detectives.

Almost immediately after Mailhot confessed, Lee began to see a change in his personality. It was like a weight had been lifted off Mailhot's shoulders, and in a strange way he was actually relieved. Mailhot became much more cooperative and free to talk. He was actually very helpful. He didn't have to watch every word, or remember what he said from one minute to the next, so the police wouldn't find out what he had done. In a way serial killers want people to know what they did.

After Mailhot confessed, Lee asked him to go into detail about how he murdered Audrey, Christine and Stacie. It was now up to Lee to get as much information from him and relay that to the other officers at the crime scene. Coincidentally, just about the same time Mailhot was confessing, the police officers who had been searching Mailhot's apartment for evidence that he assaulted Teese and Jocilin were ready to wrap up. They had no idea they were going to be looking for evidence of a triple homicide. But as soon as he confessed, Gerry Durand and the other BCI officers got the word that he had killed three people in his apartment and they were told to wait for a new search warrant, which would let them look for evidence of the murders.

"What happened?" Lee asked, trying to compose himself.

Mailhot told Lee it just went too far.

"Okay. You're doing the right thing, okay? You know what? A lot of people are going to be thankful for this. A lot of families are going to be so happy to know what happened and they're finally going to get peace. Okay, you've gotta think hard. You're the only one that's gotta tell us where the girls are. How did you fit them in trash bags?" Lee asked.

"Cut 'em up."

"You cut them all up?" Lee asked, not quite believing what he was hearing. "Where?"

"My house—in my bathtub."

"What did you cut them up with?"

"A saw."

"What kind of saw?"

"Just a regular saw you can get in Lowe's—just a woodcutting saw," Mailhot said matter-of-factly.

"Are we talking electric?" Lee asked, trying to come to terms with what Mailhot was telling him. Trying to figure out how the hell this monster cut up three human beings with a regular woodcutting saw.

"No, just a handsaw."

"Handsaw?" Lee asked, still trying to comprehend what he was hearing.

"Hm-hmm."

"Each girl was cut up?" Lee asked.

"Hm-hmm."

"Three?"

"Three."

As Lee was questioning Mailhot, Nowak came back into the room and asked Mailhot if he wanted a soda or cigarette or something. Mailhot said he'd just like a cup of water, if the detective didn't mind. But he could wait if it was too much trouble. The scene in the interrogation room was surreal. The cops couldn't believe they were dealing with a polite serial killer.

"Unfortunately for me—when he confessed, it had

been my turn to be out of the room," Nowak recalled later. "Me and Eddie thought that these disappearances were connected, but we didn't have anything else other than these other girls who were attacked, so we said, 'Let's take a look at this guy.' So we were going into it with an open mind. If he didn't do it, we didn't want to pin it on him. But it was good that it ended up being him, but when we first started questioning him, we didn't really give too much thought to the fact that this was the guy who was doing it."

As Nowak went out to get Mailhot some water, Lee continued asking Mailhot about how he murdered Audrey Harris, Christine Dumont and Stacie Goulet.

"You put them in what type of trash bags?"

"Trash bags."

"Where did you get them?"

"Like, at Wal-Mart—the drawstring kind."

"Did you already have those trash bags?"

"No. Actually, yeah, I did. I had them the first time."

"Okay, the first time you already had the trash bags—after the first time, did you go out and buy them?"

"I already had them."

"Who was the first girl?" Lee asked.

"She was," Mailhot said, pointing at Audrey's photo.

"Do you remember what date this happened on?"

"That happened last year—like February or March."

"She was cut up and put in a trash bag and she was disposed of where?"

"Um, in Woonsocket, in Rock Ridge Apartments and Brunswick bowling alley."

"Okay. So different parts—different places."

"Yeah."

"This second girl, Christine Dumont, where is she?" Lee asked, holding up Christine's picture.

"Same thing," Mailhot said. "I did the same thing for all three."

"When did this one happen?" asked Nowak, who had just walked back into the room.

"That was earlier this year."

"Do you remember what month?" Lee asked.

"I believe it was either February or March. I think it was March."

"This girl?" Lee asked, pointing to Stacie's picture.

"Probably about a month ago."

"Okay, same thing? You cut her up and put her in bags?" Lee asked.

"Hm-hmm."

"All the girls were choked? Do you remember what night you picked up [Stacie Goulet]?" Lee asked.

"I don't remember the exact night."

"Any events going on at that time that might help you remember?"

"It was late. It was just about a month ago."

"Okay, around Fourth of July?"

"Probably around Fourth of July—probably right around that time. I'm not sure."

"Where did you pick her up?"

"Arnold Street. Actually, no, I picked her up in front of Warehouse Liquors in Woonsocket."

"Okay, this young lady right here, the first one, okay? Audrey Harris—how many pieces did you cut her up in?" Lee asked. "And let's describe how you actually went about this."

"Yes."

"Head?" Lee asked.

"Limbs, head, torso cut in half from the waist."

"Okay, and each one was placed in one bag?"

"No, each one was placed in several bags, probably like four or five bags."

"Reason being?"

"To make it smaller."

"When did you come up with this idea?"

"Like, a couple days after I did it."

"Where was she?"

"She was in my bathtub."

"How was she in your bathtub?"

"I put her there after I choked her."

"Why? Did you keep her preserved or anything like that?" Lee asked, wondering how Mailhot lived with the smell of the decomposing body.

"No."

"No? But you were able to stay in your apartment with her in your bathtub? Did you sleep there while she was there?"

"While she was there? Yes, I did," Mailhot responded. "There was no smell given off from her or anything like that."

"And then you come up with the idea to dispose of the body?" Lee asked.

"How did you come up with the idea of cutting them up?" Nowak asked.

At that point the detectives figured it was better to let Mailhot tell them his story. So for the next four hours Mailhot calmly detailed how he murdered the three women in cold blood. Audrey Harris was the first woman to meet her death at the hands of Jeffrey Mailhot;

Christine Dumont was the next to die; Stacie Goulet was Mailhot's last victim.

Nowak told Mailhot the detectives wanted him to tell them everything beginning with the first time he ever saw Audrey, Christine and Stacie. Nowak reminded Mailhot that the interrogation was being recorded and that the detectives would be taking notes.

"So as you go along if we see anything we have to ask—I'm going to try not to ask a lot of questions, but I want you to go right through the story."

"Okay. I had been going to the K2U in Woonsocket with a couple of my friends that night. It was a Thursday night. I don't remember the date. This was last year. It was right around the time the Station [nightclub] fire happened. We had been hanging out at the K2U and I had gotten intoxicated and then we parted ways."

"Where did you part ways?" Nowak asked.

"At K2U—we'd come in separate vehicles. I didn't come with them. I had just met them there."

"Okay. What time did you part from K2U?"

"I'd say probably, like, eleven," Mailhot said. "I can't be sure of the exact time."

Mailhot then told him how he first saw Audrey when he was on his way home from the strip club and stopped to pick her up.

"How long after you left K2U—"

"Did I pick her up?" Mailhot asked, finishing Nowak's sentence.

"To the time that you picked her up?" Nowak decided to ask the question his way.

"It was, like, probably ten, fifteen minutes."

"All right, that's it?"

"Yeah."

"So you pretty much drove straight [home]?"

"I just drove straight home, yes."

"You know the city of Woonsocket pretty well and you know all the streets, Arnold Street, High Street, stuff like that. You know where all of that is?" Nowak asked, referring to the area in Woonsocket known for prostitution. "That's your neighborhood?"

"Yeah, I mean, I know streets I'm familiar with. I'm not too good at retaining a lot of street names."

"Okay," Nowak said. "If I ask you about a street, and if you don't know where it is, let me know."

"Right."

"So you left K2U, which is on Front Street, right?"

"Yes."

"Then you drove from K2U to Arnold Street and you found her on Arnold Street."

"She was right around the area where Joseph's breakfast place used to be on Arnold Street," Mailhot said. "It was right around that area I picked her up."

"Okay. How did that go, when you picked her up?"

"Um, I just saw her walking, so I pulled up alongside her and she got [in]."

"Did she know you? Did you know her?" Nowak asked.

"No."

"No? She just got in?"

"She just got in."

"She say anything?"

"Yes, she asked me if I wanted to party and stuff."

"What did you tell her?"

Mailhot said he told Audrey that he wanted to party and they could go back to his place, which was nearby on Cato Street. Audrey agreed. Mailhot explained that when he picked Audrey up, he only planned to have sex with her. He told Nowak they agreed on a price of $30 for straight sex.

"And this time what were you thinking you were going to do with her?" Nowak asked, trying to find out if Mailhot planned to kill Audrey.

"I was thinking I was going to have sex with her."

"And you had offered that, you said that to her?"

"Yes."

"Did you say what type of sex?"

"Yeah, just sex."

"Straight sex?" Nowak asked.

"Straight sex."

"Okay, and she agreed?"

"Yes—yes, she did."

"Did you pay her?"

"Actually, I went to go get the money and then she turned around and I choked her."

"You choked her in the truck?" Nowak asked, trying to get the story straight.

"No, oh no, I went to pay her when we were in the house."

Once in his apartment Audrey asked for the money upfront. Mailhot went to his bedroom to get the money, but then something went horribly wrong and Audrey ended up dead.

"When we got into the house, I gave her a little tour of the house and we went into my bedroom," Mailhot explained. "She got undressed. I got undressed. I was wearing a pair of shorts and she was totally naked. Then she asked me for the money and I went to go give her the money, and then she turned around and I started—that's when I went up from behind and started choking her."

"How long from the time you got in the house to the time that you started choking her?"

"Probably about seven, eight minutes."

"And what did you do [during that time]?"

"We were just talking."

"What did you talk about? Do you remember?" Nowak asked.

"I don't remember too much—I was pretty drunk that night."

"Really drunk?"

"Yes."

"You don't remember the conversation? Did it get heated or anything?"

"No, there was no arguing or anything like that."

"No arguing whatsoever?"

"No."

"Earlier in the night?" Nowak asked.

"No."

Nowak thought the reason Mailhot decided to kill Audrey was because he didn't have the money to pay her, but Mailhot said that wasn't the case.

"You had the money with you? There wasn't an issue that you couldn't pay or anything?" Nowak asked, trying to make sense of the murder.

"No."

Nowak then asked Mailhot to explain to him exactly how he killed Audrey, which he did. Mailhot even demonstrated the choke hold he used. He explained that she struggled a bit and they both ended up on the floor. Mailhot continued choking her for another thirty seconds or so before he finished her off by smothering her with a pillow.

"Did she say anything like, 'What the hell is going on?' Did she look at you? What happened?"

"Well, no, I didn't see her face 'cause she was facing away from me, and all she was doing is gagging."

"Hm-hmm."

"I didn't hear her saying anything."

"Was she kicking, scratching at you, or anything?"

"Yes, that's when I dragged her to the floor."

"How long and then what?"

"And then I had her remaining in the choke hold until—until she stopped moving."

"How long did you actually choke her before you had to take her to the floor?"

"It was like within seconds—probably like ten seconds."

"Was there any struggle at all?" Nowak asked. "I mean, I watch movies and you can see it on TV and stuff, you know. They go up and they grab them and [they] can go out right away? Was it like that?"

"No, no, she struggled a bit."

"She struggled a bit?"

"That's why I went down on the floor with her to try and keep her from struggling."

"Yeah. Now when you got down to the floor, what happened then?"

Mailhot said he kept the choke hold on Audrey for about another twenty or thirty seconds.

"And what was she doing at that point?"

"She was, you know, kicking and scratching, trying to get away still, but you know, when I got her to the floor, she . . . was losing her breath, struggling," Mailhot said. "She eventually stopped struggling about probably, like, twenty to thirty seconds after I got her to the floor, and then I let go and that's when I looked at her. I saw her eyes were just staring up—she wasn't looking at anything and there was blood coming out of her mouth and she was gagging with, like, blood bubbles coming up. And so that's when I figured she was dying."

"But you didn't think she was dead?" Nowak asked.

"No, 'cause she was still, like, breathing—I figured maybe she was still alive, so that's when I got the pillow and I suffocated her with the pillow."

"And, then, well, how did you know she was dead?" Nowak asked.

"I mean, I wasn't sure after I took the pillow off her. I just kind of looked at her and then just kind of sat back for a few minutes in disbelief of what had happened."

Nowak wanted to know if Mailhot had planned to kill Audrey or if he just felt like he had to satisfy an urge that had been building.

"It was an urge—it was no particular reason why it happened."

After Mailhot realized he had killed Audrey, he paced around his bedroom, trying to figure out what to do. He checked on Audrey again after a couple minutes and knew she was dead.

"So you sat with her, how long out in the kitchen floor?" Nowak asked.

"This was actually—I did this—this was in my bedroom."

"Okay, in the bedroom. How long did you sit with her? She's on the floor of the bedroom."

"She's on the floor of the bedroom," Mailhot said, echoing Nowak's words.

"You already killed her—brought to the ground, pillow over her head, took the pillow off—"

"No," Mailhot said, interrupting the cop.

"Realized she was dead how?"

"After I took the pillow off, I, you know, stood back for a few minutes, just kind of looking and pacing around, not knowing what to do," he explained. "I went and checked on her after a couple of minutes and I just knew she was dead. She hadn't moved, she hadn't breathed—nothing—all the breathing and everything stopped," he said.

"Okay, then what did you do after that?"

Mailhot explained to the detectives as much as he could remember about how he killed Audrey Harris. About ten minutes after Mailhot murdered Audrey, he dragged her lifeless body into his bathroom, put her in the bathtub, then put her clothes in a trash bag in the kitchen.

"Okay, so you put her in the bathtub. How much time would you say had gone by up to this point from the time you picked her up, which is sometime around eleven o'clock?" Nowak asked. "I mean, obviously, I don't expect you to know seconds, but just give it a guess."

"I would say probably, like, forty minutes or so—somewhere around there—forty, forty-five."

"All right, so you put her in the bathtub and she's still—you had never undressed, right?"

"No, she had already undressed herself," Mailhot reminded Nowak.

"Where did her clothes go?"

"In my kitchen trash bag."

Unlike some serial killers who keep souvenirs, Mailhot didn't keep any of Audrey's possessions. He threw them all away.

"So you threw it away with the regular garbage—all of her clothes?"

"Yes."

"Did she have any jewelry, ID, anything like that?"

"I think she had some, like, braids in her hair."

"Did you take those off?"

"No, I left those."

"She had no jewelry on, or nothing like that?"

"Not that I can remember. I don't believe she had any rings or anything like that."

"No wallet?"

"No."

"Okay. But everything she had you threw away, or did you keep anything?"

"Everything—I threw away."

"Do you remember her size?" Lee asked.

"She was pretty petite, probably like my height. She probably weighed about a hundred and five, hundred and ten pounds, maybe."

"Okay, what color?"

"She was black."

Nowak explained to Mailhot that some of the questions he and Lee were going to be asking were going to be redundant.

"I am going to ask them over and over again—two reasons for that. One is I've been working all day and I'm not the brightest bulb around, to be honest with you, and two, I want to make sure I cover everything," Nowak explained. "So it's not that I am thinking you are lying or anything, I'm just asking you because I want to be sure, okay? And I want you to be sure. I don't want you telling us anything that didn't happen and I don't want to write down or perceive something that didn't happen, okay?"

"Yes."

"All right, so we have her in the tub, she's naked. You've

disposed of everything she has—you take nothing from her."

"Right."

"You don't put anything in a drawer or anywhere or nothing."

"No."

"All right, she's naked. You put her in the tub. What do you do then?"

"Then probably about ten minutes later I passed out."

"From?"

Mailhot was about to say from the alcohol, but he changed his mind.

"Passed out or fell asleep—went to sleep."

"Where did you fall asleep?"

"In my bed."

"So as soon as you put her in the tub, you walked out and laid down in bed?"

"I was so drunk, I was about ready to pass out anyway," Mailhot said. "I just went to bed."

"Okay, so you went to bed and you got right to sleep, you said. You kind of passed out right away?"

"Yeah, I was so drunk, I pretty much had no choice. I was just that lit."

"Okay, so now you're asleep, you wake up the next morning, which you believe is a Friday, and . . . ?"

The next morning, Mailhot said, he woke up with no memory of what had happened the previous night. But when he went into the bathroom and saw Audrey's body in his bathtub, it all came flooding back to him. Realizing he needed time to figure out what to do, he called his boss at Avery Dennison and said he was taking a sick day.

He left Audrey in his bathtub and drove to Wal-Mart, where he bought a roll of heavy-duty plastic wrap and a roll of carpet. He brought the plastic wrap and carpet home, rolled Audrey's body first in the plastic, and then in the carpet, and put her in his GMC Jimmy and drove around town trying to find a place to dump her.

The cops wanted to know what happened to that truck, because it might contain evidence prosecutors could use to convict Mailhot.

"Where is that now?" Lee asked, interrupting Mailhot.

"I sold it," he said. "I traded it in for the vehicle I have now."

"Do you know who you sold it to?"

"I forget right now the name of the dealership, but the license plate holder on the back of my truck, I believe, has it," Mailhot said. "I believe it's something Hyundai—like Torres Hyundai or something like that. But it's written on the license plate holder on the back of my current truck now. That's where I traded it in."

After the interruption Mailhot continued his story and explained to the cops how he had cut up Audrey's body and disposed of it in area Dumpsters.

Fourteen months later, Mailhot picked up Christine Dumont, and two months after that, Stacie Goulet. Mailhot brought the women back to his apartment, presumably to have sex, then choked them, dismembered their bodies in his bathtub, put their body parts in plastic bags and tossed them away like trash in neighborhood Dumpsters. He also got rid of their clothes, and the saw he used to cut up Christine, but for some reason he kept the saw he used to dismember Stacie. In fact, he put that saw, which had a picture of a shark on its wooden handle, in the basement with some other tools behind his washer and dryer.

As Mailhot spoke, Lee and Nowak peppered him with

questions. They wanted to know how a seemingly normal guy—a guy who had never even had a speeding ticket—became a serial killer.

"Were there any other girls?" Nowak asked.

"No, that's about it. . . . I have no reason to lie now."

"That's right," Lee said.

"I have choked other girls."

"Any others die?" Nowak asked.

"No, none have died."

"And have you ever disposed of a body other than cutting them up?" Lee asked.

"No."

Mailhot explained that he cut up Audrey's body so he could get rid of it. He said he was scared and didn't want anyone to find out what he had done.

"But then it happened again," Lee said.

"Yeah."

"Why did it happen again?"

"Again I was drinking."

"Okay."

"I was drinking all three times when it happened."

"Okay, but you did the same thing with each of the girls?" Lee asked.

"Yes."

"And they were all in the same locations—the Dumpsters?"

Mailhot said he threw some of the bags in various Dumpsters in the area, including at the Plaza Village, the Brunswick bowling alley and Rock Ridge Apartments.

"Did you hang on to anything—any part of their body?" Lee asked.

"No."

"Any clothing or anything?" Nowak asked.

"Got rid of all the clothing," Mailhot said.

"I'll be right back. I'm glad you got this off your chest," Lee said as he got up and walked out.

"I'm sorry I lied to you guys."

"Jeff, listen, we deal with this stuff a lot, okay? We understand that these things happen, okay? We understand that . . . things like this happen. Now you've come this far, okay? And, again, I really do appreciate what you're doing and I hope you feel a little better that it's off your chest, because it must have been horrible eating at you," Nowak said.

"I know you guys have a lot of work to do. I know there's a lot of questions to ask," Mailhot said.

"There's other girls that haven't turned up," Nowak said.

"Hm-hmm."

"Are there more?"

"No there's not. I'm not going to confess to three and not confess anymore, okay?"

"I understand. I just want to let you know where I'm coming from. We had one, well actually her body was found down the street from where you used to live."

"Okay."

"And you know nothing about that?" Nowak asked.

"Those are the three right there," Mailhot said, pointing to the photos of Audrey, Christine and Stacie on the table.

"When you disposed of them, like, did you do it all? Did you just throw all the body parts in and just drive around the city?" Nowak wanted to know.

"Yes."

"Or did you take two [trash bags] and then go back to the house?"

"No, I did them all at once."

"You did them all at once? How long would it take you to make the whole round?"

"Probably like half an hour maybe."

"Half an hour?"

"Just driving around the city—like all of them were in Woonsocket."

"During that time, did anybody ever stop to ask you what you were doing?" Nowak asked. "Did you ever come close to getting caught or anything? Nobody? Never saw a cruiser roll up and say, 'Hey, what are you doing?' Nothing like that? Never saw a civilian say, 'Hey, get out of our Dumpster' or whatever?"

"No."

"Did you ever see anybody walking around?"

"No."

"What time of night was this?" Nowak asked.

"They were all around, like, eleven at night—eleven to midnightish."

"The first—the first one, you said you waited until the next day to do it—the other two, how long did they stay with you?"

"Well, the first one stayed with me for a couple days. . . . The last two stayed with me for a day. I did it during the night and then I disposed of them the next day."

"Okay, and when did you actually start to dismember them?" Lee asked.

"It was probably, like, five or six o'clock in the afternoon."

Lee asked Mailhot if he had been reading about the disappearances of the women in the newspapers or watching it on television. Mailhot said he hadn't heard anything about the women because he wasn't really a "news person. I mean, I turn on the news, here and there, but I've never seen or heard of them mentioned."

"Did you ever fear the police [were going to find out] that they were missing? So you never checked the newspapers or anything, knowing where they were?" Lee asked.

"Did any of the other girls ever bring it up?" Nowak asked.

"What's that?"

"Did any of the prostitutes that you picked up ever bring it up?" Nowak repeated.

"No, no."

"You had no idea that people were looking for these girls?" Nowak asked.

"I had a feeling. I mean, they must have known, had family and stuff that was looking for them, but I didn't know. I never heard or seen anything on the news about it, and I had never heard from any of the other prostitutes about these girls being missing."

"That's surprising, surprising," Nowak said.

"Yeah."

"What did you think about that?"

Mailhot said he figured something might be up when he tried to pick up another prostitute and she ran away from him.

"Well, I knew there was one prostitute that I tried to pick up once and she, like, ran away from me, so I figured that might have something to do with it," he said. "I figured she might have heard something."

The detectives wanted to know if Mailhot had murdered any other women that he hadn't yet told them about.

"But you're absolutely sure there were no other girls," Nowak said.

"Those are the three."

"Any down in Lincoln, any of the stuff happen when you lived out there?" Lee asked.

"No."

"Would you agree that it's kind of an odd coincidence that we're in this situation today and one of the [missing] girls is from out in your neck of the woods up there in Lincoln?" Nowak asked.

"Yeah, but like I said to him, I'm confessing to three murders right now," Mailhot responded. "I'm not going to not confess to a fourth one. I understand exactly what you said about families and friends needing closure. I know."

Mailhot said he wasn't going to admit to killing just three women if there were others.

"No, we're not asking you or want you to admit to anything that you didn't do," Nowak said. "Absolutely not."

"No," Mailhot said, agreeing with Nowak.

"I mean, that would be a cruel thing, right? To give the families of these three some final closure, but not close the door on any of the—" Lee said as Nowak finished his sentence.

"Rest of them," Nowak said.

"Yes, yes," Mailhot agreed.

"Are the other missing girls—any idea, you know, where they are?" Lee asked. "Their families are entitled to the same closure."

"Yes, I understand. I'm not gonna hide that at all. It's just these three right here," Mailhot said, pointing to the pictures of the dead women. "Those are the only three I've ever killed."

"Did you ever consider coming to the police after the first one?" Nowak wanted to know.

"Yes. [But] I was too afraid. Like right now, my life is over, you know?"

"Did you take any steps to tell anybody?" Nowak asked.

"No."

"Nobody then?"

Mailhot told Lee and Nowak that he never told anyone what he had done—not even when he was drunk. He said he wanted to, but he never did.

"Did you ever lay hints to anyone?" Nowak asked.

"I don't think so."

"Being in a drunken state, you never told anybody?" Lee asked.

"No, I didn't."

"I saw a lot of pictures from the bar—you know a lot of guys that you hang out with—you never told any of them? Anybody?"

Mailhot said he never told anyone.

"So it's a secret that you've been keeping to yourself that's been eating away at you," Lee said.

"What about the second girl? Did you consider coming to us? What were you thinking after the second girl—about coming to us?" Nowak asked. "Did you say like, 'Holy shit, not again,' or what was your reaction?"

"Yeah, it was that."

"Did you consider coming to anybody or telling anybody about her?"

"Yeah, I considered telling people about all three. I was considering going to see, like, a psychiatrist, or maybe just tell a couple of my friends that I really trust."

In the end Mailhot never told anybody about the murders.

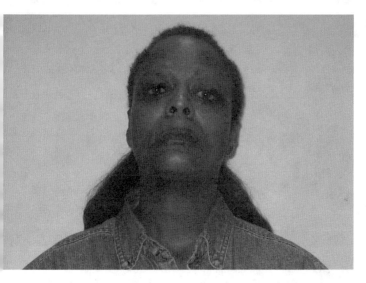

Teese Morris. *(Photo courtesy of the Woonsocket Police Department)*

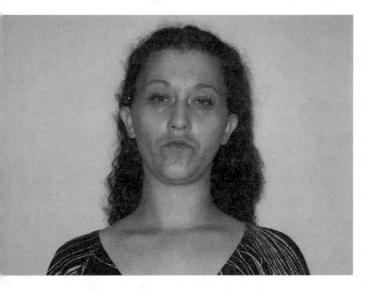

Jocilin Martel. *(Photo courtesy of the Woonsocket Police Department)*

From left to right: Lieutenant Steve Nowak, Captain Ed Lee, Jr., and Detective Gerard Durand. *(Photo courtesy of the Woonsocket Police Department)*

The building where Jeffrey Mailhot lived.
(Photo courtesy of the Woonsocket Police Department)

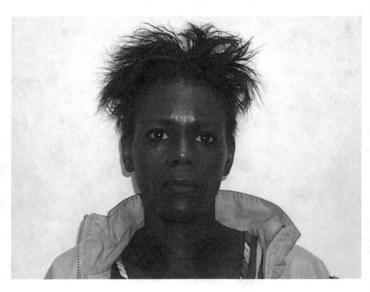

Audrey Harris. *(Photo courtesy of the Woonsocket Police Department)*

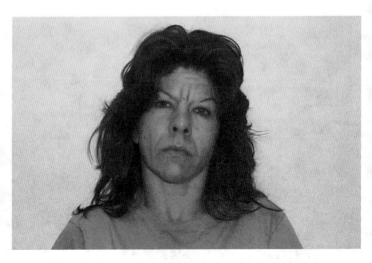

Christine Dumont.
(Photo courtesy of the Woonsocket Police Department)

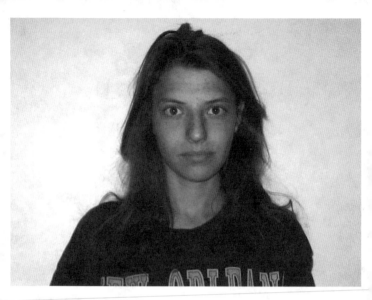

Stacie Goulet. *(Photo courtesy of the Woonsocket Police Department)*

Jeffrey Mailhot. *(Photo courtesy of the Woonsocket Police Department)*

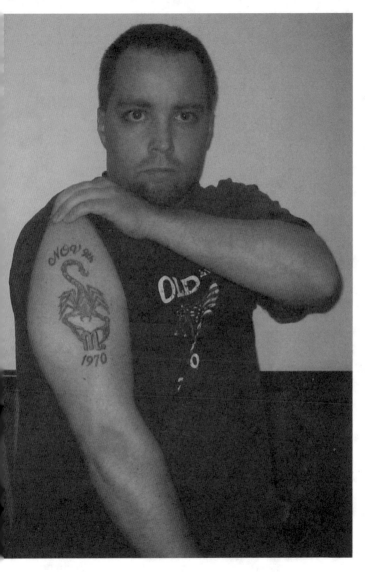

Jeffrey Mailhot displaying his tattoo for the police.
(Photo courtesy of the Woonsocket Police Department)

Mailhot's kitchen.
(Photo courtesy of the Woonsocket Police Department)

Mailhot wore some of these clothes when he dismembered Audrey
Harris. *(Photo courtesy of the Woonsocket Police Department)*

The Kid Rock T-Shirt Jeffrey Mailhot was wearing when he dismembered Audrey Harris. *(Photo courtesy of the Woonsocket Police Department)*

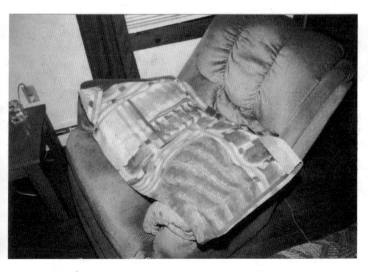

The pillow Mailhot used to snuff the life out of Audrey Harris. *(Photo courtesy of the Woonsocket Police Department)*

The bathtub where Mailhot dismembered his victims.
(Photo courtesy of the Woonsocket Police Department)

Even Mailhot's cleaning supplies were stored neatly under the kitchen sink. *(Photo courtesy of the Woonsocket Police Department)*

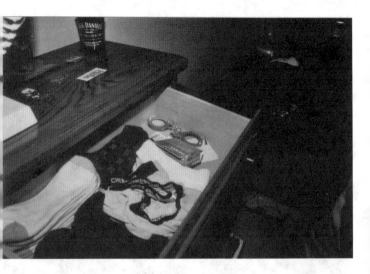

Mailhot's socks and underwear were neatly folded in his dresser drawer. *(Photo courtesy of the Woonsocket Police Department)*

Mailhot's living room, with Steve Nowak in the background. *(Photo courtesy of the Woonsocket Police Department)*

The handsaw Mailhot used to cut up Stacie Goulet.
(Photo courtesy of the Woonsocket Police Department)

The nicks made in Mailhot's bathtub when he dismembered his
three victims. *(Photo courtesy of the Woonsocket Police Department)*

Police look for the remains of the three women at the Central Landfill. *(Photo courtesy of the Woonsocket Police Department)*

...ice sifting through the trash and garbage at the landfill hoping ...find the remains of the three murdered women. *(Photo courtesy of the Woonsocket Police Department)*

Police search for the remains of Audrey Harris, Christine [
and Stacie Goulet at the Central Landfill in Johnston, F
Island. *(Photo courtesy of the Woonsocket Police Departn*

Police find the cut up remains of Stacie Goulet at the state landfill.
(Photo courtesy of the Woonsocket Police Department)

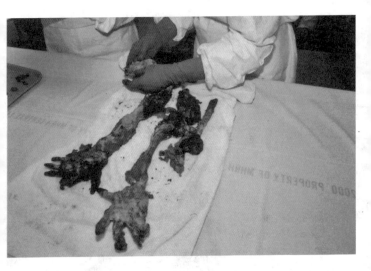

Stacie Goulet's dismembered arms.
(Photo courtesy of the Woonsocket Police Department)

Assistant Attorney General J. Patrick Youngs III. *(Photo courtesy of the Woonsocket Police Department)*

Mailhot's attorney Robert Mann *(left)* and Mailhot at his sentencing. *(Photo courtesy of the Woonsocket Call)*

Mailhot, who was crying, and his attorney Robert Mann at Mailhot's sentencing. *(Photo courtesy of the* Woonsocket Call*)*

Ray Boerger, Stacie Goulet's father, at Mailhot's sentencing.
(Photo courtesy of the Woonsocket Call*)*

Madeline Desrochers, Christine Dumont's sister, at Mailhot's sentencing. *(Photo courtesy of the* Woonsocket Call)

Left to right: Ed Lee, Jr., Steve Nowak, and Jocilin Martel at Mailhot's sentencing. *(Photo courtesy of the* Woonsocket Call)

Chapter 10

The detectives, however, were still not convinced that Mailhot had only killed three women. The way they figured it, he probably started off by just disposing of the bodies, and worked his way up to dismembering them.

"Did it get easier each time to dispose of the bodies? Or harder each time, huh?" Nowak asked. "You figure we're probably looking for others too. I mean, to be honest with you . . . there's reasons why we asked you where you learned to start cutting them up to hide them," Nowak explained. "'Cause usually it doesn't start right off the bat like that. Usually people do what you said—roll them up in a rug and throw them somewhere, because they're scared. They usually [think], 'Holy shit. What the hell did I get myself into?' It usually takes a while to progress to cutting them up."

Mailhot repeated that the reason he cut the women up was because he was afraid of getting caught. He wanted to get rid of the bodies before anyone found out he had killed them.

"It's over now, but do you feel this would have

happened again?" Lee asked. "Do you think this would
have happened again? You can't help it. It's not the alcohol either, is it? It's something inside."

"I guess. I think the alcohol may trigger it, but it's
something inside me."

"Something inside of you?"

"Yeah, I couldn't tell you in words what it is, but I do
have a big problem."

"Yeah," Lee said.

"I have a problem."

Mailhot admitted that although alcohol may have
triggered his actions, it wasn't the cause of them. He
said whatever was inside him that made him kill had
started during adulthood, not when he was a child.

"Let's face it, you said every time it's because of drinking, but it's not because of drinking, because the first
time that this happened with Audrey, you [would] have
dropped it," Lee said. "You would have put down the
bottle. You know?"

"Yeah."

"How often do you drink?"

"I drink on weekends. I'm not an alcoholic."

"So it's something else that's driving you other than
the alcohol. So let's clarify that," Lee told Mailhot.

"I agree. I agree."

"So you agree that it's not the alcohol."

"No, no, this is much deeper."

"It's not your intoxicated state that would have you
do this," Lee said.

"No."

"It's—it's you."

"When did this thing inside of you start?" Nowak
asked.

"I really don't know."

"Since you were a kid?"

"No, no."

"Has it grown stronger since then?"

"No. It was at some point in my adult life."

"Did you ever have a problem with women before?" Lee asked.

"I never had a serious problem with women. I've never actually been in a serious relationship. I've never lived with a woman. I've gone out. I've had girlfriends for, you know, months at a time and stuff, but never anything serious. I've always kind of, like, backed away, 'cause I always felt there was something about myself that I knew—I mean, I wasn't worried about hurting them, but I knew, like, there was something about me that wasn't normal."

"When did you first know that . . . something inside you wasn't right? Twenties, thirties? How old are you now?" Nowak wanted to know.

"Twenties, thirties. I'm thirty-three right now. Somewhere in, like, [my] twenties."

Lee and Nowak then began to question Mailhot about the murder of Audrey Harris. Mailhot told them he didn't want to choke her, but once he realized what was happening, he was scared to death and knew he had to finish what he started.

"Let's talk about how they were getting choked," Lee said. "What happens? You pick her up, bring her to the apartment and then let's explain in detail what happens then."

"This is the [first one]?" Mailhot asked.

"Audrey Harris," Lee responded.

"Yes, we were just going to have sex and then I just choked her."

"How did you do it?"

"I came up from behind her and I put my arm around her neck and wrestled her to the ground and choked her, and then she was still breathing and so I stuffed a pillow over her face until she died."

"Okay, so it wasn't an accident," Lee said.

"No, no."

"You choked her."

"I mean, I didn't want to do that."

"Okay."

"But then once I realized what was happening, I was just scared to death."

"You had to finish," Lee said.

"I had to, yes. I had to finish."

"Okay, and you put a pillow over her head until—" Lee didn't have a chance to finish his sentence before Mailhot responded.

"Until she died. Until she stopped breathing. Until she died."

"That pillow still at your apartment?"

"Yes."

"Where? Where is it?" Nowak asked.

"I believe it's in my living room."

"What's it look like?"

"It's, like, a multicolored pillow. It's, like, blue, tan—it's the only pillow in my living room."

The cops asked Mailhot if Audrey said anything to him while he was smothering her. Audrey wasn't doing any talking, he said. After he choked her, he said, she was spitting up blood and she had her eyes open. That's when he realized she was dying and he knew he had to finish her off. Same thing with Christine Dumont, except he didn't use the pillow.

"We came back to my place and we were in my kitchen and I just did it again."

"You came up from behind?" Lee asked.

"Yes."

"Okay, and then?"

"The same thing—I just wrestled her to the ground and choked her until she died."

"Okay, no pillow this time?"

"No."

"This time you just held on until you knew she was no longer with you?"

"Yes."

"Until she was dead?" Lee asked. "So you squeezed her until you knew she was dead."

"Hm-hmm."

"This wasn't an accident?"

"No."

"You—you made sure that she died?"

"Yeah."

"In your choke hold this time?"

"Yeah."

"No pillow after? [Then] what did you do?"

"Then I disposed of the body, like I said. I put her in my bathtub and the next day I cut her up and dumped her."

"Okay. Stacie? Stacie Goulet—you've already said you picked her up on the way home and brought her back to your house. What happened?" Lee asked.

"Pretty much the same thing that happened with that one," Mailhot said, pointing to the photo of Christine Dumont.

"With Christine?" Lee asked.

"Choked her, and with Christine, yes."

"You choked her?"

"Yes."

"The same choke hold?" Lee asked.

"The same choke hold," Mailhot repeated.

"Until she—"

"Until she died," Mailhot said before Lee could finish the sentence.

"How did you know they were dead?"

"I just left them laying there, and, I mean, I could just tell they were dead."

"Did you check? Did you know how to check for a pulse or anything like that? Did you check if they were breathing?"

"I kind of felt if they were breathing or not, and there was no breath."

"So, like the others, like Christine, this was no accident."

"No."

"You squeezed her until she died? You choked her until she died. Until you were certain she was dead? Is that correct?"

"Yes."

Now it was Nowak's turn to get some answers.

"How could you control it with the other girls? The girls that you choked that didn't go this far?" The cops still weren't convinced Audrey, Christine and Stacie were this guy's only victims.

"I don't know. It was just a situation-by-situation thing, I guess. I don't know."

"Were there some that you wanted to kill?"

"No."

"All the ones that got away you allowed to get away?"

"No, no, the ones that got away, they struggled free. And the ones that passed out and I let back up, and I stopped and they left."

"Did you think they were dead?" Nowak asked.

"I didn't think so, 'cause they were still kind of breathing."

"Okay, and what happened when they woke up?"

"They got up and they were confused and said, 'Oh, my God.' You know, they couldn't believe what happened."

"Why didn't you finish the job on them?"

"I don't know. I just don't know."

"Did you tell yourself you wanted to stop then?"

"Yeah."

"Were there some that, had they not fought with you, they wouldn't be here either?" Nowak asked. "They'd probably be in trash bags?"

"Could be, yeah."

Lee then asked Mailhot if he remembered one of the women who woke up naked on the floor and found something "sexual" on her chest. Lee asked Mailhot if he had ever masturbated on any of the women.

"No. No. I never did."

"No? Never? How about any of these girls?"

"No. I never masturbated. I never got any sexual pleasure out of it."

"Well, with any of the girls?"

"No."

Mailhot admitted Audrey got naked, but that was because they were planning to have sex. But he said he didn't undress her; she took off her own clothes before he choked her.

"Well, she was there as a prostitute," he said. "And she had undressed herself."

"Before you choked her?" Lee asked.

"Yes."

Now Lee wanted to find out more about the choke hold Mailhot used on his victims. Mailhot explained that it was just a "normal choke hold," something that just came naturally to him. It wasn't something he researched on the Internet. Then Mailhot demonstrated his choke hold for Lee and Nowak.

"I just come up from behind them and put my arm around their neck, like this."

"Okay, is it always that arm?" Lee asked, referring to Mailhot's left arm.

"Ah, yes, it is."

"Are you left-handed?"

"Actually, I'm right-handed."

"You're right-handed, but you used your left. What did you do with your right hand? Stand up and show us. Did you do anything special with your body?"

Mailhot stood up to demonstrate his choke hold.

"I hold on, like this," Mailhot said, holding his left arm in front of his chest like he was gripping one of the women. The he clasped his left wrist with his right hand.

"I just reached like this and just kind of, like, leaned back."

"What does the leaning back do?" Lee asked.

"It stops them, you know, like they're struggling, so it kind of, like, puts more pressure on their neck."

"And you never learned that anywhere? That's something you just picked up?"

Mailhot said he was never shown the choke hold, nor did he ever pick it up from watching wrestling or karate.

"That's not where I got it from," he said. "I just wanted to suffocate them."

Nowak told Mailhot he still couldn't understand why he let some of the women go.

"I mean, you're telling us some of them would be in body bags, had they not fought with you. . . . Why did you let some of them go?"

"I just didn't want to kill 'em."

"Did you realize something was going on at that moment, but you didn't realize it with these other girls?" Nowak asked. "Was there anybody else?"

"No."

"It doesn't matter now."

"I would tell you. I have nothing more to hide."

"Any that you may have blocked out?"

"No."

Mailhot told the cops that he was living on Cato Street when he first started choking the women and that was the only place he had ever choked or killed anyone.

"How many girls have you choked, including the three that have passed away, altogether?" Nowak asked.

"I couldn't give you an exact number. I would say probably upward of about, like, ten, twelve."

"Including those?" Nowak asked, pointing to the pictures of the three dead women. "Do you remember where all these happened?"

"In my apartment."

"All of them happened in your apartment?"

"Yes."

"Not anywhere else?"

"No."

"But we've got some stories from girls who were choked in other places."

"No," Mailhot repeated. "I've only choked them when they've been in my apartment."

"When did you usually pick up these girls?" Nowak asked. "On weekends, right?"

"Yeah."

"You're a working guy?"

"Hm-hmm."

"Did you go out, like, drinking with the plan to say, 'Hey, you know what? I'm going to have a few beers. I'm going to pick up a chick and bring 'em back to my place,' knowing what you're going to do all along?"

Mailhot explained that on his way home after a night out drinking beer and shooting pool with friends, he'd see a girl and decide to pick her up. But he said he never went out with the intention of killing anyone. It just happened.

"I never went out there with the intention of, you know, tonight I'm going out and killing somebody," he said. "I never went out with that intention."

"It just happened?"

"It just happened."

Chapter 11

Lee and Nowak knew they were in it for the long haul. They wanted to make sure Mailhot was going to tell them everything about the murder of the three women, so they tried to make him as comfortable as possible.

"You hangin' in there okay?" Nowak asked.

"What's that?"

"You hangin' in there okay?"

"Yeah."

"You feeling a lot better?"

"I am feeling better—nervous, obviously."

"Obviously, you're going to be nervous," Nowak said. "But you feel better and you've gotten it off your chest. And, again, we're going to continue talking to you, obviously."

"Yes."

"Because we're going to want to know everything that happened."

"Yeah."

"And we're going to continue to ask you about other girls," Nowak said.

"Okay."

Nowak told Mailhot that he really appreciated the fact that he was telling them what he had done to the women.

"I think you're a good man for doing what you're doing. I really do, no matter what you've done," Nowak said, trying to make Mailhot think that he was on his side.

Mailhot, however, had a different view of himself.

"I'm not a good person. You know what I mean? A good person doesn't do this shit, you know?" he said.

"You've got issues, but you're going to be fine, okay? We're going to help you through it and there's a lot of people who are going to help you through it," Nowak said. "But there may still be more that you need to tell us, okay? And we want to know that, all right?"

"I'm gonna tell you. I know I lied before . . . but, on my life, those are the only girls I've killed."

"Okay."

"And I have choked out more, like I said, but I have never killed anybody else."

"Okay."

"Thank you," Mailhot said.

"Okay, relax. It's tough, you know. It's tough."

"You've been doing this a long time, right?" Mailhot asked Nowak.

"Hm-hmm, a little while."

"Have you ever seen anybody do what I do?"

"I've seen people do some bad things."

"But, I mean, just be like all fucked-up about it, you know?"

"Yeah, absolutely. I mean, it happens," Nowak said. "This is a crazy world, man. Bad shit happens all the time."

"Yeah, but you know what the fucked-up thing is? I

mean, nothing really bad ever happened. I mean, yeah, my parents died, but people's parents die every day and they don't go around fucking choking girls out."

"I'm going to have to be honest with you. We're not psychologists here, we don't know what happened," Nowak said.

"Right."

"Ah, we don't know why you did it. I mean, you don't know why you did it, so there's no way I'm going to be able to tell you why," Nowak said. "The problem is that you did it and what we need to do is find out [about it]. We obviously recognize that you have a problem, or you've admitted that you have a problem. . . . You're actually helping now. You're in the process of healing now by helping the families of those girls, okay? And helping these girls because they need a proper [burial], they shouldn't just be going off into the wind, okay?"

"Yeah."

"But what we want to know is, [are] there others? That's what we're trying to get at, okay? There's other girls that you've attacked."

Mailhot again admitted that he had attacked and choked other women, but reiterated that he never killed anyone else. He also said he never thought about killing Audrey before he actually started choking her. He told the detectives he didn't remember every girl he choked, but he did remember Audrey, Christine and Stacie because they died.

"Did you ever think about it beforehand—before the first girl happened?" Nowak asked.

"No."

"You never thought about it?"

"No. That first girl that I choked, she was the first one that I ever did that to."

"Okay. We're going to be talking for a while, obviously, okay? And there may be others that come in. But can you remember every girl that you choked out?"

"I don't remember every one. I mean, I remember those three specifically because they died."

"Okay, so, obviously, those are very important to us," Nowak said.

"Okay."

"We can't stress this enough, you know. We can't be any more honest—if there's others, you've got to tell us," Lee said.

"I swear there are no more, just these three," Mailhot said. "I mean, like you said, you noticed [my reaction] right away when you put those pictures down."

"Yeah," Lee said.

"I couldn't believe you had the three of them right there," Mailhot said, referring to the photos of the three women Lee had placed on the table at the beginning of the interview.

"Oh no," Lee said.

"And I was like, 'Oh, my God.' It just brought back the fact that I really did that. But I'm not going to waste your time anymore by not . . . telling you [if] there was anybody else."

"Okay," Lee said.

"Those are the three. Those are the three," Mailhot repeated.

At this point Nowak asked Mailhot if he wanted a soda. Mailhot said he didn't drink soda, but he would like water or juice. So Nowak went out to get Mailhot some juice and Lee a cup of coffee.

"Would you be able to take us to those Dumpsters?" Lee asked.

"Yeah."

"You were last there only what?"

"Like, within the last month."

"With Stacie?"

"Yeah."

Mailhot said he dumped some of the trash bags containing the body parts of all the women in a Dumpster on the left side of the Brunswick Walnut Hill Bowl bowling alley on Diamond Hill Road in Woonsocket, as well as other area Dumpsters. However, he didn't know which parts of which women went in which Dumpsters.

"Let's clarify with Stacie?"

"Hm-hmm."

"What Dumpsters was she in?"

"Um, Brunswick."

"Where is that located?"

"Brunswick bowling alley on Diamond Hill."

"Yeah, but where's the Dumpster?"

"It's in the back of the place," Mailhot said. "If you drive around into the parking lot and you're facing the front of the building, it's, like, around the side, on the left-hand side of the building."

"And you recognize that same Dumpster? Has it always been in the same spot?"

"Yeah."

"Okay, for Stacie, what did you put in that Dumpster? Do you remember what body parts?"

"Actually, I don't remember, 'cause it was just a bunch of bags at that point and I just put them in there."

"Which vehicle were you driving for Stacie?"

"The Blazer—my current vehicle."

"The Blazer that's right out in front of your house right now?"

"Yes, yes."

"Registration on that? Do you remember?"

"It's the same."

"The plate number—do you know your plate number?"

"Um, OU-145."

"Okay, and that's the car you used for Stacie?"

"Ah, and for the second one."

"Christine?"

"Yes."

"Audrey?"

"Audrey was my GMC Jimmy that I traded in for my Blazer."

"Okay. All right, so you don't know which parts you put of Stacie where?"

"No."

"How many parts do you think Stacie was in?"

"She was in, uh, six parts."

"Six parts, and let's go over the parts, which would be?"

"The head."

"Head," Lee repeated.

"Arms."

"So we're talking the arms counted as one or . . . ?"

"Ah, two, each arm, yeah, right arm, right leg, left leg and the torso," Mailhot said.

"Are all the girls the same?"

"No, what's the name, Christine? The second one, she was almost the same as her, except I cut her torso in half."

"So she's in how many parts?"

"She's, um—seven."

"Seven parts, which are head," Lee said.

"Head, two arms, two legs, and torso in half."

"Why her torso in half and not the other girls?" Lee asked.

"Um, the first one, Audrey, I did her torso in half too."

"Okay, so seven parts for Audrey?"

"Actually, there was more parts for her, 'cause I cut her hands from her arms and her feet from her legs."

"Okay," said Lee, who was really having a hard time believing what they were talking about.

"So, like, eleven or twelve for Audrey," Mailhot said.

"You just counted them up," Lee said. "What is it?"

"Let me see—two feet, two hands, two arms, two legs, a head and a torso in half—so that's eleven."

"Okay, and why not her torso in half?" Lee asked, pointing to Stacie's photo.

"I don't know."

"She was the last—you didn't feel the need to make it any smaller? Obviously, the first one, Audrey, you cut up the most."

"Yes."

"Why is that?"

"'Cause I wanted to make sure it was small enough that I could dispose of the bags."

"So eleven parts of Audrey—eleven Dumpsters, or some in the same?"

"No, some in the same," Mailhot said. "I mean, eleven parts, but a lot of them, like their hands and their head, went in the same bag and, uh, the feet too, so there was five parts in one bag and I think that each half of the torso was in a bag each, and the legs, I can't remember how many bags I used for that."

"A question on the first girl—you said you took her out of the tub," Nowak said.

"Yeah."

"And you put her in the rug."

"Hm-hmm."

"And where did you take the rug to?"

"I just put it in the back of my vehicle at the time."

"Which is the old truck?"

"The old truck."

"Now, you have her in the back of your truck?"

"Yeah."

"Put her in the back of the truck and what happened then?"

"I was just driving around," Mailhot said. "I was just looking to see if I could find somewhere I could dump her, and I was too scared to take her out and dump her somewhere, so I just brought her back to my apartment."

"And what did you do with her?"

"And then that's when I took her out of the carpet— actually, I just left her in the carpet in my kitchen and I was trying to figure out what to do, or how I could get rid of her without anybody knowing, and then that's when I came up with the idea of cutting her up."

"What did you cut her up in?"

"In my bathtub, in my apartment."

"Where did the rug go?"

"Ah, it went in the trash."

"The regular trash?"

"Yeah—no, actually, not my trash. Honestly, I can't remember. I think I dumped it—I think there was a Dumpster in Milford, [Massachusetts]."

"When you're cutting these girls up, what do you do with the blood?" Lee asked, taking over the questioning as Nowak got up and left the room.

"There wasn't that much blood."

"Was there debris left over when you sawed them?"

"Yeah."

"Okay, and what did you do with that?"

"I'd clean it up and flush it down the toilet."

"The toilet or the tub—trying to get it down the drain or—"

"Well, whatever won't go down the drain in the tub, I flushed it."

"A lot of debris went down the drain of the tub?"

"Yeah, blood and—"

"And the toilet?"

"Yeah."

"How about the sinks?"

"No, just the toilet and the tub."

"What were you wearing when you'd do this?"

"Just shorts—a pair of shorts and a T-shirt. I think I might have been wearing a T-shirt for the first girl, but not for the last two."

Lee asked Mailhot what he did with the clothes he was wearing when he cut up the women's bodies.

"Where is that clothing that you'd wear?" Lee asked.

"It's in my house."

"Okay, blood?"

"Ah, no, I don't think so."

"You never got blood on you when you cut these girls up?"

"I got blood on me, but I washed it off."

"You washed your clothes off?"

"Yeah."

"Okay, but you had blood on your clothes."

"Yeah, a little, yeah."

"You didn't throw the clothes out?"

"No."

"Okay, so the first girl, Audrey, what were you wearing then?" Lee asked again.

"I was wearing a pair of shorts and, I believe, I was wearing a T-shirt."

"Shorts and a T-shirt. What color were the shorts? Do you remember?"

"It would be either gray or black."

"Okay, do you know where they are right now?"

Mailhot said the shorts and T-shirt he was wearing when he cut up Audrey were in his bedroom, either in one of his dresser drawers or on the floor of his bedroom if they were dirty.

"I was in your apartment," Lee said. "Your bed was unmade and there was some clothes on the floor and, I believe, there was a black pair of shorts and a T-shirt. Are those shorts the one?"

"They might be, yes. Were they black?"

"I believe they were."

"Did you wear the same shorts for all three girls?"

"Yeah, I think so. I either wore the gray or the black shorts."

"Gray or the black shorts for all three? And the gray ones are where?"

"They're also in the house. They're either in my dresser . . . the middle drawer. I might have worn them again and they might be in my laundry basket or on the floor in the bedroom," Mailhot said, explaining that he wore the shorts so he wouldn't get blood on his clothes. "They're in my bedroom somewhere."

"How about the T-shirt that you were wearing—same one for all three girls?"

"I just wore it for the first girl."

"And where's that T-shirt?"

Mailhot said that T-shirt—the black one with red, white and blue lettering and Kid Rock's name on it—was on his bed. He said he didn't throw his clothes out, because he figured they'd be okay to wear again if he washed them.

"Where do you normally do your wash?" Lee asked.

"Downstairs, in the basement there's a washer and dryer—that's where I did the washing."

"Any shoes on?"

"No."

"Are you inside the tub with the [bodies]?"

"Yes, no."

"When you are dismembering them, what do you do?"

"I'm standing outside the tub while they're in there and I have whatever part I'm cutting—like, when I'm cutting the arms, I drape it over the side of the tub and I'm cutting it that way."

"So, if you draped it over the side of the tub, then actually you're, like, keeping it all in the tub. Is it fair to say that blood's coming out of the side of the tub onto the floor?"

"A little bit, yeah."

"And then you'd have to wash that floor area up?"

"Yes."

"Okay, so there's been blood on that floor, right?" Lee asked.

Before Mailhot could answer, Nowak, who had come back into the conference room, asked him if he was ever interrupted by a telephone call or a knock on the door when he was in the bathroom mutilating any of the three women. Mailhot said he was never disturbed while he was cutting them up.

"You were pretty lucky that way," Nowak said.

"Yeah."

Nowak also wanted to know more about the saw that Mailhot used to hack up Stacie.

"It was a wooden-handled—like a woodcutting saw, and I think it's called, like, shark tooth or something. It's got a shark handle on it."

"Did you clean that saw?"

"Yeah, [with] just soap and water."

Mailhot said he got rid of the first saw—the one he used on Audrey Harris—in a Dumpster at Avery Dennison, where he used to work. He tossed it out about a month after he killed Audrey. He said he might have thrown the second saw—the one he used to chop up Christine—in the Dumpster at the Brunswick bowling alley or the Rock Ridge Apartments, but he wasn't sure.

"Did you wear gloves at all?" Lee asked.

"No."

"No?"

"Oh, I'm sorry. For the first girl, yes. I wore plastic, like, latex gloves. The disposable kind."

"Where did you get those?"

"I think I had gotten those from where I work at Avery Dennison," Mailhot said. "I take a box every week. That's where I got those."

"You still got a box of those gloves in the house?"

"I think I do," he said. "I think they're under my kitchen sink."

"With Audrey, you wore gloves, but the second two, you didn't wear gloves. Any reason why?"

"I had a couple drinks while I was doing it to calm my nerves down."

At about 10:42 P.M., Lee stopped the tape so Nowak could take Mailhot to the bathroom. Lee left the room as well and didn't come back for a while. When Nowak and Mailhot returned a couple minutes later, Nowak again asked Mailhot if he had anything else he wanted to get off his chest.

"I told you everything."

"You feel bad about it?" Nowak asked.

"Yeah, I still don't feel good about it, but I feel better because I talked about it. . . . And I just want to thank you guys for being professional, the way you have."

"No, listen we understand, we've seen this stuff, all right? It's okay," Nowak said.

"It's not okay. It's not okay."

"We've seen this," Nowak repeated. "You're going to get through this, okay? You're going to get through this. We're just the first people that are going to be here to help you; there are going to be a lot of people here to help you? Okay?"

An emotional Mailhot started to cry.

"There are going to be a lot of people to help you and we are going to help you get through this—they are going to help you get through it. Okay? Hang in there. Obviously, this is something that you are going to be dealing with for a while," Nowak said. "But it's the first step."

"I know."

"Okay, so we want you to hang in with us, all right? You know, if you need to sit down, take a break, relax, kick back for a second, you know, to collect your thoughts, it's fine," Nowak said. "We want you to help yourself. We want you to help these girls. Like I told you, and Detective Lee told you, that's what we're looking for here."

"I'm not hiding anything anymore," Mailhot said. "I'll tell you everything."

"All right. What Detective Lee's going to do when he

comes back is, we're going to go through each girl, okay? And we want you to try to remember as much as you can, no matter how minute," Nowak said. "We're going to try not to jump around, okay? We're going to try to stick to girl, to girl, to girl, okay? We're going to try to get you to tell us what happened with each one, you know? And if it takes an hour on the first girl, then it will take an hour. If it takes five minutes on the first girl, it doesn't matter. What we want to know is everything you can remember, to help us, to help yourself, to help the families of these girls, to help these girls themselves. . . . They deserve to have the truth told, okay? So everything that you can remember, however minute, you've got to let us know, okay? Do you understand all that?"

Mailhot said he understood.

Chapter 12

After Mailhot again gave Nowak and Lee the gory details of how he dismembered Audrey's body and tossed her away like yesterday's trash, the cops wanted to know where he dumped Stacie Goulet's body.

"I want to go over a few things now," Lee said. "Where's Stacie? She's the last one?"

"Mmm-hmmm."

"Let's go over the Dumpsters again and you can show us where they are."

Mailhot said he remembered where all the Dumpsters were and he could lead the cops to them. He said the first Dumpster he used to dispose of Stacie's cut up body was in back of the Brunswick bowling alley, near a lake. Mailhot said he threw three bags containing various parts of Stacie's body in that Dumpster.

"I just brought them and then just threw them in," he said.

"All right, but you don't remember what specific parts you put in?"

"No."

Mailhot said the second Dumpster was at the Rock Ridge apartment complex, at the end of a long, winding road. He said he used those two Dumpsters, as well as one at the Plaza Village and another in Milford, Massachusetts, to get rid of the bags containing the body parts of Audrey and Christine.

Lee asked Mailhot if, in the process of cutting up the bodies of the women, he cut off any identifying marks, like tattoos or birthmarks, or if he pulled out their teeth to make it more difficult for police to identify them.

But that wasn't Mailhot's style. The only reason he cut them up was to lighten the load and make it easier for him to carry the trash bags. He added that he didn't always put the same number of body parts in a bag.

"You know we're going to try to find these bags," Lee said.

"Yeah."

"Do you have any way we can help these families out by trying to locate these bodies?" Lee asked.

"I don't know what to do. I mean, that's the last thing I did with them, you know—trash gets taken away. I'm not sure where it goes."

"You didn't hang on to anything?"

"No."

"Anything at all?"

"I didn't hang on to any clothing. I threw the clothing away from the first girl and actually [from] all three, but, uh, the last two, she was wearing some, like, black—I don't know—like, black jogging pants, and she had on, like, a black tank top that I left on," Mailhot said. However, it was unclear if he was talking about Christine or Stacie.

"So all their clothing was in their bags with their bodies, or is there any other clothing?" Lee asked.

"No, the clothing—I didn't put [that] with the bodies."

"Where is the clothing?"

"The clothing is with the regular trash. It went out with the regular trash."

"From your house?"

"Yes. Oh . . . oh no, no, no, no. I'm sorry, with the first girl I actually dumped the clothing in another section of Rock Ridge."

"In a Dumpster?"

"Yes."

"And that would be Audrey?"

Lee asked Mailhot what kind of clothes Audrey was wearing the night she ran into him.

"I think, she had a coat, a shirt—I think she was wearing jogging shorts. I can't be sure at this time."

The cops then wanted to know a little something about what happened to Christine.

Mailhot said he actually met Christine on two occasions. The first time was at a local bar. After talking to her for a little while, Mailhot asked if she wanted to go back to his house. She agreed and once there she gave him a $20 blow job.

"And nothing happened that night?" Lee asked.

"No, she just left, and that was the end of that."

Lee started to ask Mailhot if he remembered what Christine had been wearing the first time he met her. Mailhot said he was having a hard time remembering, because he didn't pay much attention to clothes. Suddenly Mailhot got a little woozy.

"You okay?" Lee asked.

"Just a little dizzy."

"Take your time," Lee said, asking if there was something about the women's clothes that was making him sick.

"No, no, no. I'm actually having a really hard time, you know. I'm struggling really hard to remember. . . . I honestly didn't pay much attention to the clothes."

"You're doing a great job, you know. Take your time," Lee said. "Take all the time you want."

"I don't want to say something, like, if I'm not really sure, and I don't want to tell you something that's not [true]. You know what I mean?"

"Yeah, exactly," Lee said. "We don't want you to do that either. So take your time, but anything comes to mind you think of—but where were the clothes? Do you remember where you dumped them?"

"Honestly, offhand, I don't remember where I dumped them. I can't remember right now," Mailhot said, although he already told the detectives that he threw the clothes out with his regular household trash.

"Are they still in the house by any chance?"

"No, no, no, they're definitely gone."

"Okay. Want to go to Stacie and her clothes?"

"I pretty much kept all her clothes on her. . . . She was wearing, like, a black tank top type of shirt, and, like, black jogging pants, like windbreaker material pants. Actually, she had a pair of sneakers that I put in my garbage and went out with my garbage. . . . The trash was picked up the day after I choked her."

"You cut through her clothes?" Lee asked.

"Yeah, I cut around the pants. I mean, they were pretty light."

"Yeah, you didn't use a saw for that—to cut around her pants?" Lee asked.

"No, I used a box cutter knife."

"Where's that?"

"I have a red toolbox in my kitchen."

"On the side of the refrigerator?"

"Yes."

"And the box cutter's in there?"

"Yes."

"Did you cut her skin with that at all?"

"When I went to cut the pants, I probably caught her skin with it."

"Okay, why do you say 'probably'? You saw cuts there?"

"No, I didn't see the cuts. I mean, I felt [them]. I didn't see any blood."

Mailhot said the only tools he used to cut the women were the handsaws and the box cutter. He disposed of two of the saws and kept the third in his basement.

At that point Nowak wanted a little more information about exactly what happened to Stacie.

Mailhot explained that before he killed Stacie, she gave him a blow job, but he didn't reach orgasm.

"What happened?" Lee asked.

"I was drunk. I had a couple beers, and usually when I do, I don't finish."

"Did she just stop? She just stopped, or did you tell her to stop? Were you mad that she stopped?" Nowak asked, thinking maybe Mailhot killed Stacie because she decided to stop servicing him.

"No, no. She just stopped because she was doing it for a while and nothing was happening, so she said she couldn't do it all night because she had to go."

"Was she waiting when you grabbed her?" Lee asked.

"Yes."

"So, no other tools at all?" Lee asked.

"No."

"No pair of underwear or anything that was left behind?" Lee asked, jumping from one subject to the next.

"No."

"You weren't thinking about keeping anything just to remember them for some reason?" Lee asked, knowing if they couldn't find the bodies of the three women they needed something to tie them to Mailhot.

"No."

"Jewelry?" Nowak asked.

"That never crossed your mind?" Lee asked, continuing where Nowak left off.

"Did any of them have any jewelry?" Nowak asked before Mailhot had a chance to respond to Lee's question.

"Not that I recall—the only thing I can recall is Audrey had some type of braids in her hair."

"What did you do with them?" Nowak asked.

"They're still on her head."

Lee next asked Mailhot to describe any tattoos or other distinguishing marks the women had on their bodies.

Mailhot said Christine Dumont had one or two little tattoos, but he didn't remember what they were or where they were located, although he thought they could have been on her lower back or maybe her shoulder. He didn't think Audrey Harris or Stacie Goulet had any tattoos.

"How about any other features that stand out? Anything about these girls that you fixated on or remember about them, their bodies, their breasts, anything?" Lee asked.

"No."

"No, nothing? Feet, nail polish?"

"No, I never looked at details like that."

"Even when you were cutting off their hand or foot, you didn't notice anything like that, any nail polish or anything?"

"No, I was just trying to get through it. I was trying really not to look, as much as I could."

"How long did it take to dismember Audrey?"

"From start to finish, probably, like, a few hours."

"More than two hours?"

"Yeah."

"Two or three?"

"Probably right around three."

"Did you take any breaks?"

"Yeah. I would have a beer just to try and calm my nerves down."

"How long were your breaks?"

"Probably, like, ten, fifteen minutes."

"On all? Pretty much the same routine on all three?"

"Just about."

"Did you get more proficient [each time]?" Lee asked.

"I didn't, not really. I mean, I just kind of did the same thing for all three, you know, just walking away for a little while, you know what I mean?"

"When you cut off a limb, was there a certain spot that you would start on?"

"Yeah, I cut off, like, the arm at the shoulder, you know right below the shoulder."

"Did you do all three the same way?" Nowak asked. "Did you cut them up the same way? I mean, as far as the process—did you start at the same place?"

"Ah, yeah."

Nowak then asked Mailhot to describe exactly what he did and how he did it.

Mailhot explained that he put the dead women in the bathtub, but before he laid the heavy black plastic sheeting on the floor, he removed the little blue rugs that were around the toilet and near the sink. Next he grabbed a trash bag out of the box, opened it and placed it on the floor on top of the plastic wrap, so that when he was through cutting a body part, he would put it right in the bag and wrap it up so he wouldn't mess up the floor.

"I didn't want a mess that I'd have to, you know, have to clean up."

"Okay, so where did you start on the body?" Nowak asked.

"I think with the first one I started with the head and the hands, then the legs, and then I cut the torso in half. It was pretty much the same for all of them, you know. I mean, I would start off with maybe a leg or arm, but the torso was always the last thing."

"And the reason that you started with the head and hands?"

"There was no real particular reason."

"What was the overall reason why you were cutting them up again?" Nowak asked. "Like I told you, things are going to get redundant. We're going to go over it."

"Just to, you know, get rid of them less conspicuously," Mailhot responded.

"And the head was always first?" Lee asked.

"No, I never really picked anything to be first. I think I started with the head with the first one, and then the second one I think I started with the arms, and then I did the head and then the legs and torso. . . . If you're asking me if it was like, you know, some kind of ritual I had or anything, there was nothing."

Lee and Nowak wanted to know what Mailhot did to mask the smell as he was dismembering the women. The only thing he said he used was some bathroom air spray to cover up the smell from Audrey's decomposing body.

"Did you have to cover your nose or anything like that?" Lee asked.

"Yeah, kind of, and that's why I was using a lot of the spray."

"What did you use to cover your nose?"

"Just my hand."

"Did you vomit at all during this?" Nowak asked.

"No, I thought I was going to, but I came close."

"But you didn't?"

"No."

Nowak wanted to know what was going through Mailhot's mind after he finished cutting the women up and putting them in the trash bags.

"Did you already know where you were going to dump them?"

Mailhot said he just started driving around late at night, looking for places to dump the bags.

"Did you ever almost get caught dumping a bag? Anybody say something or ask you, 'What are you doing in our Dumpster?'" Lee asked.

"No, no."

"What was the certain time of night that you would do these dumpings?"

"Late, about ten or eleven at night—right around there."

"Okay, was that for all three?"

"Times vary. I think the first one was probably, like, ten or eleven," Mailhot said. "The other ones may have been a little sooner, maybe, like, nine o'clock. But it was always dark out. But it was never later than, like, eleven o'clock."

"Any particular reason why that time of night?"

"I wanted to, you know, just wanted to throw 'em out while it was dark out."

Usually, after he threw the bags out, Mailhot drove around for a while, then drove back home. Although the night he tossed out the bags containing Audrey Harris, he went to a local bar and had a couple beers before going home. Mailhot told the cops he never talked to anyone about what he had done.

"Did you have the Internet during any of this?" Lee asked.

"Yes."

"Did you talk or chat with anybody about it?" Lee was looking to find evidence of Mailhot's crimes tucked away in his computer's hard drive.

"No. I don't go in any chat rooms or anything like that."

"Any sites you've every looked up to assist you in dismembering or covering up smells or anything like that? You never looked that up."

"No. I mean, I guess I kind of got the idea from an episode of *The Sopranos*."

"What idea?" Lee asked.

"Of cutting up."

"Which one?"

"There was an episode where they killed a guy and they got him in the bathtub and chopped him up a little bit before they got rid of him."

"How long ago did you watch that episode?"

"Probably, like, a couple of years ago."

"Been thinking about it since then?" Nowak asked.

"No. I hadn't thought of doing it to anybody," Mailhot said. "It was just a way of getting rid of what I had done."

"So you realized what you did and you said, 'Oh shit, I gotta get rid of it' and—pow—that pops into your head and [you said], 'Hey, I saw this [show] once'?" Nowak asked.

"Well, that was for the first one and that was after having her for a couple of days, and then, you know, thinking what can I do to make this go away, and then that popped into my head."

"But you never got it on the Internet?" Nowak asked.

"No."

"Do you want to know why we're asking, to be honest with you?"

"Why?"

"Somebody around your house just said what he did probably had something to do with the computer," Nowak explained.

"Oh."

"Did you ever do anything on your computer that would make somebody say that?"

"Say what?"

"Say the reason you were getting arrested was because of your computer? Any reason that anybody would come up with that?"

"No."

"Ever do anything on your computer?"

"Look at porn with somebody on your computer or something like that?" Lee asked.

"No, I mean, I've downloaded some porn, you know

normal stuff—lesbian porn, stuff like that. Nothing, nothing, nothing—no killing, no freaky stuff," he said. "No."

"I think you obviously know we can check you history—look at everything you ever looked at on the Internet," Lee said.

"Yep."

"I mean, it's really—it's not a big deal."

"Right, no," Maihot responded.

"Just curious," Lee said.

"No, I never looked any of that up on the Internet. When I did it with the first one, I didn't have any computer at the time," Mailhot explained. "That happened last February 2003 and I bought my computer that summer. I think it was, like, July or August of 2003, I bought my computer."

"Okay."

"You got that *Sopranos* movie at your house?" Lee asked.

"No, it was an episode on HBO."

"Okay, so the thought of cutting someone up never [occurred] to you until after?"

"Right."

"This is going to sound like a messed-up question," Nowak said. "[But] while these girls were there, did you ever tape, audio/video, or take pictures before or after anything?"

"No."

"One of the things we noticed in your apartment was that you got a lot of pictures. They all have girls in them too—a lot of girls."

"Yeah, well, a lot of those pictures—it's just hanging out with friends and stuff like that."

"Were any of those girls in any of those photographs—wherever you are—prostitutes?" Nowak asked.

Mailhot explained that he went on a Carnival Cruise to Cozumel and the Cayman Islands with his friend Scott, and the girls in the pictures were just girls they met from Tampa, Florida.

"Did you go with any prostitutes on the vacation?" Lee asked.

"No."

"Down there, you didn't get any sex?" Lee asked.

"Well, I got sex from the two girls we met."

"How did everything go with them—no problems?"

"Yeah, no problems."

"No choking?"

"No choking."

"Did you think you got away with it?" Nowak asked. "Be honest with me."

"Yeah."

Mailhot said he didn't even think the police were looking into the murders of the three women because none of the other prostitutes he talked to ever mentioned it.

"So, did you think when you're ready to choke a girl, best do it with a prostitute because they wouldn't be missed?"

"Yeah, I figured, you know, hey, they're out on the street and they're just doing a trick to get their next fix of crack or coke or whatever they do. I thought, you know, maybe they really wouldn't be missed."

"What did you think about a prostitute?"

"I just thought [a prostitute] was someone who really needed help and is kind of like—"

"Lower than a normal human being?" Lee asked before Mailhot finished his thought.

"Maybe, in a way, maybe—just like the world doesn't need them as much, maybe."

"Do you dislike them?"

"I don't dislike them."

"Did you ever have a problem with a prostitute?"

"No."

"Did they ever give you a hard time or make fun of you?" Lee asked. "You said you had a problem one time performing."

"No, I've had problems performing when I've been drinking, you know what I mean? I mean I can perform, but I can't finish."

"No one's ever given you a hard time? Put any pressure on you?"

"No."

"Make you resent prostitutes a little bit?"

Mailhot said it was just the opposite. In fact, the prostitutes he'd been with when he couldn't reach orgasm were actually very understanding. They just told him they couldn't stay with him all night until he finished, but they weren't mean about it.

At that point Lee and Nowak were called out of the room for a short period of time. When Lee returned, he asked Mailhot how he was doing.

"You all right?"

"No, I'm not. I'm obviously not all right in the head. Someone who's all right doesn't do these things."

"It's over, all right," Lee said.

"It's over, but it's just beginning too," Mailhot said.

Again Lee left the room.

"Hey, Jeff, quick question, have you been with any other prostitutes since?" Lee asked when he came back in.

"No, that was the last one," he said, referring to Stacie.

"That's the last one? You haven't picked anyone up? You haven't had the urge to pick anyone up?"

"No."

"No, but you probably were going to eventually?"

"There was probably a good chance I would. Can I ask you a question?"

"Sure."

"What do you think is going to happen to me?"

"As far as what?" Lee asked.

"As far as this. I mean, what's going to be the end result for me? 'Cause I'll be honest with you right now, I really think I deserve to die, and I pretty much want to, and I've wanted to for a while now."

"Have you tried to commit suicide?"

"No, I haven't, but I've really thought about it."

"Listen, let's get through this now, okay? I know there's a lot going through your [mind]. You've given us a lot of information and you've cleared your conscience," Lee said.

"Yeah, but you know what? I'm not doing any good alive. I mean, really, especially now. I mean, everybody in my family, everybody is going to know this about me," he said. "I've been sick of life for a while, and now there's no reason for me to be around anymore."

Lee told Mailhot that there was a reason for him to continue living—to bring closure to the families of the dead women.

"You know you've done some bad things, but here's your opportunity to do some good things, okay? Try to make it all right, okay?"

"I want to help you guys makes this right for the families and everything, but after I do, I just want to die. I just want to be done with it, you know what I mean? And like I said, this isn't something I'm thinking now because of all this. This is something I have been thinking about for a long time—for years now. I'd say, probably the last six, seven, eight years."

"Why?"

"Not because of anything bad happening to me. I've had a very fortunate life. My parents got divorced when I was nine and they both died at a young age, but they both loved me."

Mailhot said everyone in his family loved him and would do anything for him. The sad part, he said, was despite their love he had been slowly alienating himself from them.

"I just don't want to go on anymore. I really, really don't. I know I owe it to these families to do my part to help you guys do what you have to do."

Lee told Mailhot he had to be strong and keep it together to help the families.

Mailhot said he told a good friend of his named Wendy Livingston how he felt inside and that he wanted to end his own life.

"Did you confide in her about the girls?"

"No."

"Were you thinking about it?"

"Yes, I was thinking about it, but I didn't want to."

Mailhot said he'd felt like killing himself for a long time and maybe in some way those feelings had something to do with why he killed Audrey, Christine and Stacie. Mailhot stressed that he never told Wendy anything about what he did to the three women.

"It really didn't have anything to do with the girls," he said. "I was just confiding in her how I felt on the inside."

"Have you felt like this for a long time?"

"I've felt like this for a long time."

"And you've only acted on it in the last year?"

Mailhot said that maybe in some way that he didn't understand, the fact that he felt so bad inside might have had something to do with why he started killing prostitutes.

"But I've felt this way for a long time and I've never considered killing anybody else but myself," he added. "I've never wanted to end another life but my own."

"Okay," Lee said.

"And Wendy can tell you about the conversation we had."

"Did you ever tell her you did some bad things?"

"No. I never got into any of that. She doesn't know any of this."

"Why should I take you at your word?" Lee asked. "I know you've been great with us, but why should I take you at your word. I mean, how can you stress to me that there are no other women?"

"I don't know any way that I can make you believe it. I really don't. All I can tell you is there are no other women. Those are the three right women, right there," Mailhot said, pointing to the pictures of the women on the table. "The only women I have ever murdered. The only people I've ever murdered. I've never murdered anybody else."

Mailhot swore he never murdered any other women or men, for that matter. He said admitting to one or more murders at that point didn't really matter.

"It's not going to make my life any easier or harder, you know what I mean?"

"Okay," Lee said.

"My life is already over, man, and I really want it to be over. I really do."

"You know that's for other people to decide, but that's not something we're going to do right now," Lee said. "This is your chance to do something good, which you have been doing, okay."

"And I will. I'll do whatever you guys need me to do."

"And I appreciate that and I'm sure the families will appreciate it," Lee said.

"I apologize for lying in the beginning."

Lee next asked Mailhot to sign a consent form allowing the police to search his vehicle and his apartment with the understanding that any incriminating evidence could be used against him in court. Mailhot read the consent form aloud and then signed it.

Chapter 13

With the housekeeping chores out of the way, Lee again asked Mailhot if he had killed any other women, which he hadn't yet mentioned.

"No, no, there's no more that passed away. I mean, like, I said a couple of them I thought I recognized that I thought I may have taken home, but to be honest with you, I can't be sure," he said. "The only ones I recognized for sure were those three."

Lee asked him if he wanted to look at the pictures of the other women again. Lee wanted to know about the women who were able to get away from Mailhot after he choked them.

"I'll look through it again. I know I picked her up," he said, pointing to the photo of another woman. "I can't be sure when I picked her up."

"Let the record show that he picked out Maria Feliciano, twenty-five," Lee said. "Do you remember anything specific about Maria?"

"No. I mean, she just looks like somebody that I may have picked up."

"Okay."

"Do you remember about the one we talked about earlier—about the girl being naked on the floor when she woke up?"

"Yes."

"Does that ring a bell?"

"No," Mailhot said.

"No?" Lee asked, confused because Mailhot just said he did remember.

"No. The only thing I remember about that girl is she was about my height—maybe about an inch or so shorter than me and she was pretty heavyset," Mailhot said. "That's the only thing I remember right now about her."

"Do you remember having a violent struggle with a black girl, not necessarily with Ms. Harris, but that other black girl you ended up in the bedroom with?"

Mailhot said he remembered having a violent struggle with the heavyset black girl.

"I don't remember exactly when that happened, to be honest with you. It [happened] in the bedroom," he said. "She got away from me after I wouldn't let her go. She was begging me to let her go."

"What did she say?" Lee asked. "Do you remember what she was saying for you to let her go?"

"I think she called me 'master' at one point. 'Please, Master, please let me go, don't hurt me,' something like that."

"Did she try anything more personal to try to persuade you not to choke her?"

"I think she offered to give me my money back and stuff."

"She mentioned that she had kids?"

"She might have."

"Do you remember her leaving anything at the house?"

"She may have left earrings or something like that."

"Do you have any idea when this happened?"

"I think it was probably last year sometime. Probably around, like, October, November."

"Where did you pick her up?"

"I think it was Arnold Street. If it wasn't Arnold, it was, like, right around that area."

"You don't remember her leaving any clothing behind—any other personal items?"

"Actually, I think she left a jacket behind that I tossed in the garbage. Yeah, she did leave a jacket behind."

"Any other items?"

"Not that I can remember."

"Okay. And that altercation took place in the kitchen?"

Mailhot explained that it took place in his bedroom.

"We were on the bed, she broke free. She managed to struggle free and she was standing in the bedroom. She's like, 'Please, let me go. Please, please, Master, please,' and I let her go."

"Do you remember someone coming to your house the next day to retrieve items with the boyfriend, uh, pimp?"

"No."

"Do you recall asking her if she was with anybody or was anybody outside?"

"I might have asked her."

"What would be that purpose?"

"Just to see if she was waiting for anybody, because I think that I remember that she said she had to go because she was in a hurry to go somewhere, and I think I said something like, 'Why do you have somebody coming here or coming to pick you up?' or 'Are you in a big rush?' or something along those lines."

"Did she have anything to eat or drink at your house?"

"Um, she may have had a beer. She may have opened a beer. I don't remember for sure."

"Would you describe her again?" Lee asked.

"She was, you know, black and she was pretty heavy-set."

"Facial features, eyes, anything stick out a little bit?"

"Um, no."

"Do you remember her name?"

"No."

"Where'd you pick her up again?"

"Either Arnold Street or, like, right in the surrounding area."

"Any of these girls ever fight you back and cut you or anything like that?"

"Maybe they left a couple scratch marks or something."

Mailhot said one of the women gouged his eyes to get away from him. When that happened, he let her go.

"So bad injury?"

"No."

"Did you have to seek medical attention for that?"

"No. When she tried to stab me to get her finger in there, I let her go."

"Okay. Do you remember another girl passing out, and when she came to, you let her go?"

"Hmm."

"What makes you decide whether they're going to live or not?"

"I honestly don't know. It's just a random thing."

"Did she turn around and run out of the apartment?"

"No, I think when she was leaving, I think, I was walking her out and I got behind her and I started choking her."

"But what happened? Was that the first time you choked her?"

"Yeah."

"But you let her go without further incident?"

"Yes, I let her go, and she was out on the floor for about probably a minute or two, and then she came to, got up and just left."

"Do you remember what time that was?" Lee asked.

"What time of night?"

"What time of year?"

"Oh, I can't be sure on that."

"Any other altercations that stick out with girls—any violent struggles?"

"No. Uh, there was one other one that struggled and got away."

"You weren't thinking about sending her away, especially when she's going to call the police?"

"At that point I kind of freaked out. I just wanted her to go. I was just doing whatever I could just to get her to leave at that point."

"What are you thinking when you're driving around and you're going to pick up prostitutes? Are you thinking of the sex aspect of it, or are you thinking more of the choking? Does that come into play when you're out there?" Lee asked.

"I'm just, you know, thinking about having sex and maybe getting a blow job."

"I mean, what were you thinking when you were picking up Stacie, the last one? I mean, you already killed two girls—what's in your mind? I'm just trying to understand—to see what's going on, that's all. Does it come into play sometimes?"

"I think so, yeah."

"Is it a rush?" Lee asked.

"It can be, yeah."

"When's the biggest rush—what part of it?" Lee asked.

"I would say the actual getting them into my place."

"Yeah, the lure. Once they're in the door and the door shuts," Lee said. "Every one of them occurred in your apartment, the choking?"

"Yeah."

"Have you ever choked anyone outside of that apartment?"

"No."

"Maybe you could say it like that. . . . Maybe it's because I know that building. There's no one else in that building with me, so it's like privacy."

"How come?"

"There was an old lady that used to live in the apartment next to me and she passed away after the first three years I was there," Mailhot explained. "Then after that, my landlord didn't rent out the top-row floors at all."

"How'd she die?"

"Heart attack or something. She was, like, eighty-something, I think. I think she was my landlord's aunt."

Lee wanted to know if Mailhot had ever thought about moving to a new place after he murdered Audrey, Christine and Stacie. He admitted he thought about it, because he figured if he left the apartment, maybe things would change.

"I don't want to be the kind of person that does this kind of thing," Mailhot said, adding the only reason he stayed was because the rent was only $310 a month.

"But like you say, it was actually the rush—once you actually get them in the door. Do you think of your apartment in any certain way, or the house—how it's empty like that, almost like a dungeon or whatever?"

"No. I just think that if something were to happen in there, you know, there's nobody in the house—so, most likely, nobody would hear or see anything."

"Yeah. And you don't have people that visit you that often?"

"Not at nighttime, not usually," Mailhot said. "Nobody usually comes unexpectedly."

"What about your windows? Like I noticed in the past few days, your windows are really open."

"Yeah."

"When you're bringing someone in, do you make it a point when they're there to shut your windows or anything for the sound?" Lee asked.

"No. I never really planned on bringing somebody in—it's never like a really big plan."

"Is that why the choke? Sound?"

"No, really. It's just the way of doing it, I guess."

"Tell me about the choke," Lee said. "Any rush come with it?"

"No, I guess what I was looking for was to end their life."

"How come?"

"To be honest with you, I really don't know. I mean, I'm no friggin' psychologist," Mailhot said. "I don't know, maybe it's something to do with taking these bad feelings out on somebody else and maybe . . . that will make me feel better. But it doesn't and I still did it anyway."

"You don't know where those bad feelings come from?"

"I think it's nowhere specific—it's nothing that happened to me as a kid or anything."

"Nothing traumatic in your childhood."

"Nope."

Mailhot said the only traumatic thing that ever happened to him was when his parents died of cancer. He said he was depressed after that, but he didn't think that was where the bad feelings came from.

"I know there are good people in the world, but I just feel the way things are going in the world and just all the things you see—I know it's stupid for me to say this, but all the killings and all the drugs. I mean, the world is just somewhere I don't want to be anymore. I really don't," Mailhot said. "And I'm pretty much living out my life right now. I'm not going to do anything special with my life. I'm not really special. I'd like to have a million dollars and do all kinds of things, but I'm not motivated enough to make it happen, you know what I mean? And I know I'm not doing any real good and I'm not really a family guy. I mean, I love my family, but I really don't enjoy going to visit family members and stuff like that for the most part.

"It's like over the last seven or eight years, these feelings have grown stronger and stronger. I kind of like to isolate myself in my apartment and just watch TV and I won't answer my phone when people call me. I just don't want to have anything to do with anybody, you know what I mean?"

Lee then asked Mailhot if he had any other family. Mailhot told him about his aunt Lucille, who lived in nearby Pawtucket.

"She's the most wonderful woman," he said. "She's the nicest, kindest woman, and there's no reason on earth that she deserves a nephew that she loves so much who doesn't contact her whatsoever. I mean, it probably breaks her friggin' heart, you know. But, yet, I don't call her anyway."

"Did you stop calling her after the first murder?" Lee asked.

"No."

"Did that have anything to do with it?"

"No, I mean, in the end it had a little something to do with it, but it's not the real reason," Mailhot said. "I've felt this way. I've been isolating myself more even, you know, before this started to happen."

"Who do you feel bad for, the actual girls that are dead or the families?" Lee asked.

"Probably the families," he said. "Because, I mean, the way I looked at it—I mean, I know their families love them and everything like that, but the lifestyle they had—I mean, they were just going down the toilet anyway," Mailhot explained. "I mean, they weren't doing any good. I mean, they weren't doing themselves any good. They're just, you know, into that world of drugs and prostitution. In a sick way I was thinking maybe I was doing them a favor."

"Yeah," Lee said.

"Because they're killing themselves anyway, you know. That's actually the way I looked at it, kind of— they're just out there spreading diseases and stuff like that."

"Is that something you were worried about?"

"To be honest with you, no," Mailhot said.

"Does that make you mad?"

"I mean, a little, but it's not the main thing."

"Did you ever catch any [disease]?"

"No. I mean, the last time I was tested was when I had a physical for the job I'm at now."

"Did you have an AIDS test?"

"No."

"So you weren't worried about being with these girls?"

"I mean, they check for that when they do a blood test on you, right?"

"Yeah."

"Yeah, they gave me a blood test at work."

"Is it something you were worried about?" Lee asked.

"To be honest with you, no."

"So, not really much feelings toward them."

"No, I mean, I feel bad for it, but like I said, I think they're better off in a way."

"What made you talk to us about it?"

Mailhot said he just wanted to get everything off his chest and be totally honest. He said he wanted to do what was right for the families—to give them closure.

"I don't want to hide anymore. I don't want to have this shit inside me anymore," he said. "I really just want to be done with everything. I want to do what I have to do to help the situation in any way I can, and then I want that to be my last act, you know what I mean. I want to do what's right for those families. I know it's not going to bring their family member back, but like you said, do as much good for them as [I] can because of the bad I've done."

"That's very important," Lee said.

"I'm not expecting any forgiveness or anything from them," Mailhot said. "I'll do what I can to help you guys do what you need to do to help them get closure."

As Mailhot continued to look through the book of photographs of other prostitutes, he recognized a name.

"Do you know if she has a sister or relative named Jessica, because I recognize the last name?"

"As a prostitute?"

"No, I went to school with her."

"Hmm, I don't know for sure," Lee said. "Let me check into that for you, though."

"You don't have to. I was just curious if you knew off the top of your head."

"Yeah. Did you go out with her or something?"

"No, she was just a girl I knew from school."

"Do you think you told me enough specifics about the other girls that were choked and that were able to escape?" Lee asked after a long pause.

"Yeah. I pretty much told you everything I remember. I told you about the girl that said she phoned the police from her cell phone," Mailhot responded. "I choked her and she passed out on the kitchen floor. She got up a couple of minutes later and she took off, and then the one, the black girl in the bedroom, that struggled and got away and I didn't mean to let her go. That's the only ones I can remember that [got away], and then the one that gouged my eyes."

"What did she look like?"

"She was tall and thin and had kind of shoulder-length brown hair."

"Where did you pick her up?"

"She was walking down Arnold Street."

"Have you ever heard about the missing girls?" Lee asked, referring to some other area women who were missing.

"I've never heard."

"On the news or anything like that?"

"No, no."

"Are you sure about that?"

"Positive. I mean, I swear if I did, I would help you out.

I mean, there's no reason for me to hold anything else back right now," Mailhot said. "I mean, I'm confessing to three murders right here."

"Okay."

"If there was a fourth or a fifth—"

"But you've got to understand there's other unsolved ones out there and you know—"

"And I know I'm a suspect," Mailhot said, finishing Lee's sentence. "I know no matter what I say, nobody's ever going to know for sure until somebody actually gets caught or confesses to it or whatever."

"Yeah," Lee said, agreeing with Mailhot.

"But I take full responsibility for [those] right there," he said, pointing to the photos of Audrey, Christine and Stacie. "That's what I've done. Those are the murders that I've done. I've never murdered anybody else."

Lee and Nowak next asked Mailhot if he had ever murdered any woman from outside Woonsocket.

"Have you been anywhere else?" Nowak asked.

"Have I been anywhere else?" Mailhot repeated, not quite sure what Nowak was getting at.

"Have there been any other girls anywhere outside of Woonsocket?" Nowak asked.

"No, no."

"Have you ever been to Massachusetts?" Lee asked.

"I've been to Massachusetts, yes."

"Ever pick up any hookers in Massachusetts?"

"No."

"Worcester?"

"No."

"Remember that conversation, we want to get over here and you did a hell of a good job getting over here," Nowak said, referring to the fact that Mailhot decided to start telling the truth. "The sergeant did a hell of a job working with you to get over here, but we need to be one hundred percent certain that we're here."

"I keep telling you that I've told you everything."

Nowak then asked Mailhot why he decided to start murdering people at that stage of his life.

"I don't know," Mailhot said.

"It doesn't make sense. Do you know what I'm saying, now at thirty-three to wake up and have [the urge to kill]?" Nowak continued.

"I haven't had urges to kill anybody," Mailhot responded.

"When did you first start getting those urges?" Nowak asked, not really paying attention to Mailhot's previous answer.

"Like, the first time that it happened with that first girl—I mean, it was an accident. I wasn't out to really kill her. I wasn't out to kill her. The second and third ones, yes. The first one, no. I didn't want to kill her. I didn't intend to kill anybody."

"Remember we talked about the girl found near where you used to live?" Nowak asked, still trying to determine if Mailhot had anything to do with the murders of any other women.

"Yes."

"Did you ever hear about [her]?"

"No."

"You never read about that in the newspaper or heard that on the TV or anything?"

"No, I never heard."

"Don't you live around a [gun] club area?" Lee asked.

"What?"

"Rod and gun club area?"

"No," Mailhot said.

"You ever been up there?" Nowak asked.

"I've been to Lincoln Woods before, but I'm not familiar with the rod and gun club."

"Have you ever gone out in the woods at all in Lincoln, besides Lincoln Woods?" Nowak asked.

"No. When I was a kid, I used to live in Lincoln, but the last couple of years, I haven't been up there."

"Do you go by there? Do you still have relatives that live up in Lincoln?"

"Yes, my stepmom lives there."

"Where you used to live?"

"Yeah."

"Same house?"

"Same house."

"Okay. And how long did you go there?"

"Not too often, maybe once a month or so."

"Are there any other girls?" Nowak asked, one more time.

"No, there are no other girls," Mailhot said. "I'm being honest with you. There's no other girls."

"Nowhere? How about outside of Rhode Island?"

"No, besides those three, there is no other girls, period, period."

"So, basically, you told us first it was an accident," Nowak said. "Then you said, 'Hey, this ain't too bad' and then [you killed] the others."

"Yeah."

"That's pretty much what happened?"

"That's it."

"I'm not saying it would never have happened again," Mailhot said. "It very well may have—the pattern I was on."

"Absolutely, we talked about that," Nowak said.

"I admit that, but there are no other girls."

Nowak again asked Mailhot if he had ever killed anyone else.

"Like I told you, you're a good guy," Nowak said. "You're a good guy at heart, because you're coming out and you know what happened was wrong and you're telling us about it and you're trying to make amends. You've had thoughts for the families. If you're not telling us something . . . that's going to eat you up for the rest of your life."

Mailhot again said he told them everything.

"There's nothing else to confess—nothing else," he said. "I've spilled my guts. I've told you everything there is to tell."

"Okay," Lee said. "What we're going to do now is, I'm going to do one more consent if that's okay with you? And that would be a swab of your mouth for DNA down the line. Is that okay with you?"

Mailhot said it was okay.

"How do you do that? You just take a sample of my mouth?"

"I don't even know if they're going to do it today," Lee said.

"I'm telling you guys. I really appreciate you being professional and everything," Mailhot said. "Like I said again, I'm sorry I started to lie to you in the beginning, but I've told you everything and I've never killed anybody else. Those three victims, those are mine. That's it. I have choked other women, but I never killed another woman. Like I said, not to say that it would never happen again, because it probably would have. It probably would have. I'm really sorry you guys have to be in the presence of somebody like me. It's got to make you sick to have to be with people like me all the time—deal with the worst of humanity."

"Well, something good happened tonight," Lee said. "It's been a long night and I appreciate your honesty. Are you sure there is nothing else that you want to get off your chest?"

"No," he said. "I mean, you guys were right. I'm glad I was able to talk about it."

"What did I tell you?" Lee asked. "It's going to be like the weight of the world taken off your shoulders."

"I know I have a lot of consequences to deal with, but it did feel good to say it."

"Okay, good. We appreciate that," Lee said. "This will conclude the interview. It's now [July 17]. It's 0204 hours in the morning. That will conclude the interview."

The cops then took Mailhot downstairs to process him into the system. Nowak then wrote up an affidavit for a search warrant for a judge to sign that would allow police to search Mailhot's apartment for evidence that he murdered Audrey, Christine and Stacie.

In the affidavit Nowak explained that he and other members of the Woonsocket Police Department had been assigned to investigate several attacks on local prostitutes. He said that during the course of the investigation police interviewed several known prostitutes, including Jocilin Martel. He said Jocilin told police that sometime during the first week of June 2004, she was picked up by a clean-cut man who took her to a house on Cato Street. She said the house was lime green with dark green shutters. She said there was a wall in the front of the property, with stairs leading up to the front door.

Nowak told the judge that Jocilin said when she and

the man got inside the apartment, he started to choke her, but she stuck her thumb in his eye and was then able to escape. Nowak said police used cable company records, driver's license records and vehicle identification records to identify the man who lived in the apartment as Jeffrey Mailhot. He said Jocilin was able to pick Mailhot out of a photo lineup.

In addition, Nowak explained to the judge that another local prostitute, Teese Morris, told police she was attacked in a similar manner on February 15, 2004. Nowak said Teese told police that she was also picked up by a clean-cut guy on High Street. She said the guy took her back to his house on Cato Street. When they were in the apartment, Teese said, the guy went up behind her and attempted to choke her, but after a violent struggle, Teese said, she was able to break free. However, the man grabbed her and once again started choking her.

Nowak told the judge that Teese begged for her life and the guy finally let her go, but she left some personal belongings in his apartment, including a medium-length brown wig, a blue sweater and a small black pocketbook containing personal papers and photographs. He said Teese then called the police to accompany her back to the apartment to retrieve her belongings, but they couldn't get into the apartment. Like Jocilin, Teese also identified Jeffrey Mailhot as the man who choked her.

Additionally, Nowak told the judge that two other prostitutes also told police they were attacked and choked by a man fitting Mailhot's description. One of the women identified the house on Cato Street as the house where she was attacked, but she was unable to pick Mailhot out of a photo lineup. Nowak said the police weren't able to find the other woman to show her the lineup.

As part of the warrant Nowak told the judge that on July 16, 2004, armed with a warrant to search Mailhot's apartment for evidence of the attacks on Jocilin and Teese, he and Lee set up surveillance on Cato Street. He said when Mailhot got home from work, they arrested him and brought him back to the station, where he was given his Miranda rights and then confessed to murdering three women, cutting them up with a handsaw, putting them in trash bags and disposing of them in various Dumpsters in the area. Nowak told the judge that Mailhot said he flushed excess human tissue, fluids and bone down the bathtub drain or the toilet.

After reading the affidavit, the judge okayed the search warrant.

Chapter 14

Lee and Nowak knew the Mailhot case was one of the biggest cases Woonsocket had ever seen and they wanted to make sure the detectives worked together and did everything by the book. They didn't want a repeat of what had happened some years earlier—a murder case that nearly brought the entire department to its knees. And a murder case that people were still talking about during the Mailhot investigation, Lee said.

"We were all talking about the Tempest case and saying we didn't want a repeat of that," Lee said later. "We wanted the people of Woonsocket to have faith in us. We wanted them to know we were going to do everything we could within the law to solve the murders of the three women."

The case Lee was referring to that brought disgrace down on the department was the 1982 murder of twenty-two-year-old Doreen Picard. The case went unsolved for years. Almost immediately after Doreen was murdered, rumors began to circulate about a police cover-up.

In 1992, Raymond "Beaver" Tempest, Jr., nicknamed

after the child star of *Leave It to Beaver*, was convicted of second-degree murder for killing Doreen with a metal pipe, ten years earlier. He was sentenced to eighty-five years in state prison.

At the time of the murder Beaver's father, Raymond Tempest, Sr., was a high sheriff in Providence County, and the former second in command of the Woonsocket Police Department. Beaver's brother, Gordon, was a police detective in Woonsocket in the 1980s and then promoted to lieutenant.

In 1993, Gordon was convicted of perjury for trying to cover up the murder and lying to the grand jury. And because of that conviction, Gordon was fired from the police department. Robert Monteiro, Raymond Tempest, Jr.'s brother-in-law, was also convicted of perjury for lying to the grand jury.

After the brothers were convicted, people realized that the rumors were true—some members of the police department had helped cover up the crime. At best, the theories went, the detectives messed up their investigation. At worst, people felt that the police deliberately covered up the evidence.

During the Mailhot investigation Woonsocket police learned that the New England Innocence Project, a Boston-based prisoner's advocacy group, had asked the court for permission to test evidence from the Picard murder case for DNA. The advocacy group believed Tempest had been unjustly convicted. And a Rhode Island Superior Court judge ruled that there was enough evidence to warrant new DNA tests.

For Lee and Nowak, that meant that the police hadn't done their jobs and they were determined to make sure they handled the Mailhot case the right way.

In late 2004, a prisoner's advocacy group petitioned the court to test some of the evidence used in Tempest's trial, contending he was unjustly convicted. In March 2005, superior court judge Daniel J. Procaccini ordered the DNA testing to take place at Orchid Cellmark Labs in Dallas, Texas. Tempest was the first prisoner in Rhode Island for whom DNA tests were ordered in his bid for a new trial.

In his order the judge, who noted that no eyewitnesses testified at Tempest's trial, said, "This court cannot think of a case more appropriate for DNA testing than one re-lying mainly on circumstantial evidence."

Under Rhode Island state law DNA tests can only be done in cases where someone was convicted based on weak circumstantial evidence and where DNA test-ing was not available during the original trial.

The judge ordered DNA testing on the murder weapon—a twenty-eight-inch length of pipe—clumps of hair found in Picard's hands, her fingernail clippings, as well as some bloodstained pillowcases and curtains found near the crime scene.

As of this writing, although the results of the tests were in the hands of prosecutors and defense lawyers, there was no indication of exactly what they were going to do with those results.

Before the Mailhot case, Lee said, the Tempest case was the most widely publicized case in Woonsocket, and it put the police department in a very bad light. In order to understand Lee's concerns, you have to under-stand the case and its effect on the Woonsocket commu-nity. Things were so bad that one Woonsocket police officer told the *Providence Journal* that "officials are so scheming that the agency resembles the treacherous Italian house of Borgia of the Middle Ages."

On February 19, 1982, Picard's body was found brutally beaten in the basement laundry room of a Providence Street residence. Her landlady, Susan Laferte, was found next to her. She, too, had been viciously battered and was just barely hanging on.

Rumors ran rampant for years that Beaver Tempest was involved in Picard's murder and that his police department connections were helping to keep him out of jail.

According to the Woonsocket police, Doreen's murder may have been the result of a disagreement between Beaver Tempest and Susan Laferte over the pick of the litter of pit bull terriers.

In 1991, a key investigator in the case, Roger Remillard, who was then the police chief in North Smithfield, Rhode Island, told the *Providence Journal* that some people testified to a statewide grand jury that Beaver Tempest attacked Picard's landlady because of a feud over the puppies.

According to Remillard, a former Woonsocket police captain, Tempest and Laferte had mated her beige female pit bull, Ginger, and his black male pit bull, Bullet. He said Tempest and Laferte disagreed over whether or not Tempest would get the pick of the litter.

So Tempest allegedly attacked Laferte in the basement laundry room of her house, and he repeatedly struck her with a two-foot section of pipe, known as an antenna mast, while Laferte's dog nursed her puppies close by, Remillard said.

Picard accidentally came upon the attack when she went to the basement to do her laundry. Not wanting to leave any witnesses, Remillard said, Tempest then beat

Picard to death with the pipe. Remillard told the *Journal* there were also other motives that led police to arrest Beaver Tempest and his brother, Gordon.

In 1990, the grand jury handed down indictments that finally led to the trial and conviction of Beaver Tempest for murder. The grand jury also charged Gordon Tempest, a seventeen-year police veteran, with perjury. Prosecutors said Gordon Tempest lied to the grand jury when he said he never interviewed a Woonsocket resident about the Picard case at the police station in 1983 or 1984. During the interview the resident disputed Beaver Tempest's alibi for his whereabouts at the time of Picard's murder.

During his trial several witnesses testified that Beaver told them that he had committed the crime and that because of his family connections to the Woonsocket Police Department, he'd get away with it. But there wasn't any physical evidence connecting him to the crime. In addition, he had professed his innocence from day one.

Despite the fact that many people believed the Woonsocket police tried to cover up the crime, others said Beaver Tempest was arrested and convicted because corrupt police officers coerced witnesses, and prosecutors went out of their way to present evidence in such a manner as to convince jurors Tempest was guilty. In fact, some said the police and prosecutors knew Beaver Tempest was innocent because they knew who really murdered Doreen Picard, but they manipulated the evidence to get a conviction against Tempest.

In either case, the Woonsocket Police Department didn't come off looking so good, and Lee and Nowak wanted to make sure the department handled the Mailhot case the right way. And as they investigated the murders of Audrey, Christine and Stacie, the Raymond "Beaver" Tempest, Jr. case was in the back of their minds. During the Tempest case friends turned against friends, and police officers turned against police officers. Lee and Nowak didn't want that to happen again.

According to Caught.net, a Web site that contains the public list of judicial misconduct, prosecutorial misconduct, legal misconduct, ethics violations and civil rights violations in Rhode Island and elsewhere, the family of the real murderer—not Tempest, Jr.—was very wealthy and had strong political ties. And according to the Tempest family, police had zeroed in on another suspect on day two of the investigation.

The Beaver Tempest murder case began around 3:30 P.M. on February 19, 1982, when Woonsocket police were called to Picard's apartment building after a fifteen-year-old tenant and her father discovered Picard and Laferte in the basement.

Doreen Picard was the oldest of the four children of Ronald and Simone Picard, who lived in Bellingham, Massachusetts. As a teenager Doreen was "girlish but tomboyish," her mother told the *Providence Journal.* In high school she was on the varsity volleyball team. She also played basketball and softball and was on the cheerleading squad. When she was a senior, she was named most valuable student athlete and crowned prom queen.

After graduation Doreen worked at a company in Wrentham, Massachusetts, and at night she took courses in early-childhood development at a local college. Doreen wanted to be a teacher.

She had only lived in Laferte's building for about ten months before she was murdered. In fact, she was in the process of packing her belongings to move to a larger apartment the next day.

Initially police thought both women had been shot in the head, but later after examining Picard's body, the medical examiner said he thought they were bludgeoned with a weapon like a shingler's ax. However, four days later police found the real murder weapon—the twenty-eight-inch pipe—in the first-floor entryway.

It appeared police overlooked the pipe during their initial investigation. However, one officer, Sergeant Michael Sweeney, remembered seeing the pipe in the area on the day of the murder. Prosecutors were not aware of that information until the day Sweeney was scheduled to testify at trial. When they found out, they sent Sweeney home before he could testify. Tempest's supporters contended they did that because the cop's testimony would have damaged the state's case.

Ultimately, however, prosecutors called Sweeney to testify. He told the court that when he first saw the pipe, he didn't think much about it because at that point he was looking for a gun. But he also said he did tell a detective about the case, but he didn't remember who it was.

Tempest's backers believed that the Woonsocket police didn't conduct a very professional investigation because they overlooked, as well as destroyed, crucial evidence during the initial search. For example, they said, police allowed a woman to clean the floor in the back hallway destroying a bloody footprint that had been discovered there.

But despite those mistakes, which appeared to be the result of shoddy police work, prosecutors were still able to convince the jury that the mistakes were part of a police conspiracy to protect Beaver Tempest so he wouldn't be arrested.

Later it was also discovered that some other pieces of evidence—evidence that might have exonerated Beaver Tempest—were either lost or destroyed at the state's forensic lab, or after they had been returned to the Woonsocket police.

In order to prove his innocence, as well as to prove that there had been no cover-up to keep him from being arrested and charged with the crime, Beaver agreed to take a polygraph test, which was administered by an independent expert, who determined that Beaver Tempest was not responsible for the murder of Doreen Picard or the assault on Susan Laferte.

However, the problem was that two detectives on the case were not satisfied with the way the test was conducted and wouldn't accept the results. Tempest's supporters believed that the two detectives were covering up for someone else and that no one in the Woonsocket Police Department had covered up anything to protect Raymond "Beaver" Tempest.

For years the investigation into the murder of Doreen Picard hit a number of roadblocks, least of which was the fact that the surviving victim, Susan Laferte, said she couldn't remember anything about the incident. Laferte was in a coma for several weeks after she was beaten. When she came out of the coma, she had even forgotten her husband and two young daughters.

In 1991, there was another twist to the Picard murder case that again made people think police were covering up the case and intimidating witnesses. At that time, Daniel "Danny" Shaw, the state's star witness, changed his version of the murder. Despite having said for years that he wasn't with Beaver Tempest the day Doreen was murdered, he changed his story and told police he saw Tempest beat the young woman to death.

But Shaw, a convicted felon and admitted alcoholic, then told Woonsocket commander Rodney Remblad that he saw Beaver Tempest repeatedly beat Doreen with a two-foot pipe in Laferte's basement on February 19, 1982. According to Shaw, Tempest attacked Doreen because she caught him beating Susan Laferte. Shaw said Tempest said he had to kill her so she wouldn't tell police he had beat Laferte. Shaw told police he was too afraid to stop Tempest.

That was the break in the case the police needed.

But Beaver Tempest's supporters maintained that police coerced Shaw into lying. Just months earlier when he had testified at Tempest's bail hearing, Shaw said he saw Tempest beat Laferte, but he left the house before Picard was killed.

So why did Shaw change his testimony? He said it was because he felt guilty covering up Picard's murder and just couldn't take it anymore. Shaw also said he never told police the whole story because he thought once Beaver Tempest had been arrested and sent to jail, he would confess.

But Raymond Tempest, Jr.'s lawyer and others said Shaw's change in testimony called into question his credibility.

According to Tempest's supporters, Shaw had told anyone who would listen that Beaver Tempest didn't murder Doreen Picard, and he, Shaw, wasn't in the basement of Laferte's apartment building the day she was killed. Shaw also complained that Remblad was pestering him and trying to get him to lie and say Beaver Tempest killed Doreen. Tempest's backers alleged that prosecutors intimidated Shaw by threatening to indict him if he didn't tell the truth—*their* truth.

But from the very beginning Shaw denied he was with Beaver on the day Doreen was murdered. He did, however, say he had gone to Laferte's building with Beaver the day before the murder.

Prosecutors tried to get Shaw to say he was mistaken and he was really there the day Doreen was killed, and that he saw Beaver beat both women. Shaw continued to tell prosecutors and the grand jury the same story— he wasn't there the day of the murder.

But prosecutors weren't getting the answers they wanted from Shaw, so they continued to bring him back to testify in front of the grand jury. And each time Shaw told the grand jury that he was being intimidated and harassed by Remblad. Again prosecutors told Shaw they'd charge him with perjury if he lied to the grand jury. And again Shaw said he was telling the truth and Beaver didn't commit the murder.

Finally, though, Remblad was able to convince Shaw that he really was with Beaver Tempest and Beaver's brother-in-law, Robert Monteiro, on the day of the murder. Shaw gave police a signed statement claiming he did see Beaver Tempest murder Doreen Picard.

But Tempest's supporters said that police could have easily disproved the information Shaw gave them about the murder because it just didn't match up with the physical evidence. But, they claimed, the cops were more interested in clearing the case than they were in finding the truth.

It didn't stop there, though. The police and prosecutors let Shaw know that he needed someone to corroborate his story in order to make him more credible. Shaw knew just what to do. He approached a good friend and former drug dealer, Ronald Vaz, and said he needed him to back his story. He also told Shaw exactly what to tell police.

Vaz, a career criminal, then testified before the grand jury that Beaver Tempest told him on four different occasions that he had murdered Doreen Picard. His story did exactly what police wanted it to do—corroborated Shaw's testimony.

While waiting for the trial to start, Beaver claimed Shaw called him at home in December 1991. Beaver told Shaw he wasn't able to talk to him because he was a witness in the case. So Shaw told Beaver to just listen to what he had to say.

According to Beaver, Shaw apologized for lying to the police and the prosecutors about Beaver's involvement in Picard's murder. He said the police coerced him into saying he was a witness to the murder.

Beaver then gave the phone to his father, and Shaw told Raymond senior that the police and the prosecutors had used him to make up a story in order to strengthen their case against Beaver. Shaw claimed that most of the time when they talked to him, he was either drunk or high and didn't really know what was going on. He explained that he finally gave in and did what the police wanted just to get them to stop pressuring him.

Shaw said the police—especially Commander Remblad—manipulated him to get what they wanted. He said that Remblad told the other cops to ply him with alcohol to keep him off guard. He finally told Beaver's father that he was going to tell prosecutors that he had lied about Beaver's involvement in Doreen Picard's murder.

However, later that day, before Shaw was able to get to the office of the attorney general to retract his story, he was hit by a car and hospitalized for a week. When he was released, he went to prosecutors and told them that he was lying and that he never saw Beaver beat Doreen to death. He told them the Woonsocket police forced him to lie. The attorney general's office then went into damage control mode and began playing down Shaw's importance as a witness.

It now appeared that the case against Beaver Tempest was in trouble because prosecutors had lost their star witness. But they shouldn't have worried, because less than two weeks later, Ronald Vaz stepped up and gave a more detailed statement to police.

In that statement Vaz alleged that Shaw actually participated in Doreen Picard's murder. Vaz said Danny Shaw told him he punched Doreen in the head before Beaver murdered her. In addition, Vaz said, Beaver and Shaw had visited his house more than 50 times since the murder and each time they had told him that they were both involved in Doreen's murder. Vaz also told police that Beaver Tempest's brother-in-law, Robert Monteiro, drove Beaver and Shaw to and from Laferte's apartment building the day of the murder.

In his unsigned statement Vaz implicated everyone Danny Shaw would have testified against in court. Vaz was now the attorney general's new star witness.

In October 1991, before Beaver Tempest went to trial, the Woonsocket Police Department conducted an internal investigation into the department's handling of the Picard murder case. The investigation was conducted to determine if any officials of the department mishandled or interfered with the investigation into Doreen Picard's murder.

According to a report in the *Providence Journal,* "almost from the first day" of the investigation into Doreen Picard's murder, Detective Sergeant Ronald A. Pennington had been concerned about possible misconduct by Beaver Tempest's brother, Gordon, and other officers. In addition, Francis Lanctot, Woonsocket's mayor at the time, publicly criticized Lynch's handling of the case.

After the report was completed, Woonsocket police chief Francis Lynch was suspended—initially with pay, but then without pay—on administrative charges that he mishandled or impeded the Picard murder investigation. The allegations against him included the fact that he showed up drunk at the scene of the murder and repeatedly tried to impede the investigation from the beginning because of his friendship with Raymond Tempest, Sr.

Lynch was also charged with inadequately securing the crime scene, even though he was the ranking officer at the scene, and allowing Gordon Tempest to take over the investigation, even though he was the brother of the known suspect. According to the report, Lynch also withheld evidence from officers investigating the case and failed to cooperate with Rhode Island State Police and Providence police, who were assisting the WPD with the investigation.

As a result of the report, four police officers, including Lynch, were suspended because of allegations that police bungled the Picard investigation and undermined the prosecution's case. Lynch and two of the officers were ultimately reinstated, but Lynch retired on a disability pension shortly after his reinstatement.

Finally at the end of March 1992, ten years after the murder of Doreen Picard, Beaver Tempest's trial got under way.

During the trial one of Beaver's former neighbors testified that she overheard him admit he killed Doreen Picard and brag that he wouldn't get caught because his father had "paid off a large sum of money."

She also testified that in early 1983, she heard Tempest tell her boyfriend that he murdered Picard and beat Susan M. Laferte on February 19, 1982. The neighbor said that while she sat on her living-room sofa, Tempest and her boyfriend were in the kitchen talking. She told the jury that she heard Beaver Tempest tell her boyfriend that he attacked Laferte in the basement of her house. She said she heard Tempest admit that he beat Picard when she tried to stop him from bludgeoning Laferte with a pipe.

"'The other girl came down the stairs at the wrong time,'" the woman said Beaver told her boyfriend. She told the court that Tempest said he couldn't let Picard get away. He had to do her too. The woman also testified that Tempest bragged that he'd get away with the murder.

"He said his father paid off a large sum of money to make sure that Beaver's name was never mentioned about this," she said in court. "The murder weapon would never be found. It had been wiped clean of fingerprints and gotten rid of."

The woman, a licensed practical nurse and admitted former cocaine addict, told the court that Tempest said he attacked Laferte because she was "going to tell [his wife] something, and he and [his wife] had just gotten back together." Prosecutors claimed that Beaver Tempest had had an affair with Susan Laferte.

The woman said Beaver Tempest told her that she and her boyfriend had better keep their mouths shut or they would be seriously injured, because his father knew a lot of people.

The woman's statements seemed to back up the testimony Ronald Vaz provided at trial as well. Vaz told jurors that Beaver Tempest bragged about killing Picard and beating Laferte and told him that his brother, Gordon, hid the pipe he used.

But Beaver's attorney wanted to know why Vaz had waited nearly nine years to tell police about Tempest's statements. Vaz said it was because he was afraid for himself and his family and he didn't want to get involved while Beaver's brother, Gordon, was still on the police force. He added that he was really scared, because Beaver's father was a very powerful man who knew a lot of people.

But at the trial Beaver's father and brother disputed the testimony of the prosecution witnesses who said they helped cover up the murder of Doreen Picard. Despite their testimony, on April 22, 1992, Raymond "Beaver" Tempest was found guilty of murdering Doreen Picard. The jury didn't even deliberate for two full days.

In 1997, a report issued by an independent consulting firm was released that was highly critical of the WPD and its ability to do its job.

According to the report, *the public has not been served.* In the face of the report Commander Rodney Remblad retired unexpectedly and a state police lieutenant was appointed acting chief to begin to heal the wounds within the department and repair its damaged credibility.

Factions in the department created animosity among the members, the report read. *Several of these factions were associated with the previous chief.*

One of the issues that had damaged the department was the investigation into the murder of Doreen Picard.

Was it any wonder that Lee and Nowak wanted to make sure they handled the Mailhot case by the book?

Chapter 15

After Mailhot confessed, the police wanted to learn more about the soft-spoken man who had committed three horrific murders. They soon learned that as a kid growing up in a subdivision on Grandview Avenue in Woonsocket, he kept mostly to himself. His parents divorced when he was just nine years old. He attended Woonsocket schools and graduated from Woonsocket High School in 1989. His mom died of lung cancer in July 1988 when Mailhot was just seventeen. Then when he was twenty-two he lost his dad to the same disease.

As an adult Mailhot tried doing what he could to stand out. After living with his stepmother in Lincoln, Rhode Island, for several years, he moved back to Woonsocket and rented the apartment on Cato Street. He bought a $17,000 Harley-Davidson Fat Boy motorcycle and the requisite leather jacket. He loved to watch wrestling on television and even took up weight lifting to build up his body. For kicks he liked to sing heavy metal songs on karaoke nights at Box Seats, an area sports bar where Woonsocket cops often went to unwind. In fact,

Sergeant Steve Nowak remembered seeing him there on several occasions.

Police talked to some of his friends, including Wendy Livingston, his former girlfriend. No one who knew Mailhot could believe that he had murdered three women. He had never even had a parking ticket.

Wendy Livingston told police she met Jeff through a mutual friend, and had known him for about two years. She said they started dating in December 2003 and they broke up sometime in April 2004. She added that she'd always be friends with him. At the time police talked to her, Wendy said she hadn't seen Jeff for a couple months, although she had talked to him on the telephone.

Wendy said Mailhot was always polite and concerned and treated her and her family very well. She said he was a good guy. While they were dating, she called him "Muffin" and he called her "Butterfly."

Wendy said she liked rough sex—spanking and bondage—and she'd often ask Mailhot to choke her during sex. She also liked to be choked as a kind of foreplay before they had sex. But if Mailhot's grip got too tight, Wendy would tap him and he'd let her go. She said Mailhot would never think of hurting her. In fact, she said Jeff wouldn't even choke her as hard as she wanted him to, because he really wasn't into that shit. He liked it soft.

During the time they dated, Mailhot told Wendy that he was depressed sometimes and that he just didn't want to wake up anymore. Not that he wanted to commit suicide—he didn't have the balls to kill himself. Mailhot was depressed because his family liked him and because they were always calling him to see how he was doing. He just wanted them to leave him alone. Mailhot wanted to be more like Wendy, who was the black sheep of her family.

The cops also talked to Mailhot's friend Patrick Harrison. Harrison and Mailhot met when they worked together at Avery Dennison Corporation in 1991. Harrison said the last time he saw his friend was July 3. Mailhot had attended a get-together at Harrison's Woonsocket house. He left around 10:00 P.M. Harrison assumed he was going home because he still had his work clothes on. Harrison said that it was unusual for Mailhot to attend the party in his work clothes, because he didn't usually go out unless he had showered and changed.

Harrison said the pair was supposed to go to the ocean the next day, but Mailhot never showed up at Harrison's house. Harrison tried calling Mailhot's cell phone around 8:00 A.M., but he got no answer. Harrison said he went to Mailhot's house on July 9. He had gone to Mailhot's house to use his beard trimmer, but his friend wasn't home, so he used a spare key Mailhot kept in a black pipe by the front steps and let himself into the apartment.

The cops asked him if he saw anything out of the ordinary in Mailhot's apartment.

"No, it's just like every time I go there, you can eat off the kitchen floor," Harrison said. "His CDs, DVDs and tapes are in alphabetical order. Remote controls lined up in the middle of the coffee table. He was a neat freak."

During the interview the detectives asked Harrison if he knew his friend was picking up prostitutes.

"Honestly, I didn't think he had the balls," Harrison said. "When we went out to bars, he would not talk to any girls unless he knew them. I can't believe he did [this], and unless I know otherwise, I won't believe it. I can't believe he picked one up, never mind do anything else."

Detectives also interviewed Mailhot's landlord, Stephen Lovatt, who said Mailhot had been his tenant for about six or seven years. Lovatt said he never had any problems with Mailhot.

"In that time I have known him to be a good tenant," Lovatt said. "As far as I know, he goes to work every day. I remember one time he accidentally broke a window and I fixed it and did not charge him because he was a good tenant."

Lovatt said he didn't know Mailhot socially; he only knew him well enough to say hello when he saw him.

The police asked Lovatt if Mailhot ever did anything he thought was odd.

"He once told me that he got a computer and I told him I would help him with it," Lovatt said. "The next thing I know is that he's telling me he sold it. I then noticed computer boxes in the trash, so he must have gotten a new one. Other than that, I cannot think of anything."

Lovatt told the detectives that he never paid attention to Mailhot's comings and goings and had no idea if he ever brought anyone home with him.

The cops then asked Lovatt if Mailhot brought his own trash barrels out to the street for pickup.

"He will put his barrels near mine and I or my kids will take them out to the road," Lovatt explained, adding that he had never seen Mailhot take out any bags of trash in addition to the barrels.

The police canvassed Cato Street to get information about Mailhot from his neighbor, but they didn't have much luck. Most people were either not home or had never even seen or heard of Jeffrey Mailhot.

One resident who lived nearby said he never really saw anything suspicious going on at Mailhot's house. However, one incident did stick out in his mind. The man said he saw Mailhot pull his Blazer in front of his apartment on around June 26. There was a girl with Mailhot, he said. But Mailhot only stopped his vehicle for a second before quickly taking off again. Then he came back around the block, stopped and once again quickly took off. Mailhot again drove up in front of his house, but this time he parked the Blazer. The neighbor said it looked like Mailhot was trying to convince the girl to go into his apartment with him, which she ultimately did. The neighbor said the woman was in her mid to late twenties, with dark skin and black hair in a bun. The man said after they went inside, he went to bed and had no idea what happened after that.

Sometime after his arrest, police learned that Mailhot had responded to a letter written to him by his boss at Proma Technologies, the company where he now worked in nearby Franklin, Massachusetts, which produced technologically advanced metallized papers. So the police contacted Mailhot's boss, who agreed to bring the letter to the station.

In his letter Mailhot said he hoped no one at the company would have any accidents because they were distracted thinking about his situation. He went on to say that despite everything that had happened, he was doing okay and that he was getting an unbelievable amount of love and support from his family and friends. In fact, he was getting more support than he could have hoped for or imagined. And in that respect he felt like the luckiest person in the world.

Now comes the hard part, he wrote. *I know that everyone wants an explanation for the horrible acts that I committed.*

Mailhot said the first thing he wanted his coworkers to know was that he didn't plan to kill anyone. The murders were not premeditated, he said, adding that he would try to explain what happened without going into the gruesome details. Mailhot explained that nearly a year and a half earlier he was driving home alone after hanging out at a local bar with some friends. He said he was pretty wasted. Before he got home, he stopped to pick up a girl who was walking down the street near his house. That girl was Audrey Harris.

Mailhot took Audrey back to his house, where they had sex. After they finished, Mailhot said, Audrey told him she had given him the AIDS virus. However, Mailhot never told police Audrey claimed to have given him the AIDS virus.

At that point, I reached out and grabbed her around the neck, he wrote. *I was so drunk that I don't remember much after that.*

For the next couple days, Mailhot said, he didn't know what to do. He considered telling someone what he had done or turning himself in to police, but he didn't because he was afraid of losing his family and friends. So he thought and thought about how to hide "the horrible thing" he had done. Mailhot told his boss he didn't come up with the plan to dismember Audrey's body on his own. He explained that he had seen it done on an episode of *The Sopranos* and figured it was the only way to dispose of her body.

Over the next year I had many sleepless nights and many days of just trying to cope with what I had done, he penned.

Mailhot said he thought about going into therapy but didn't. He said he wished he had talked to someone about murdering Audrey Harris, because if he had, maybe Christine Dumont and Stacie Goulet would still be alive.

Mailhot told his boss he met Christine and Stacie the same way he had met Audrey—and on the same street. Neither of them deserved their fate, he said.

I don't know how to explain why I attacked those women, he wrote. *I have played those events over and over again in my head and the only thing I can remember thinking when I attacked the last two women was what the first woman said to me. I kept flashing back to that comment she made about giving me AIDS.*

Mailhot said he didn't want anyone to think that he was making excuses for murdering three women. He said he felt nothing but remorse and regret for what he had done and had given a full confession to the police.

I felt a lot of emotions during and after confessing my actions (sorrow, regret, fear, etc.) but mostly I felt glad and relieved to finally talk about it out loud, Mailhot wrote. *Now at least the families of the women know what happened to their loved ones and can begin the process of working through and dealing with the tragic news and try to move on. I know that the pain and loss they are experiencing will never be erased.*

Mailhot said he wanted to let his coworkers know that the person they knew at Proma was the person he really was.

I hope that you can believe that, he wrote. *I would never in my right mind hurt anyone. I know that in my heart. I also know that I need to get some serious help in order to find out what is wrong with me. I don't care if it takes the rest of my life; I want to understand how a person like me could do such horrible things.*

Mailhot said he knew he was a good person and he hoped that he would get better, no matter how long it took.

Chapter 16

Although his friends and family didn't think Jeffrey Mailhot was a murderer, he certainly appeared to fit the demographic profile of a serial killer developed by criminologists. The typical serial killer is a white male who commits his first murder when he is around thirty years old. Serial killers typically kill more than three people, and most of them just target strangers or people they may have seen around once or twice. Though a few travel around, leaving bodies in their wake, most kill within a specific area.

However, according to University of Houston criminologist Steven Egger, an expert on serial killers, there are a number of misconceptions that exist about serial killers. In his book *The Killers Among Us,* Egger lists some major myths about serial killers, which, he said, "are ingrained in the public's understanding of serial murder."

Those common myths are as follows: All serial killers had terrible childhoods, were beaten by their parents and were sexually abused. Serial killers are "mutants from hell," who do not really look like an average person.

Serial killers prey on anyone who crosses their path and really don't pick out their victims. Serial killers are able to stay one step ahead of police for a long time. The male serial killer is a sex-starved person, who kills because he had a horrible childhood and because of the way society has treated him. He has an unusual relationship with his mother, and he travels alone across the country and has an in-depth knowledge of police procedures, which allows him to elude authorities. He is an insane coward who preys who on the weak and helpless.

According to Egger, these myths are incorrect for a number of reasons. But the most important reason why the myths are incorrect is that serial killers are individuals, who have lived different lives and really don't fit the same mold.

Egger said the first myth—all serial killers had terrible childhoods and were probably abused when they were kids—is just not true. Some may have had it rough when they were kids, but you can't generalize and say they all did, according to Egger.

Egger is right on when it comes to Jeffrey Mailhot. There was no indication that Mailhot had it bad as a kid. The only bad thing that happened to him was that his parents died while he was young.

The second myth—serial killers are mutants from hell and do not resemble the average person in appearance or mannerisms—is also not true, according to Egger. He said there just isn't really any way to figure out who is a serial killer just by looking at the way he looks and the way he acts.

Most serial killers, like Jeffrey Mailhot, look and act just like everybody else. Many of them have normal jobs, get married, have children and hang out with friends. In fact, Egger said, they look and act "normal." But what makes them different, Egger said, is the horrible crimes they've committed, the often incomprehensible reasons they give for what they've done and the lack of remorse for those crimes. Jeffrey Mailhot was sorry for the grief he caused the families of Audrey, Christine, and Stacie, but he never felt any remorse for murdering the three women.

Egger said, contrary to popular wisdom, serial killers don't select their victims randomly. Instead, they usually put a lot of thought into deciding who their victims will be. Serial killers select their victims based on their own criteria, according to Egger. Mailhot selected prostitutes because he felt he was doing society a favor by getting rid of them, and because he figured nobody would really miss them.

Egger also said, despite what people think, serial killers don't have any superhuman abilities that allow them to elude law enforcement authorities. If, in fact, police are unable to apprehend a serial murderer, it's because of the system and society—not the superpowers of the killer. Maybe the police haven't had the right training or maybe there's not enough manpower to handle the case. There's also the fact that people who could help police in the investigation just don't want to get involved, Egger said.

According to Egger, another pervasive myth—serial killers all fit a similar profile—just isn't true as well. He said serial killers are individuals, and they can't all be lumped together.

Some of them can have great childhoods, great jobs, super families—or maybe they have nothing at all, Egger said. Maybe it makes it easier for society to deal with serial killers, if society thinks they're all alike. For if we don't know who they are, how can we stop them? he said. No one agency, not even the FBI, has all the answers when it comes to serial killers, he said.

Unfortunately, when it comes to serial killers, we really don't know much of anything, he said. But there is one thing that various studies have shown us—prostitutes are more likely to be the targets of serial killers than any other group of people.

Egger said one of the main reasons is that they are vulnerable because they are so available. That's because no one pays much attention to a john picking up a prostitute in an area that's known for prostitution, he said. And besides, who's going to go to the police to report a missing prostitute? he reasoned. Jeffrey Mailhot knew that, and that's why he knew it would be so easy to murder women who were known prostitutes.

Egger said most serial killers are psychopaths—people who treat their victims as objects, not as human beings, which is why many serial killers target prostitutes. Serial killers who murder prostitutes don't see them as someone's daughter or someone's wife—they just see them as trash to be thrown away, according to Egger. That's exactly the way Jeff Mailhot viewed Audrey, Christine and Stacie. And that's literally what he did with their remains.

But not everyone who kills more than one person is a serial killer. So what exactly makes someone a serial killer?

During his research into the mind of the killer, former FBI agent John Douglas came up with three categories to define the killing of multiple people: serial murder, spree murder and mass murder.

According to his biography on his Web site, Douglas was the legendary head of the FBI's Investigative Support Unit, and has hunted some of our country's most notorious and sadistic criminals: the "Trailside Killer" in San Francisco, the "Atlanta Child Murderer," the "Tylenol Poisoner," the man who hunted prostitutes for sport in the woods of Alaska and Seattle's "Green River Killer."

According to his Web site, Douglas has confronted, interviewed and studied dozens of serial killers and assassins—including Charles Manson, Sirhan Sirhan, Richard Speck, John Wayne Gacy, David Berkowitz ("Son of Sam") and James Earl Ray—for a landmark study to understand their motives and motivations.

"To get inside their minds," he said.

In order to understand Jeffrey Mailhot, we need to look at exactly what the experts have to say about serial killers.

The teenagers responsible for the massacre at Columbine High School in Colorado cannot be classified as serial killers, because they killed their victims all at once. In the case of the Columbine shootings, which happened on April 20, 1999, Eric Harris and Dylan Klebold went on a shooting rampage, and ended up killing twelve students and a teacher. They also wounded over twenty other people before turning their guns on themselves. Douglas classified Harris and Klebold as mass murderers.

According to Douglas, a mass murderer kills three or more victims at one time and in one place, although there may be a number of crime scenes. For example, a person might kill someone inside one building and then move on and kill more people down the street, Douglas said.

A spree murderer, according to Douglas, tends to do his killings within a short period of time. And he continues to kill until he gets caught, turns himself in, kills himself or commits "suicide by cop," by doing something that causes a cop to kill him, Douglas said. Although a spree killer usually picks his victims at random, he will most likely kill someone who meets his needs at the time. For example, he will kill for sex or money, or even because he's hungry, Douglas explained.

When it comes to spree killers, police usually know who they are. Take Andrew Phillip Cunanan, for example. Cunanan murdered five people, including fashion designer Gianni Versace, during a three-month cross-country killing spree in 1997. On June 12, 1997, the FBI put Cunanan on its "Ten Most Wanted Fugitives" list. The killings ended when Cunanan killed himself on July 23, 1997. He was twenty-seven.

Cunanan murdered his friend Jeffrey Trail on April 27, 1997, in Minneapolis, Minnesota. Next he killed architect David Madson at Rush Lake, near Rush City, Minnesota. Madson, who had been shot in the head, was found on April 29, 1997. Police soon connected the two murders because Trail's body had been left in Madson's apartment.

After killing Madson, Cunanan drove to Chicago, and on May 4, 1997, he killed seventy-two-year-old Lee Miglin, a real estate developer. He then stole Miglin's car, drove to Finn's Point National Cemetery in Pennsville, New Jersey, and murdered its caretaker, forty-five-year-old William Reese, on May 9, 1997.

Police theorized Cunanan killed Reese for his pickup truck, because he left Miglin's car in the cemetery. After

Cunanan killed Reese, the FBI put him on their "Ten Most Wanted" list.

Cunanan then traveled to Miami Beach, Florida, where he hid out for a couple months before killing his fifth, and final, victim—fashion designer Gianni Versace—on July 15, 1997. Then, on July 23, Andrew Cunanan committed suicide on a Miami houseboat.

Although serial killers also kill three or more people, the difference between serial killers, mass murderers and spree murderers is that there is a "cooling-off" period between the murders of serial killers, according to Douglas. That's because serial killers usually don't like to take risks; they want to be sure that if they commit a murder, they won't get caught. Jeffrey Mailhot killed Audrey Harris in February 2003, Christine Dumont in April 2004 and Stacie Goulet in July 2004.

Some experts believe that serial killers are "addicted" to killing, and once they start, they just can't stop. And a serial killer, they say, usually goes after strangers, but his victims are usually the same sex, around the same age and do the same kind of work. Douglas said serial killers are drawn to places where there is widespread prostitution, drug addicts and runaways—people that the serial killer figures won't be missed. Mailhot certainly fit that part of the profile.

According to Douglas, most serial killers feel inadequate, insignificant and powerless in one way or another. And in their minds, they can feel powerful by controlling others. Controlling another human being makes a serial killer feel important, almost as if he's accomplished something, Douglas said.

Serial killers never identify with their victims or even feel sorry for them. They figure they've been victims all their lives—dominated and controlled by other people. They believe they can be in control by calling the shots and deciding who lives or dies, according to Douglas.

Even though a serial killer will admit he murdered people, he never really accepts responsibility for it, Douglas said. He'll blame it on someone, or something else, or say he was abused as a child. And a serial killer may shed tears over what he's done, Douglas said, but the tears are for him, never for the victims.

Mailhot accepted responsibility for the murders, but he never expressed remorse for the victims. In fact, he said he felt he was ridding society of people who really didn't matter. And in his letter to his coworkers, he implied that it was probably Audrey Harris's fault he killed her and the other women, because she had told him she had given him the AIDS virus, and this had made him angry. He did, however, express remorse for the victims' families.

According to Douglas's Web site, serial killers will take trophies or keep some kind of memento of their crimes. Sometimes a killer will keep a victim's jewelry—something she was wearing at the time of the crime. It could even be something like a driver's license or other ID or even a photo the victim carried with her, Douglas explained. Some serial killers might cut off some of a victim's hair and keep it. When a serial killer commits a murder, he feels a sense of accomplishment; he feels so good that he doesn't want the feeling to end. Serial killers collect trophies, Douglas said, to keep up the fantasy of the crime.

While Mailhot didn't keep those kind of trophies, he did keep souvenirs of his kills, like the pillow he used to smother Audrey Harris, the clothes he wore when he cut up the women's bodies and the saw he used to dismember Stacie Goulet. Mailhot also apparently put a little dot of Stacie's blood on the July 4 entry on a calendar on his refrigerator.

Douglas said that during the cooling-off period between murders, serial killers will "pull out their trophies and just sit back in their La-Z-Boy chairs and relive the crime over and over in their minds." That would have been easy for Mailhot, because he actually left the pillow he used to suffocate Audrey on the chair in his living room.

Not all killers, though, take trophies. David Berkowitz, the "Son of Sam," for example, didn't take any tokens, because, unlike Mailhot, whose crimes were up close and personal, Berkowitz's crimes were very impersonal. He shot and killed his victims from a distance.

David Berkowitz was born on June 1, 1953. After his arrest in August 1977, he confessed to killing six people and wounding seven others in New York City, from 1976 to 1977. Berkowitz told police that a neighbor's dog, possessed by a demon, ordered him to commit murder. However, Berkowitz later claimed he only killed three people and wounded one other. He said the other victims were murdered by members of a satanic cult to which he belonged. To this day Berkowitz is the only person ever charged with the murders, but some law enforcement authorities believe he may be telling the truth.

Although Berkowitz didn't keep trophies, he visited the grave sites of the victims, where he rolled in the dirt and relived the fantasy of the kill, Douglas said.

When a serial killer commits his first murder, he views it as quite an accomplishment; it makes him feel so good about what he's done that he doesn't want the feeling to end, Douglas said. For killers, taking mementos keeps the fantasy alive.

Douglas also came up with terms to describe the different types of crime scenes: organized, disorganized or mixed.

According to Douglas, when a crime scene appears organized, it is usually premeditated and there is not much evidence found at the scene. Typically, an organized criminal has an antisocial personality. He knows right from wrong and is not insane. He is also someone who will not show any remorse for his crimes.

In contrast, a disorganized crime scene indicates that the criminal did not plan his crime. The disorganized criminal is more likely to be caught than the organized criminal, because he often leaves evidence like fingerprints, blood and semen at the crime scene, Douglas said. A disorganized crime scene may mean that the perpetrator is young, under the influence of alcohol or drugs, mentally ill or, for some reason, has trouble controlling the victim, according to Douglas.

There are also crime scenes that are both organized and disorganized, Douglas said. By way of example, Douglas points to the case of the murders of Nicole Brown Simpson and Ronald Goldman, for which O.J. Simpson was tried and acquitted.

Douglas said although the crime scene appeared to be very premeditated—the perpetrator brought the weapon, gloves and a hat to the scene—it also appeared disorganized, because even though the crime was planned out, the murderer didn't expect to be confronted by another person. Therefore, the murderer lost control over the situation, and the appearance of the crime and crime scene shifted from organized to disorganized, Douglas said. In addition, a mixed crime scene might indicate that more than one person was involved in the crime, he said.

Like everyone else, a killer learns from experience, Douglas said. And if you don't catch him right away, he'll probably get better at killing. The Woonsocket police were lucky they got the break that led them to Jeffrey Mailhot, because there's no telling how many more women he would have murdered if he wasn't caught. He even admitted to police that he would have kept on killing. And even if Mailhot had sought counseling to find out why he had become a murderer, he never would have gotten better.

According to Douglas, serial killers can never be rehabilitated, because they don't think the way the rest of us do. Because of that, their brains can't be reprogrammed— no matter how much counseling or treatment they have. Douglas said all you can do is write them off.

Mailhot was no different from any other serial killer in that regard.

"Mailhot had psychological problems," Sergeant Ed Lee said later. "We sat there and interviewed him and we tried to find those answers ourselves. He even said, 'My parents died at a young age, but a lot of peoples' parents die at a young age, and they don't kill people.' A lot of people say it's [a serial killer's] inability to love, because they weren't loved as a child. Obviously, he also had some obsessive/compulsive issues and some underlying mental-health issues that we don't know about."

Lee said what Mailhot described in his interview with police fit the profile of a serial killer.

"They live out this fantasy in their minds, time and time and time again, and then when they get up enough courage to act upon it, it becomes like someone smoking crack for the first time. They're addicted, and that's it," Lee said. "[Mailhot] admitted that he wasn't going to stop. It was going to be more frequent and he said it was something that he couldn't control."

Lee said what was so intriguing about Mailhot was that the people who knew him—his neighbors, his coworkers and his family—thought the police were out of their minds to think that he could murder three women.

"It was that whole 'Dr. Jekyll and Mr. Hyde' thing," Lee said. "People didn't want to believe that someone could be so friendly to them and be such a good guy, but who was actually a monster deep down inside and was capable of doing those things."

One of the most notorious serial killers in history, of course, is "Jack the Ripper." Although there have been many books written about "Jack the Ripper," his identity still remains a mystery. Because of the way Mailhot cut up his victims, a comparison to "Jack the Ripper" was inevitable. Although the two men dismembered their victims for very different reasons, they both murdered the same type of women—prostitutes.

For a six-week period in the late summer and early fall of 1888, "Jack the Ripper" murdered and mutilated five prostitutes. Jack was never caught—despite a massive manhunt by law enforcement. And unlike almost all other serial killers, including Jeffrey Mailhot, "Jack the Ripper" just seemed to vanish.

Jack stalked and killed his victims on weekends. Maybe that meant he was a regular working stiff during the week. It almost defies belief that he was never caught and that he left very few clues behind.

Like the serial killers who came after him, including Jeff Mailhot, Jack was probably a nice-looking guy, able to convince the women he ultimately murdered to go off with him.

And like today's investigators, police handling the murders committed by Jack developed a working theory of the killer, a psychological profile, if you will. He was thought to be a single white male, between twenty and forty years old. Because it didn't appear that his victims struggled with him, and because they had no defensive wounds, police figured that Jack was a normal-looking, respectable guy who overpowered his victims and killed them quickly.

The difference between Mailhot and Jack was that Jack killed his victims so he could mutilate them, while Mailhot killed to kill and dismembered his victims in order to more easily dispose of their bodies.

In 1988, one hundred years after the Ripper murders, the Institute of Forensic Sciences developed an FBI psychological profile of Jack. Those experts said "Jack the Ripper" was male, in his late twenties, and lived in the area where the murders occurred. They believed he was employed and didn't have a family, because he was out late on the weekends. And they figured he was most likely a loner.

Sounds like Mailhot. However, unlike Mailhot,

London police thought Jack might have been in some minor trouble with the law. And they thought he might have been abused by his mother when he was a child. There was never any indication that Mailhot had been abused.

London's East End and the Whitechapel section of the city, with its run-down shops and rooming houses, where Jack picked up his victims, could be compared to the area around Arnold Street in Woonsocket, where Mailhot picked up his victims.

Both men were drawn to those places because of the prostitutes that walked the streets. For Mailhot, Jack and many other serial killers, these working women were perfect victims. For one thing, they were used to going with strangers, and for another thing, they probably didn't have families who would even miss them.

Jack's first victim was Mary Ann Nichols, born Mary Ann Walker. She was forty-three when Jack murdered her in the early-morning hours of August 31, 1888. Jack slit Mary Ann's throat from ear to ear, mutilated her body and left her on the street, where she was found by a local police officer. Unlike Mailhot, Jack didn't care about getting rid of his victims.

Jack's second victim was Annie Smith Chapman, forty-seven. Annie married John Chapman in 1869 and the couple had three children, two girls and a boy. One daughter, Emily Ruth, died of meningitis when she was just twelve years old.

Sometime in 1884 or 1885, Annie and her husband agreed to separate. Some said it was because of her "drunken and immoral ways." Whatever the reason, Annie found her way to a rooming house in Whitechapel and sometimes sold herself in order to pay for her bed.

On the evening of September 7, and the early-morning hours of September 8, 1888, Annie was forced to turn to prostitution to pay for her night's lodging. But Annie went back to her room and her body was found nearby, shortly before 6:00 A.M. on September 8. Police believed she had been choked to death because her face and tongue were swollen. She had nearly been decapitated and her insides had been cut out. Her intestines had been placed on her shoulder and her female organs had been cut out and were nowhere to be found. But the killer made no attempt to hide or remove her body.

After Annie was killed, police and local residents believed her murder was committed by the same person who murdered Mary Ann. But then three weeks went by without another murder and residents were lulled into a false sense of security. But like most serial killers, Jack was just biding his time before he struck again.

And strike again he did—with even more rage. Woonsocket police always believed that had Mailhot continued his murdering ways, his attacks would have also become more violent.

Elizabeth Stride, forty-five, was Jack's next victim. Again, much like Audrey, Christine and Stacie, she had family problems and ended up living in a rooming house in Whitechapel, around 1882. By 1888, she had been arrested for prostitution and public drunkenness. On the evening of September 29 she left her rooming house and was seen at various places during the night and in the early morning hours of September 30. But the last time anyone saw her alive was about 12:45 A.M. At the time she was with a man outside on a local street. She was found around 1:00 A.M. by a man driving his horse and cart. Her assailant had slit her throat, but he had not mutilated her body.

Shortly after Elizabeth was found, police discovered the mutilated body of forty-six-year-old Catherine Eddowes. Like Jack's other victims, Catherine's throat was slit. Her killer had also sliced up her face and removed her intestines, one of her kidneys and her womb.

Then Jack took another brief hiatus until November, when he killed again with a vengeance. It was probably because he was losing his grasp on reality and no longer had much control over his actions. His need to kill grew stronger and the killings became more frequent—something that would have happened to Mailhot, had he not been caught. His need to kill would have overpowered his life and he would have had to kill more and more women just to feel normal.

The youngest of Jack's official victims was Mary Jane Kelly, twenty-five, who was murdered on November 9, 1888. Family issues had caused Mary Jane to turn to prostitution to support herself. Mary Jane was found shortly before eleven that morning. She was lying on the bed in her room. Her throat had been slit and she was nearly decapitated. Her killer had slit open her stomach and removed her breasts. Her arms had been mutilated and her face hacked so severely that she was no longer recognizable. Because there were no defensive wounds, investigators believed she had been murdered while she was sleeping.

Of course, "Jack the Ripper" was never caught and no one knows his identity. Many have speculated he was a well-known figure of the time, but who knows? Maybe he was just a regular guy, like Jeffrey Mailhot, with an insatiable appetite for murder.

* * *

Today, when most people think of serial killers, the first name they think of is Ted Bundy. Before he was put to death in 1989, Bundy confessed to murdering dozens of young women in a number of states over four years in the 1970s.

On the surface Bundy, like Mailhot, didn't fit the profile of a homicidal maniac. He was intelligent, confident, politically astute and attractive. But what caused Bundy to embark on his killing spree?

Theodore "Ted" Robert Bundy was born Theodore Robert Cowell on November 24, 1946. Born to an unwed mother, his grandparents raised him and tried to hide the fact that he was illegitimate by pretending his mother was his sister. Unlike Mailhot, Bundy seemed anything but normal as a child. He tortured animals, was obsessed with knives, engaged in voyeurism and became a compulsive thief. Some speculate it was the breakup with his first girlfriend that caused Bundy to begin his murderous rampage because his victims resembled her.

Just before he was executed on January 24, 1989, Bundy granted an interview to psychologist James Dobson. During that interview Bundy talked about how he developed his compulsive behavior and also discussed how his addiction to hard-core pornography fueled his crimes.

As with Mailhot, alcohol unleashed the murderous monster in him, Bundy said. And like Mailhot, Bundy grew up in a good home and was not abused in any way. Bundy told Dobson he didn't want anyone to accuse his family of contributing to his criminal behavior. Bundy explained that although he took responsibility for his actions, he said his introduction to pornography contributed to his violent behavior.

Bundy told Dobson that he was a normal person who had good friends. Bundy said he led a normal life, except for his destructive addiction to pornography—an addiction that he kept hidden from people close to him.

Bundy said that as his addiction to porn grew, he needed more and more explicit material. Then, he explained to Dobson, that there came a point where just looking at pornography no longer satisfied him and he realized he couldn't control his sexual fantasy any longer and he needed to find an outlet for his destructive energy.

Some of Bundy's comments to Dobson are remarkably similar to Mailhot's comments to Lee and Nowak.

Bundy said when he woke up in the morning after murdering someone and realized what he had done with a clear mind, he was absolutely horrified. He said there was no way to describe the urge to murder, and once that urge had been satisfied, how it felt to become "himself" again.

Like Mailhot, Bundy wasn't some bum or pervert whom people could look at and immediately determine there was something wrong with him. He said he was a normal person who had good friends and led a normal life, except for the fact that he had been influenced by pornographic violence to commit murder. Bundy told Dobson that an FBI study on serial murder indicates that the most common interest among serial killers was pornography. However, Mailhot and Bundy differed in that respect—Mailhot never mentioned that he was addicted to pornography or that it played a part in his murderous behavior.

Bundy, though, told Dobson that had he not been

addicted to pornography, he and his victims and their families would have been better off. He said he was absolutely certain he would not have been driven to murder without the influence of violent pornography.

When asked by Dobson if he felt remorse for murdering so many people, Bundy said he did. But like Mailhot, he seemed to feel more remorse for the families of his victims than for the victims themselves. When Dobson asked him to talk about the murder of a twelve-year-old girl, Bundy said it was too painful to talk about, but he said he hoped someday the families of his victims could find in their hearts to forgive him, although he didn't expect that.

Although Mailhot and Bundy seemed to share some similar traits, Mailhot had much more in common with another prolific serial killer known as the "Green River Killer."

Given Mailhot's statement to police that he would have continued killing if he had not been caught, it's quite possible that he could have become another Gary Leon Ridgway, also known as the "Green River Killer."

Gary Ridgway, born February 18, 1949, is one of the most prolific serial killers this country has ever seen. He was arrested on November 30, 2001, and initially charged with killing four women, whose murders were attributed to the "Green River Killer." Then two years later, Ridgway pleaded guilty to murdering forty-eight women.

Like Mailhot, Ridgway also murdered women involved in street prostitution. When Ridgway confessed to police, he told them that he had actually murdered more than the forty-eight victims he was charged with killing.

Although police could never really figure out exactly why Ridgway killed so many women, they said that some of his admissions indicated that he was deeply psychopathic. However, they said, he didn't suffer from any mental disease or defect that would absolve him from responsibility for the murders. According to police, there was nothing in Ridgway's past—except for the murders—that suggested he was mentally ill. The same could be said of Jeffrey Mailhot.

When a forensic psychiatrist asked Ridgway if he thought he had a mental illness, Ridgway replied that he used to have a problem with "killing women," the government said in its statement about the case. Asked why he thought that was an illness, Ridgway responded, "I don't. I don't know if it was an illness, or just, uh, I just wanted to kill."

Sounds a lot like Mailhot.

Like Mailhot, Ridgway was raised in a seemingly stable home, in McMicken Heights, Washington. When Ridgway was arrested, his friends and family described him as friendly but a little strange. It seemed incongruous that the same man who went door-to-door for his Pentecostal Church was also obsessed with prostitutes and had dysfunctional relationships with women, according to the government's statement.

After Ridgway's arrest both a prostitute and his second wife—Ridgway had been married three times and had a son—testified that, in 1982, he had placed them in a choke hold using a police-type hold, with his forearm and upper arm—the same way Mailhot choked his victims. Ridgway once claimed that prostitutes did to him "what drugs did to a junkie."

In 1982, Ridgway began murdering prostitutes and dumping them in the area around King County, Washington. A lot of the young women were teenagers and almost all were prostitutes, who met their fates while working the streets. For twenty years the murders and disappearances of the women were attributed to a suspect police dubbed the "Green River Killer." Although investigators believed that the Green River Killer stopped killing in 1984, Ridgway told police that he continued to kill, albeit at a slower pace, until 1998.

Both Mailhot and Ridgway ultimately decided to plead guilty to murder. Ridgway, who wanted to escape the death penalty, decided to plead guilty to aggravated murder in the first degree for all the murders he committed in King County.

In June 2003, police began a five-month interview process with Ridgway. After detectives confronted him with all of the Green River murders, as well as similar unsolved murders, Ridgway said that he killed over sixty women in King County.

Early in the interviews Ridgway said he hadn't planned to kill any of his victims, but ultimately admitted that once he managed to get a woman to his house, he killed her, regardless of how she acted or how he felt. Like Mailhot, Ridgway refused to confess to murders he didn't commit.

Ridgway told police he really didn't remember the specifics of each murder. Prosecutors theorized that his inability to recall the details of the killings was also the product and symptom of his psychopathy. He didn't remember because the women didn't mean anything to him as individuals, but rather just existed to satisfy his needs.

"[L]ike I said before, they don't mean anything to me," he told police. "And I . . . and once I've killed 'em, I didn't kept it in memory. I just knew where they . . . I dumped 'em."

During his interviews with police Ridgway explained the methods he used to find and kill his victims. Like Mailhot, Ridgway used the same methods for hunting, killing and hiding the bodies of his victims. Ridgway claimed that he only killed street prostitutes. Like Mailhot, Ridgway decided to kill prostitutes because it was so easy.

"Uh, prostitutes were the—the easiest," he told police. "I went from, uh, havin' sex with 'em to just plain killing 'em."

Again like Mailhot, Ridgway also picked up hookers because he figured police wouldn't look very hard for a missing prostitute. And he also said it would be more difficult for police to investigate the murder of a prostitute because they moved around so frequently.

Ridgway was right—police were often delayed in their investigations because most of the time nobody filed a missing person's report on a woman; and even if a report was filed on a woman, police had a hard time tracking down her last movements. And sometimes other people would say they'd seen the missing victim even after she had been murdered. In the case of Christine Dumont, the cop on duty when her sister tried to fill out a missing person's report said she wasn't missing because he had just seen her the previous night.

A victim's race didn't matter to Ridgway, nor did

it matter to Mailhot. They were equal-opportunity murderers who viewed all prostitutes as garbage.

"[J]ust . . . just garbage," Ridgway told investigators. "Just somethin' to screw and kill her and dump her."

The women Mailhot and Ridgway picked up went with them willingly because they weren't afraid of them. Women went with Mailhot because they thought he was clean-cut and attractive, and they got into Ridgway's vehicle because they figured he was such a small man, he could never be the "Green River Killer."

Both men preferred killing their victims in their homes. When they managed to persuade their victims to go to their houses, each of the men did what he could to put the women at ease by showing them around. Mailhot offered Teese Morris some food and a beer. He gave Audrey Harris a tour of his apartment. Ridgway showed his victims his son's room to reassure them that he wasn't dangerous.

"They look around and everything, they're getting more secure as you go," Ridgway said in an interview with police. "They look in the bedrooms, nobody's in there, nothin's, you know, 'There's my son's room.' 'Hey, this guy has a son, he's not gonna hurt anybody.' His name's written on the door and it's empty and it's got his bunk bed there, toys on the floor. . . ."

Although Mailhot and Ridgway both choked their victims—it was more personal that way—Ridgway murdered his victims after sex. But for Mailhot, it was never about the sex. It was about the power and control—as it was for Ridgway as well.

It appeared, however, that Ridgway was more depraved than Mailhot because he told police he often went back to the place where he had dumped a victim's body to have sex with her corpse. It was free, he said.

While Ridgway went to great lengths to dispose of his victims' bodies—sometimes he posed them, other times he covered them up—Mailhot just wanted to get rid of his victims' remains as quickly as possible.

One reason both Mailhot and Ridgway avoided detection for so long was that they did not fit the popular preconceptions of a serial killer. They weren't really loners—Ridgway was married, and Mailhot had friends and family—they controlled their anger and they didn't have a known juvenile or violent criminal history. They both also had steady jobs and were well liked by their coworkers. For thirty-two years Ridgway worked in the paint department at Kenworth Truck Company. He earned $21 an hour as a journeyman painter applying designs to trucks. The work was precise and tedious and it required a sharp eye. But it was the perfect job for a meticulous man.

When Mailhot and Ridgway were arrested, their coworkers, friends and families told police they couldn't believe these men were cold-blooded killers. Ridgway was described as a reliable employee. But attendance records revealed he was not at work on the days the victims he is charged with killing disappeared. Coworkers shared impressions of him: hard worker, smart, meticulous, nice, friendly, too friendly. Others called him odd, off-the-wall and spooky.

The problem was, the people who thought they knew those two men really didn't know them at all.

"[T]he women they underestimate me, for . . . I look like an ordinary person, . . . I, ah, acted in a way with the . . . with the prostitutes to make 'em feel more comfortable . . . ," Ridgway told police. "And, um, got on, ah, got in their comfort zone, got into the . . . ah, 'Here's a guy, he's not really muscle-bound, he's not, ah, look like a fighter, just an ordinary john,' and that was their downfall is . . . is they . . . My appearance was different from what I really was."

Those words could just as easily have been spoken by Mailhot.

Neither Mailhot nor Ridgway had any empathy at all for the women they killed. In the midst of an interview about stealing money from his victims after killing them, Ridgway said, "And, like, uh, uh, um, uh, not trying to go off the subject, but I thought I was doing you guys a favor, killing, killing prostitutes—you guys can't control them, but I can."

Like Jeffery Mailhot, convicted British serial killer Anthony Hardy murdered three prostitutes in London, dismembering two of them in an effort to more easily dispose of their bodies. Because of that he was dubbed the "Camden Ripper." Hardy was convicted in November 2003, around the same time Mailhot was murdering his victims.

Like Mailhot, Hardy had a pretty normal childhood. He did well in high school and studied engineering at a London college, where he met his wife. However, the couple was divorced in 1986. Unlike Mailhot, Hardy got in trouble with the law because he harassed his former wife and also stole a car. He spent some time in prison for his crimes.

Hardy spent the early 1990s drifting around London, drinking and doing drugs. He often lived in fleabag hotels, but he also spent some time living on the street.

Unlike Mailhot who was able to keep his mental illness in check, Hardy's bouts with the disease manifested themselves in a number of ways, including ranting, raving and acting psychotic on any number of occasions.

From 1995 to 1996, he was treated in and released from a mental-health facility. He appeared to be responding to treatment, but on April 24, 1998, he was arrested for being drunk, as well as for rape, a charge that was dropped because the victim declined to press charges.

Then on January 20, 2002, when police were arresting him for damaging his neighbor's home, police discovered a dead prostitute in Hardy's bed and arrested him on suspicion of murder. In a strange turn of events, medical examiners determined that the woman died of natural causes and police were forced to drop the murder charges against Hardy.

Then on December 30, 2002, a homeless man looking for food in a trash bin on Royal College Street discovered a bag containing human remains. He took the bag to a nearby hospital, where officials called the police.

When police searched the area, they discovered eight more bags containing the body parts of two different women. They also discovered a trail of blood that led them directly to Hardy's front door. After gaining access to his apartment, police found a hacksaw with human skin in its teeth, an electric jigsaw, as well as a considerable amount of blood in the bathroom. They also found a woman's torso wrapped in trash can liners.

Police apprehended Hardy the next day and took him into custody. Police said the two women, as well as the woman who died in Hardy's bed, were prostitutes who plied their trade to feed their crack cocaine habits. Authorities then reinvestigated the first woman's death and charged Hardy with three murders.

Anthony Hardy pleaded guilty to all three murders and was given three life sentences. At his sentencing the judge said, "Only you know for sure how your victims met their deaths, but the unspeakable indignities to which you subjected the bodies of your last two victims in order to satisfy your depraved and perverted needs are in no doubt." And the chief inspector on the case said, "Hardy is manipulative and evil. He is highly dangerous to women."

Those words from the judge and the inspector could just as easily have been applied to Mailhot.

Then there was serial killer Robert L. Yates, Jr., a middle-aged father of five, a decorated military helicopter pilot, and National Guardsman, who was convicted of fifteen murders, but thought to have killed as many as eighteen women. Like Mailhot's victims, Yates's victims were also involved in drugs and prostitution.

And like Mailhot, Yates came from a stable, loving home and led a relatively ordinary life, except for his extraordinary military career. Yates grew up on Whidbey Island, Washington, where his mother died while he was still in high school. (Mailhot's mother died when he was in high school as well.)

After Yates graduated from high school, he enrolled at Walla Walla College, but he dropped out after only two years. Then, in 1975, he was hired as a guard at the Washington State Penitentiary in Walla Walla. He worked there for six months. In 1976, he married a woman named

Linda, and then enlisted in the army and worked as a helicopter pilot for nineteen years.

While in the U.S. Army, Yates received a number of awards and medals. When he left the army, Yates got a job as an aluminum smelter and also joined the Washington National Guard, where he achieved the rank of chief warrant officer 4 and flew helicopters. Like Mailhot, Yates was well liked by his peers and thought to be very good at his job.

While they were investigating the murders of a number of women, beginning in the early 1990s, police zeroed in on Yates and discovered that there was a one-year period from spring 1997 to spring 1998 that Yates had been unable to fly the helicopters because of a medical condition. They also discovered that a number of prostitutes were murdered during the time when he wasn't flying.

Mailhot and Yates had something else in common—they both liked to drive through the red-light district in their neighborhoods picking up prostitutes.

Much like Mailhot's family and friends, none of the people who knew Yates believed him capable of such heinous crimes. In fact, when Yates was arrested, his family issued a written statement describing him as a *loving, caring and sensitive son, a fun-loving and giving brother, an understanding, generous and dedicated father, who enjoys playing ball, fishing and camping with his kids.*

Yates, forty-eight, pleaded guilty, in 2000, to the attempted murder of one woman and the murders of ten other women in Spokane County from 1996 to 1998. He also admitted to murdering two other women in Walla Walla. Yates was sentenced to 408 years in prison.

Prosecutors in Pierce County, Washington, also charged Yates with the aggravated murders of two other women, Melinda Mercer and Connie LaFontaine Ellis. At trial prosecutors told jurors that Yates killed for the thrill of it and because he enjoyed sex with his dead victims. Although Mailhot didn't have sex with the women he murdered, he also killed for the thrill of it.

Yates and Mailhot were alike in so many ways that Yates's statement to the jury could have been written by Mailhot.

Yates told the court that he prepared his statement so that he could say everything that was in his heart. The first thing he did was apologize to everyone he had hurt by his evil deeds. But he never apologized to his victims.

"'To all my victims' families, to my family and to the people in the community, to the families of Melinda Mercer and Connie LaFontaine Ellis, I know you are suffering great anguish. I find no words to comfort you, to explain, justify or soften all the evil, pain, separation and death that I've caused,'" Yates read aloud. "'The world is a frightening place, and I've made it more so for many. I've caused so much pain and devastation.'"

Yates said hundreds of people were hurting and grieving because of his acts. He said he let sin enter his life and take over his soul until it caused him to commit murder. He said sin blinded him and he was powerless to defeat it.

"'There were times—long periods—when in between my horrific crimes, there were periods of relative calm,'" he said. "'Nothing evil happened. But that sinful nature, which wrought so much recent violence, never really left.'"

Yates said he couldn't rid himself of his sinful nature.

He said his guilt was like a disease eating away at his soul. Like Jeff Mailhot, Yates said it was something he just couldn't share with anyone else.

"'I lived a double life,'" Yates said. "'I stayed in denial—denial of my needs, denial that someone, somewhere, could help me. Through my denial, because I couldn't face the truth, I thought I could be self-correcting, that if I kept it all to myself, someday it would all go away. That's denial. By my denial, I blinded myself to the truth—the truth that no one is so alone in this world as a denier of God. But that was me, alone and in denial.'"

Finally Yates said he began looking at all the ugliness inside him and exposing it for what it really was. He said the best thing that could have happened to him was to be arrested and held accountable for his actions. He said it was time for him to stop being in denial and face the truth.

"'If God is the creator of this universe, then there are no unimportant people, and I took the lives of these loving, wonderful, important people from you,'" Yates said. "'I feel your hurt every day and it won't go away. It never will. I've devastated your hopes and dreams. I've left you with only photographs and memories instead of warm family gatherings, cherished hugs and future happiness. The opportunity to say farewell or clear up misunderstandings was not afforded you.'"

Like Mailhot would do at his sentencing hearing, Yates again apologized to all the people he had hurt—everyone except the victims themselves.

"'Nothing I have said here today will justify or excuse my wrongs or even make sense of them. My compassion goes out to all I've hurt. . . . There are so many innocent victims in all of this—families, friends and communities, my family, who had nothing to do with any of this. I'm so very, very sorry for what has happened. There are inadequate words for me to express my guilt, my shame and my sorrow for having devastated you in taking away the wonderful people, the wonderful, loving people, the warm human beings you cared for so much. It's my prayer that you will look to God to help fill the hollow I've left in your hearts. I apologize to all of you, and I thank the court for allowing me to speak.'"

Yates currently is on death row at the Washington State Penitentiary in Walla Walla, Washington.

Mailhot, Ridgway and Yates all thought they were doing a good thing murdering prostitutes and getting them off the streets.

But why did Mailhot, Ridgway and Yates kill? They didn't suffer from the same kind of mental illness as Anthony Hardy did, so they couldn't use that as a reason for murder. Instead, they murdered their victims deliberately and methodically. Although Mailhot expressed genuine remorse for the families of his victims, neither he nor Ridgway nor Yates expressed remorse for the women they murdered.

They killed because it was what they wanted. They killed because they could. They killed to satisfy their evil desires.

Chapter 17

While Lee and Nowak were continuing to interview Mailhot, Durand received word that the suspect had confessed to murdering three prostitutes and dismembering them in a bathtub with a "shark saw."

After hearing that, Durand immediately went upstairs to Mailhot's bathroom and looked at the edge of the bathtub. What he saw seemed to confirm Mailhot's story. There was a group of three marks facing in one direction and two other marks about six inches away from the first group, facing in the other direction. There was also a wider and longer mark on the face of the tub and a pinkish stain on the beige bathroom wall that looked like someone had wiped something off from it.

While waiting for the search warrant that would allow him to look for evidence relating to three murders, Durand photographed the basement area and began making a diagram of each room in Mailhot's apartment. A little after 4:00 A.M., Durand was notified that a judge had signed off on a new search warrant based on Mailhot's confession. At that point he began vacuuming Mailhot's couch, den rug, bedding, bathroom floor and an area under the kitchen table. He also took the bedding and bed pillows, as well as the floral pillow from the recliner in the den—the pillow Mailhot used to smother Audrey Harris—and ultimately brought them back to the lab.

Lieutenant William Labossiere and Detective Claire Demarais, of the Rhode Island State Police, were also brought in to help Woonsocket police look for evidence. When Labossiere and Demarais arrived at Mailhot's home, they were briefed on the investigation and then got to work.

On the refrigerator in the kitchen Labossiere noticed a piece of paper with the dates of several holidays written on it.

"On this paper was a reddish stain near the notation for the July Fourth holiday," Labossiere said.

In the bathroom Labossiere saw what looked like blood spatter stains on the floor near the doorway, around the base of the toilet and on the lower portion of the outside of the bathtub. An area on the wall above the toilet tank appeared to have been wiped down, leaving a pink discoloration. There were several streaks of color on the edge of the fiberglass bathtub, as well as on the inside of the tub.

Labossiere and Demarais went down to the basement, which was divided in half. One half of the basement, which appeared to be for storage, was a mess. Jeff Mailhot kept his workout equipment in the other half of the basement, which also contained a washer and dryer, stereo equipment, a furnace and a water heater. Along the far wall behind the washer and dryer, police notice several boxes. On top of one of the boxes was a hacksaw and blades, a handsaw, which was covered with a cardboard sheath decorated with a picture of a shark, and a hatchet.

Shortly after police started searching the basement, Durand received a telephone call from another detective, who said Mailhot had just confessed to killing three prostitutes with a "shark saw."

The detectives then examined the bathtub for other marks and notches and photographed the notches on the outside and inside rims of the tub. They also took pictures of the notches and scratches they found on the inside of the tub. Then they photographed and took samples of what appeared to be blood spatter on the outside base of the tub. The officers also took samples they thought might be blood from several other areas in the bathroom, including the floor, the wall between the bathtub and the toilet, behind the toilet and the floor in front of the toilet.

The forensic team also cut out the drainpipes in the cellar that connected to the bathroom, as well as the drains in the bathroom, and took swabbings from the pipes and the traps of the drains. Before they disassembled the tub, toilet and floor, they sprayed luminol on the bathtub and floor. The bathtub and the floor near the tub and toilet glowed blue, indicating the presence of blood. But the grout between the tiles on the floor and a curved swipe mark near the sink really fluoresced brightly. The police knew they had hit pay dirt.

The investigators cut out a piece of the wall behind the toilet that appeared to have a discolored swipe mark on it. They also seized the toilet and dismantled and seized the tub and shower stall. When they removed the base from the bottom of the tub, they discovered a reddish brown substance that ran along the length of the base. Once the bathtub and shower stall were removed, police called a member of the Woonsocket Fire Department, who arrived with a "hooligan" tool to remove a section of the tile floor near the tub. The police first took the evidence back to the station, then brought it to the Rhode Island State Health Laboratory to be examined.

While Labossiere continued processing the bathroom, Demarais and Durand went to the Woonsocket police station to process Mailhot's 2004 Chevrolet SUV. After photographing the SUV and listing everything inside it, the detectives noticed a stain on the rear passenger-side wheel well. They tested the stain to see if it was blood, but it wasn't. They sprayed luminol in the vehicle, but again they didn't find any blood.

When he finished processing Mailhot's vehicle, Durand went back to Mailhot's apartment to continue looking for evidence to connect him to the murders of Audrey, Christine and Stacie. While there, Durand confiscated a black plastic "drop cloth" roll, a roll of gray duct tape, an opened box of thirty-gallon Hefty Cinch Sak trash bags, a pail and two mops from a storage closet in the apartment. He also seized a utility knife from a red toolbox, which was in the kitchen. When he was finished, Durand brought everything back to the police station.

While doing some paperwork at the station on July 21, Durand and Detective Lieutenant Timothy Paul got a call to go to Mailhot's apartment. When they arrived, they learned that workers from the Woonsocket Sewer Department (WSD) had placed a remote camera in the eight-inch sewer pipe that led down Cato Street, near Mailhot's address. The workers showed the police video of some live segmented worms in the gunk in the pipes.

They explained that it was unusual to find worms there. After seeing the worms—known as protein worms—investigators directed the sewer workers to dig up the street so they could find out if the pipes contained genetic material from any of the three murdered women.

When the pipe was partially exposed, police dug up the soil from underneath and around it and sifted it for possible evidence. When enough of the pipe had been exposed, Durand wrapped it with plastic and duct tape to preserve any evidence. The pipe was then cut and Durand also wrapped the three ends of the Y connection of pipe with plastic and duct tape. The pipe was removed from the hole, and Durand and Paul took it to the state medical examiner's office.

But on the way they got called back to Cato Street because the plumbing company that was scoping the sewer pipe that led from the street to Mailhot's house found a large amount of something that looked like hair. They also found a mass of sludgelike material that the plumbers said was uncommon. Then using a snakelike video camera, which was placed into the pipe, police also located another mass of matter and more worms.

Police seized all the materials and even swabbed the camera for possible evidence. They ultimately transported everything to the medical examiner's office. However, no DNA from the women was ever found on the pipes or anything that had been inside the pipes. And it was later determined that the protein worms had been feeding off the protein shakes Mailhot used to drink.

Later that day Woonsocket police located the GMC Jimmy that Mailhot owned when he murdered Audrey Harris. Police discovered that the SUV was owned by Brian Duffy, proprietor of Quality Van Sales in Norton,

Massachusetts. When detectives met with Duffy, they
learned that he had bought the vehicle at auction and
had had some bodywork done on it before painting it in
camouflage colors and giving it to his son as a birthday
present.

Duffy told police the SUV was in bad shape because
his son had used it as an off-road vehicle on the forty-
five acres of land behind his Attleboro, Massachusetts,
home. The cops made arrangements to seize the vehicle and obtained Duffy's permission to search it.

When they went to pick up the vehicle, police spoke
to Duffy's son, who told them that he got the truck for
his birthday on February 2, 2004, and used it for joyrid-
ing with friends on his family's property. He said he had
vacuumed the SUV a couple times since he got it. He
told police he used a Sears sixteen-gallon wet/dry
vacuum, but he had never emptied out the contents of
the machine since he had the vehicle. Police confiscated the vacuum because they thought it might contain
evidence of Audrey's murder.

Police brought the vehicle and the vacuum back to
the station to process them, but like Mailhot's Chevy
SUV, they, too, were clean.

During the investigation Massachusetts state trooper
Jon Provost was asked by his superiors to assist the
Woonsocket police in their investigation. Provost's job
was to check out some of the Dumpsters where Mailhot
said he tossed the remains of the three women. Provost
checked out the four Dumpsters behind the Bugaboo
Creek Steak House on Route 109 in Milford, Massachusetts, where Mailhot said he dumped some of Christine's body parts on April 24, 2004.

Provost met with the manager, who showed him where

the Dumpsters were located. The restaurant's four containers were located about thirty feet away from the building. However, two of the Dumpsters located closest to the building belonged to the Dollar Tree store, another business located in the same building as Bugaboo. The other two belonged to Bugaboo, along with two other containers made especially for the disposal of grease.

All of the Dumpsters were serviced by BFI in Auburn, Massachusetts, while the grease containers were handled by Baker Commodities, Inc., in North Billerica, Massachusetts. Provost contacted the disposal companies to determine how soon after April 24 the trash and grease had been picked up and where they had been taken. It's unclear when the trash was picked up, but the grease was picked up on April 22, May 10, June 4 and June 28, then taken to Baker's facility to be processed and shipped overseas.

Provost didn't find any evidence that Mailhot had dumped Christine's remains in any of the four Dumpsters.

A couple days later, however, Bugaboo's general manager called Provost and told him that a couple months earlier one of the restaurant's employees found a power saw in one of the restaurant's Dumpsters. Because it still worked, the employee, who also worked as a carpenter, took it home. Provost met up with the employee at the restaurant and took the saw from him. The employee wasn't sure exactly when he found the saw, but he told police after he removed it from the Dumpster, he brought it inside the restaurant to see if it worked. It did, so he brought it home. Provost confiscated the saw and ultimately transported it to the WPD. The saw, however, had not been used by Mailhot to cut up the bodies of the three women.

Chapter 18

After Jeffrey Mailhot confessed, it was up to Ed Lee to coordinate assigning the people to do certain tasks, like finding the Dumpsters where Mailhot dumped the bodies and body parts, and tracing the trash to the Rhode Island Central Landfill in Johnston.

"We were really only looking for Stacie, because of the time period," Lee recalled. "We knew Audrey and Christine were long gone, but maybe there was a chance Stacie could be found in a Dumpster and in the landfill."

Wearing protective gear and equipped with garden rakes, twenty or so volunteers from the WPD, as well as the RISP and the city of Woonsocket, began the unenviable ten-day task of digging through tons of compressed garbage in sweltering July heat.

"We had a state police dog looking for a scent," Lee said. "And he had some certain areas of interest. but you're looking at a football field full of compressed trash—one hundred yards and fifteen feet deep—and on top of all the trash, they put a kind of mulch and continue to layer it. The people who ran the landfill told us that Audrey and Christine were down so far that their bodies were decomposed with bacteria or burnt off with methane and it would have taken a monumental effort to locate them, so it was out of the question to even think we were going to find them. But they said maybe we would get lucky and find some of Stacie's remains. But her body parts could be in different parts of the landfill, depending on what Dumpster he had put them in and when those Dumpsters were emptied."

Mailhot had told the cops what to look for—black plastic bags, with yellow drawstrings—so the volunteers spent their days digging through garbage, looking for those bags.

"It was one of the dirtiest, grossest tasks we've ever taken on," Lee recalled. "When the excavator goes in and pulls away the dirt and goes down deep into the trash, the smells were awful. None of my officers threw up, but a state trooper did. We wore gloves, masks, but still the smell got through. And when you went home at night, you'd have to throw away whatever you were wearing that day, because you could not get rid of the smell. It was summer, it was hot—mid July. The whole time I was there—we were saying we are never, ever going to find anything."

But as the week progressed, the Rhode Island Resource Recovery employees helped the cops work up a system to make it easier to search.

"They would dig out a certain section, put it in the back of one of these massive dump trucks, bring it down to the bottom of the hill, dump it, and a team of officers, investigators and volunteers were able to go through that trash, scoop it up and put it back in another location," Lee said.

Finally, on day ten, Steven Fairley, a cadet from the police academy sifting through the trash with his rake, just happened to see a human skull and hair in a trash bag.

"He called over the lieutenant, who called the chief, and then the chief told me and Steve," Lee said. "Steve and I flew down there, and the guys were jubilant. They were celebrating, because—literally—we found the proverbial needle in a haystack. It was unbelievable. There was a head and arms in the bag—the bag was ripped open, but there was enough there to identify her through DNA. We stopped then, even though we wanted to find the bodies for the other families, but it would have taken so much more work. The other families were upset, but we had to explain that it just would have been an impossible task, if there was even anything left."

The discovery of Stacie's remains was huge for the police. It was the evidence that was going to back up Mailhot's confession at trial and put him away for a long time.

"We thought this was going to trial, but I don't think he had any intention of going to trial," Lee said later. "He said he wanted to help us bring closure to the families and then he wanted to die. But I had to explain to him that there wasn't any death penalty in Rhode Island. I said, 'We'd like to oblige you, but we can't.'"

Durand was at the police station when he got word that police had recovered a skull, hair and possibly some hands, at the Johnston landfill. Durand gathered up his equipment and went to the medical examiner's office with Detective Ron Tetreau.

Shortly after they arrived, Lee and Nowak and a member of the ME's office arrived from the landfill with the remains, which were in a black garbage bag with yellow ties, similar to a Hefty Cinch Sak. Dr. Elizabeth Laposata, the medical examiner, then began to examine the contents of the bag. She first tried to determine if she could identify the remains using fingerprints. She exposed both hands, and Durand examined them to see if he could locate any ridge skin for possible fingerprints. Although he couldn't find any ridge skin on the fingertips, he was able to see some faint ridge skin on the thumb area of the palm of the right hand. When Laposata examined the skull and hair, she located a tooth, which she said was an incisor. She also found a hair scrunchy, which was still attached to the victim's hair.

Durand and Tetreau went back the next day to the medical examiner's office to witness the postmortem examination of the remains. Before the police arrived, Laposata had separated the remains and X-rayed them. When Durand and Tetreau got there, the ME started by examining the two black plastic garbage bags, as well as a heavier black plastic material that was similar to a plastic drop cloth. There was also a piece of gray duct tape stuck to the plastic drop cloth and some trash, including several plastic bags, pieces of plastic and a small ripped piece of latex or rubber in the trash bags. The piece of latex appeared to be the wrist end of a rubber glove.

Laposata next examined the hands and arms. She told police that it looked like each of the humerus bones had been cut. Each humerus bone was separated from the elbow and cut farther up toward the shoulder area. Durand was able to locate some faint ridge skin on the second joint of the left ring finger. He inked and rolled it and was able to get a very faint fingerprint, which he planned to reexamine later. Laposata then examined the skull and hair. She found a skin fragment with a fingernail tangled up in the hair. The skin had some ridge characteristics, so Durand inked it and rolled it and was able to see some fingerprint ridges.

At that point Durand and Tetreau brought the garbage bags, the plastic drop cloth, the right hand, the left hand and the ridge skin fragment to Ed Downing, the fingerprint examiner at the state crime lab. Unfortunately, he couldn't find any ridge detail on the fingers of either hand, so he gave the hands back to Durand and Tetreau. However, he kept the garbage bags, as well as the drop cloth with the duct tape. He wanted to see if there were any fingerprints on the duct tape and he was also going to try and match the black plastic drop cloth with the black plastic drop cloth police had confiscated from Mailhot's apartment.

When they were finished, they went back to the medical examiner's office to bring back the hand and arm, but they kept the skin fragment. While there, they learned that after the ME cleaned the humerus bones, she observed marks that looked like saw marks on them. She also found another skin fragment, which was turned over to the police, who took it back to the station and secured it with the rest of the evidence. On Monday, they took the saw they had seized from Mailhot's apartment, picked up the humerus bones from the medical examiner's office and took them to the state crime lab.

Through DNA testing the medical examiner ultimately indentified the remains as those of Stacie Goulet.

Chapter 19

On July 23, seven days after Mailhot had been arrested for murdering Audrey, Christine and Stacie, his high-profile court-appointed defense attorney, Robert Mann, filed a motion to reduce Mailhot's bail. Mailhot had been held in the Adult Correctional Institutions in Cranston, Rhode Island, on $200,000 cash bail since July 16.

Mann had represented some of Rhode Island's most notorious murderers, including serial killer Craig Price. Price, a teenage football player, known as the "Iron Man," lived in Warwick, Rhode Island. In the summer of 1987, the five-ten, 240-pound African American teen broke into his neighbor's house and stabbed twenty-seven-year-old Rebecca Spencer fifty-eight times. He was thirteen years old.

Two years later he butchered another neighbor, thirty-nine-year-old Joan Heaton and her daughters, Jennifer, ten, and Melissa, eight, with Heaton's own kitchen knives. Price stabbed Jennifer sixty-two times. A police investigation led detectives to Price, who, like Mailhot, calmly confessed to the four murders.

* * *

On July 30, 2004, Mailhot, dressed in blue prison clothes, appeared in district court in Providence to face three counts of first-degree murder. At that time his bail was revoked and he was ordered held without bail at the ACI. The hearing lasted just two minutes. Mailhot just gave his date of birth and his address—the Adult Correctional Institutions—before he was taken from the courtroom and brought back to jail. He did not enter a plea to the charges. Only Stacie Goulet's parents attended the hearing.

After the hearing William Shea, then Woonsocket's police chief, told reporters that investigators were fairly certain that Audrey, Christine and Stacie were the only women Mailhot had murdered.

"Mr. Mailhot basically worked an ordinary job," he said outside the courtroom. "He went to work all the time. No police or criminal record. Originally he didn't appear as though he would be capable of it."

Shea said in the twenty-five years that he had been a Woonsocket police officer, the murders of the three women were the most horrific murders the department had ever seen. At a news conference later that day, the Rhode Island attorney general said he hoped the charges would bring some solace to the families of the victims.

But solace wasn't what one family member was thinking about. At the news conference Madeline Desrochers, Christine Dumont's sister, said if Mailhot was found guilty of the murders, she wanted an "eye-for-an-eye" justice.

While police continued their investigation, Stacie Goulet's family, at least, was able to bury her. On

September 21, about one hundred of Stacie's family and friends gathered at a funeral service at the T. Lauzon Funeral Home in Woonsocket to say a final good-bye to her. Stacie's casket was closed.

The Reverend Don Parker, interim pastor at St. James Episcopal Church, told mourners that Stacie was a good daughter and mother, who had gone home and met Jesus when she died.

"If asked, I'm sure Stacie would have said she would have liked to have lived for another seventy-five or eighty years," Parker said. "But on one summer night, through violence, her life was ended. God will wipe every tear from her eyes."

After the service Stacie was buried at a cemetery in Bellingham, Massachusetts, just over the Rhode Island border.

But the families of Audrey Harris and Christine Dumont weren't able to put them to rest. Without a body or a death certificate, their relatives had no way to hold a funeral. Audrey's mother, Claudette, and Madeline Desrochers, Christine's sister, met with members of the Rhode Island Attorney General's Office to discuss how they could obtain death certificates for the two women.

Under state law a certificate of "presumptive death" can be issued, but only under the most extraordinary circumstances. The attorney general's office told Claudette and Madeline that the statute had never been used in the case of a homicide. It seemed the last time a certificate of presumptive death was issued was nearly five years earlier after the crash of EgyptAir Flight 990, which crashed into the Atlantic Ocean, off the coast of Nantucket Island, Massachusetts, on October 31, 1999. All

217 people on board were killed and many of the bodies were never found.

According to the statute, the superior court would have to order the medical examiner to issue a presumptive death certificate, but the attorney general would have to start the process. At the time, although sympathetic to the plight of the families, the attorney general wanted to make sure none of the evidence against Mailhot was revealed before the case was presented to the grand jury. The problem was, if the attorney general initiated a petition for presumptive death, he would have to release some of the same information needed to get an indictment against Mailhot. And he was afraid if the evidence was released too early, it would compromise the state's case.

"We're trying to balance the real concerns of the families, who are hurting very much, and the concerns of prosecutors, who are trying to bring the killer to justice," a spokeswoman for the attorney general told the local newspaper, the *Woonsocket Call.* "Right now our first priority is bringing who we think the killer is to justice. We think the best way we can offer a small measure of solace to the families right now is to do the best we can to present the case to a grand jury."

Finally—without a death certificate—Audrey Harris's mother, Claudette, held a memorial service for her daughter in December 2004 in St. James Baptist Church in Woonsocket. Mourners brought teddy bears, Audrey's favorite collectible, with them to the service.

And as of December 2007, Madeline Desrochers said she still hadn't received Christine Dumont's death certificate.

Chapter 20

At the beginning of January 2005, Mailhot was arraigned in Rhode Island Superior Court on charges that he murdered Audrey Harris, Christine Dumont and Stacie Goulet. In addition, Mailhot was also arraigned on two counts of felonious assaults for the attacks on Teese Morris and Jocilin Martel. Mailhot pleaded not guilty to all the charges and the judge remanded him back to the Adult Correctional Institutions, where he was to remain held without bail until his pretrial hearing on April 5. The judge did not set a trial date during his arraignment.

At that time state prosecutors announced that they were going to seek a sentence of life without parole, the state's maximum sentence, for Mailhot if he was to be convicted of any of the first-degree murder charges. Rhode Island does not have the death penalty. By making the case a life-without-parole case, prosecutors were letting Mailhot and his attorney know that they would be unlikely to accept a plea agreement from

Mailhot—unless he was willing to spend many, many years behind bars.

However, Mailhot finally decided to accept responsibility for murdering Audrey, Christine and Stacie, and he pleaded guilty on February 15, 2006, in Rhode Island Superior Court in Providence to three counts of first-degree murder, one count of assault with the intent to commit murder and one count of felony assault.

At Mailhot's sentencing hearing Rhode Island assistant attorney general J. Patrick Youngs, III said if there had been a trial, his office would have introduced evidence of Mailhot's involvement in the disappearances and murders of Audrey Harris, Christine Dumont and Stacie Goulet, as well as the assaults on Jocilin Martel and Teese Morris.

Youngs told the court that the investigation into the disappearances of the three women led investigators to Jocilin, who then told police about her experiences with the man who lived on Cato Street.

"Jocilin Martel described the assault against her in June of 2004, wherein she accompanied a man, the defendant, to his apartment . . . ," Youngs said. "Ms. Martel was choked, but she managed to break free. Frankly, she shoved her thumb into his eye. She described in detail the man, the building and the apartment."

Youngs told Judge Mark Pfeiffer that after talking to Jocilin, the police looked through their records and discovered that Teese Morris had also been assaulted in the same apartment on February 15, 2004. Both women then identified Jeffrey Mailhot as the guy who attacked them, and after getting a warrant, the police arrested him. Then during a very lengthy interrogation, Mailhot finally admitted killing Audrey, Christine and Stacie and described how he lured them back to his apartment, choked them, dismembered their bodies in his bathtub, placed them in garbage bags and scattered their remains in Dumpsters throughout the city.

"Then there was an exhaustive search by the Woonsocket police and state police at the central landfill," Youngs told the court. "The search went on for ten days. It was a miracle they found body parts, which were [identified] by DNA as Stacie Goulet. The investigation also produced a surveillance video from Lowe's hardware store in the city of Woonsocket on the Fourth of July, the day after Stacie was missing. Mr. Mailhot was on video buying a saw at Lowe's. That saw is found in the basement of his apartment. That saw matches the grooves in the bathtub and matches the grooves in Stacie Goulet's arms that were found at the landfill."

The prosecutor added that blood that matched both Audrey and Christine was found in Mailhot's bathtub. However, he reminded the court, neither of those two women had ever been found.

"Your Honor, had all of this been presented to the court, the state would have proved beyond a reasonable doubt that Mr. Mailhot did, in February 2003, murder Audrey Harris. On or about April 3, of 2004, murdered Christine Dumont. On or about the Fourth of July, 2004, murdered Stacie Goulet. In June of 2004, assaulted Jocilin Martel with intent to murder. And on or about February 15, 2004, committed a felony assault on Teese Morris. All of these assaults and murders occurred in the city of Woonsocket at [address on] Cato Street."

The judge then asked Mailhot if he accepted each of those statements. Mailhot said he did.

After Mailhot admitted what he had done, the court

heard from Jocilin and Teese, as well as from the families of the murdered women.

Jocilin said she was grateful for the opportunity to express herself to Mailhot on her behalf, as well as on behalf of Audrey, Christine and Stacie, who could no longer do so.

"I believe God spared my life so I could be here today and testify against Mr. Mailhot so he cannot kill anybody no longer," Jocilin said. "My mother, my one-year-old son, Andre, are also grateful I am still alive."

Jocilin told the court the whole experience had been very traumatic for her, her family and all the people who loved Audrey, Christine and Stacie. She said she would always remember the three women.

"Mr. Mailhot, I hope that you get all you deserve today because a lifetime of suffering couldn't be enough," she said.

The next to address the court was Audrey's mom, Claudette Harris, who thanked Jocilin for coming forward with the information that led to Mailhot's arrest. Then Claudette spoke directly to Mailhot.

"Jeffrey Mailhot, you deliberately sought out and killed a part of us, my daughter, Audrey Harris," she said. "And now her children, Anthony, Damica and Sean, do not have a mother. Her brother, Timothy, and sister, Alisha, miss her, and so do her entire family."

Claudette told Mailhot that all the families wanted to see him rot in prison for the rest of his pitiful life.

"I want to know, where did you dump Audrey's

body?" she asked "Only you have the answer. And I would like you to tell me where to find her remains."

Claudette said mere words couldn't express the way she felt about him.

"You sit here quiet, trying not to be noticed," she said. "But I'm here to tell you that all eyes are on you nonstop and everyone will continue to keep their eyes on you until the day that you die. Jeffrey Mailhot, God have mercy on your soul."

Youngs asked the judge if he could read into the record, two letters written by Christine Dumont's nieces, who were in the courtroom, but didn't want to speak.

The first letter, entitled "Did You Know," was written by Christine's niece Amanda, and was addressed to Mailhot.

In her letter Amanda asked Mailhot if he knew that her aunt was a terrific mother and a good person who would go out of her way to help people. She asked if he knew that her Aunt Christine had beaten death twice before she ran into him.

Amanda also asked Mailhot if he knew that he broke her heart. She told him because of what he did she would never see her aunt laugh or cry again.

"Did you know that you took that away from me?" she asked. "I don't think you do. So I just thought you should know that. As for you, I hope you either die in jail or rot in hell."

Youngs said the second letter was from Christine's niece, Michele.

In her letter, Michele told Mailhot that she wanted him to know the impact he left on her family. She said he had no right to take her aunt away from her family. She said Christine was not a piece of trash even though Mailhot disposed of her that way.

Like her sister, Michele told Mailhot that before drugs took over her life, she was a good mom, daughter, sister, aunt and friend. And she told Mailhot that he could never spend enough time in prison to pay for what he did to her family and to the families of Audrey and Stacie.

Michele said Mailhot would still get to eat, sleep and breathe everyday, but her Aunt Christine would never get to do that again. Michele said her aunt would never see her family or children again.

"You got life and she got death," she said. "I believe in an eye for an eye and a tooth for a tooth. You should be put to death. You are the devil in disguise. May you rot in hell," Michele said.

Then Christine's sister, Madeline Desrochers, addressed the court.

Madeline told the court some of the things she remembered about her beloved sister.

"I remember when my mother brought my sister home for the first time. She looked like a little doll," she said. "I remember the day she went to school for the first time. She thought she was a big girl. I remember when she got her first boyfriend. She thought she was so grown up. I remember when my sister got hit by a train when she was fifteen and she fought for her life and she made it."

Madeline said she remembered when her sister was eighteen and got a boyfriend and thought she was in love.

"His name was Joe. She spent twenty-three years of

her life with him," Madeline said. "I remember when she told our whole family, she was going to have a baby. She was so very happy. My sister was a great mom. I remember when she used drugs for the first time. She did not know how to get off. The drugs started to run her life. For ten years my sister struggled with addiction. I remember when my sister called me from the hospital bed to tell me she was kidnapped and beaten in the head with a crowbar and she was left for dead. She fought that and she made it."

Then Madeline recalled the day Christine's son told her the family hadn't heard from her in two days. She said she knew something was wrong right away. And she remembered when the police knocked on her door and told her that her worst nightmare had come true.

"And I remember the next day the police officers came and told me what you did to her, when and where you put her," Madeline told Mailhot. "Now I have to remember her in my heart because I cannot go anywhere to visit her to tell her I still love her. My sister was still fighting for her life every step of the way and you had to take it away from her. My sister's life was not yours to take. My sister still had a lot of fight and life left in her. And seven months from now, my sister would become a grandmother. She would have loved that and been so happy. My sister was a great person—full of life. And I believe she would have won her fight someday, but you made sure she will never fight again. As for you, I believe God will take care of you until your judgment day. I believe you will rot in hell, where you belong."

* * *

The next to speak was Raymond Boerger, Stacie
Goulet's father.

Boerger told the court there was always a hole in his
heart not knowing Stacie when she was young.

"She was thirteen when she came into my life and
filled my heart with joy and laughter," he said.

Boerger said when he first heard Stacie was missing,
he started looking for her day and night. Then one night
his wife, Debbie, told him that the police wanted to talk
to the family about Mailhot murdering Stacie.

"When the police arrived that day and they told me
and my family that you, Jeff Mailhot, confessed to murdering all three women, chills and shakes came through
my body and I began to cry and my hands became fists
of rage," Raymond said. "I think, 'How could you do
such a horrific thing?' Hearing police say that you, Jeff,
have no record and seemed to be so smart in school and
have a good job. You sure became a local freak with a
twisted mind. What you did to my daughter, Stacie, my
heart became an empty hole again. Like my wife says,
I can forgive you, but I will never forget you for what
you have done because I have a son named Jeffrey, and
I call him Jeff. And every time I say that name, I will
always be tormented by what your dangerous hands did
to my daughter and the others. If you have any feelings
about losing your parents, then you know how I feel
about losing my daughter. If you don't know how it
feels, then you are a coldhearted person and you deserve to be in jail."

Raymond told Mailhot that at Stacie's funeral her
children asked over and over if they could see their
mother. But all he could do was tell them that her coffin
was locked and he couldn't open it.

"That was the most devastating thing I have ever heard in my life from two little children," he said. "It hurt me to see my grandchildren in so much pain. And you didn't only hurt my grandchildren, but you hurt myself and other families that loved Stacie very much. And because of you I will never hear her or see her warm smile. I will never be able to give her a hug or tell her I love her, because you brutally, viciously stole her from my heart. And you treated her like garbage. She wasn't garbage. You may have torn apart our families, but you didn't make us weak. You made us stronger, for we know we will see her in heaven someday."

Raymond told the court that Stacie didn't have a drug record; she got caught up in the wrong scene at the wrong time. He told Mailhot that he was just a cold-blooded killer. He said Mailhot's family must be very disappointed in him because he was going to be locked up for the rest of his life, even though he was considered the smart one.

"Where did the smartness go?" Raymond asked. "All you did was embarrass your family, your friends and hurt your loved ones. And my only question for you is, are you sorry about the murders or are you sorry you got caught? I think you're sorry you got caught, because you had no intentions of stopping. And I'm glad you're locked away for the rest of your life so you won't murder anybody anymore. "

Raymond then showed Mailhot pictures of his family—the family he said Mailhot destroyed.

"Stacie didn't deserve to die by your brutal hands," he said. "And I hope that your days in jail will do something for you, because I got to remember for the rest of

my life what you did. I'm sure your parents ain't going
to see you in heaven. You better get a book and pray."

Stacie's mom, Debbie Boerger, was the last family
member to address the court.

"First I would like to set the record straight about
who Stacie really was," she said. "My daughter, Stacie,
was never arrested for drugs. And about her living a
high-risk lifestyle, that wasn't her either. She got caught
up in a situation she knew was wrong. She was chang-
ing that situation around to get her life back on track
until the brutal, violent murder that took her life away.
The day the police came and told me you admitted to
murdering Stacie was the day you ripped my heart
apart. You took away my only daughter, who meant
everything to me."

Debbie said although she and Stacie didn't always
agree on everything, she never thought her life was going
to be cut short by a vicious man, like Mailhot. Debbie
said she was looking forward to many happy times with
Stacie, who, she said, was kindhearted and smart.

"She wasn't only my daughter," Debbie said. "She was
also a mother of two, a friend, a sister, a cousin and aunt
to many people who loved her very much. She always
smiled even when things were tough. She would say to
me, 'Mom, things are going to get better. You'll see.' Because of you my daughter will never see better things
happen. Myself and many others will never understand
how you could do such a horrific act of violence."

Debbie told Mailhot that she was sorry that his parents died when he was young. But she also wondered

what they would think about what he had done, if they were alive.

"Your life here on this earth now lies in the hands of the court," she said. "If it were up to me, even if the death penalty was allowed, it wouldn't be good enough. I don't know if you knew that Stacie was three months pregnant. When you took Stacie's life, you took her unborn baby's life too."

Then Debbie told Mailhot that because of him Stacie's two children will have to live without their mother for the rest of their lives. She said she didn't understand how Mailhot could have murdered Stacie and the other women. And she told him his fate was in God's hands, even while he was still on earth. She said she turned to her faith to help her find a way to forgive him for what he had done.

"God always says we must forgive those who have wronged us," she said. "To remain unforgiving shows we do not understand that we ourselves need to be forgiven. It took me a lot of praying and church counseling to be able to say today, 'Yes, I forgive you.' But I have one question for you. Did you forgive yourself? I have heard that you tell people that you are sorry. It's one thing to say you're sorry and mean it, or just say it because that's what you think we need to hear.

"One thing I have learned from you is looks can be deceiving," Debbie said. "Let me tell you something, Jeff, God looks at the heart of a person and only God knows whether you're truly sorry and if you mean it. Many people have asked me how I cope with this whole ordeal. I was angry, hurt and numb inside, all at the same time, until one day God spoke to me and said Stacie has given her life to Jesus and now she lives her life in heaven. So

I know that when I die I will see my daughter again. And I give thanks to the Lord God Almighty. And my closing remarks, I would like to say, Jeff, read the Bible. Turn away from your sinful nature and change your ways, and turn your life to Jesus Christ and know that he is real and that he is there for you and that he can give you eternal life forever because Jesus loves you."

The court then sentenced Jeffrey Mailhot to two consecutive life sentences and an additional ten years in state prison. However, he could be eligible for parole in 2047, when he's seventy-seven years old.

After he was sentenced, Mailhot addressed the court.

"I would like to make an apology statement to the families here and also to my family," he said. "There is nothing I can do that's going to take away the pain of the actions I have done. I just hope God can give the families, not only the victims' families, but my family, also, peace to be able to move on from this and knowing I am going to be paying for this for the rest of my life. That's all."

Chapter 21

After Mailhot was sentenced, Jocilin said she had come forward because she wanted to help police put Mailhot away so he wouldn't hurt anyone else. She believed God helped her get away from Mailhot so she could save other women. She also said she wanted to live with her mother in Woonsocket and take care of her eleven-year-old son. And she wanted to stay clean.

But despite her near-death experience with Mailhot, the lure of the drugs pulled Jocilin back to the streets, and once again put her in harm's way. A little over a month after Mailhot was sentenced to spend the rest of his life in jail, Jocilin again narrowly escaped death at the hands of a john she met on Arnold Street.

It was about 9:00 P.M. on Tuesday, March 28, 2006, and Jocilin was walking alone on Arnold Street heading toward Church Street. After she passed an auto repair shop, she ran into an African American man who propositioned her. She agreed to go with him and they walked down an embankment to the railroad tracks.

Once they got there, the man took out his wallet and Jocilin noticed that there wasn't any money in it.

Realizing something just didn't seem right, Jocilin had a change of heart and started to walk away. But before she could get very far, the man grabbed her from behind by pulling her hair, which was in a bun. He dragged her down another small embankment closer to the tracks. Jocilin started screaming for help and struggled to get away, but the guy smacked her in the face a few times while she was on the ground, then started choking her.

Still screaming, Jocilin started kicking at the man. Enraged, he picked up a big wooden stick and started beating her with it. As he beat her, he yelled at her to stop fighting and give in if she wanted to live. Jocilin tried to keep fighting him off, but finally she gave up, exhausted. But she continued to scream for help. Her assailant told her if she didn't shut up, he was going to kill her. Then he got on top of her, unzipped his pants and told her to perform oral sex on him. Fearing for her life, Jocilin did as she was told. However, the guy couldn't get an erection. After a while the man made her stop and let her get off the ground, telling her if she knew what was good for her she wouldn't try to escape and she wouldn't scream for help.

They both walked back up the embankment and onto Arnold Street. When they got to a local dive called Buddy's Café, Jocilin ran in the front door and started crying and yelling for the bartender to call the police. At that point Jocilin's attacker took off running down Arnold Street. One of the guys in the bar drove Jocilin home. A couple days later she went to the hospital to get treated for her injuries. Hospital personnel called the police, and Patrolman David Paradis was dispatched to take Jocilin's statement.

In his report Paradis noted that Jocilin's left eye had been badly injured and was swollen shut. Her arms were scratched, her neck was bruised and her face was also badly swollen.

Police went to the area where Jocilin was assaulted—coincidentally, right near the Cato Street apartment where Mailhot had attacked her—and photographed the scene. But they didn't recover any evidence that would lead them to her attacker.

Unfortunately, Teese didn't learn any more from her brush with death than Jocilin had.

On July 26, 2007, Teese was again arrested for prostitution. For several months before she was arrested, Woonsocket police had been monitoring the area around Blackstone Street, near Gordy's Pub, which had become a hotbed of prostitution. Officers from the department's vice squad had seen an increase in the number of prostitutes hanging around, as well as johns driving laps around the area trying to pick them up.

On more than one occasion Detective Daniel Turgeon ran into Teese and told her to stop loitering. On Tuesday, July 24, 2007, at about 5:00 A.M., police flooded the neighborhood to get rid of the prostitutes, including Teese, before they conducted a "john sting"—an undercover operation using male and female police officers as decoys to trap the men trying to pick up prostitutes.

Turgeon asked Teese to leave, which she did, but she returned several minutes later. Again Turgeon asked her to leave or he was going to arrest her. Teese flipped him the bird and told him to fuck himself, then walked away.

Wanting to keep up the pressure on the prostitutes and johns, and because most of the prostitutes knew who they were, detectives from the Woonsocket Police Department contacted detectives from the Central Falls Police Department (CFPD) and asked them to continue the undercover surveillance.

Around 9:20 P.M., on Thursday, July 26, Central Falls' detectives were driving down Blackstone Street in an unmarked car, and Teese was standing outside Gordy's Pub. As the detectives drove by Teese, they slowed down. Thinking they were just johns, Teese walked over to them, opened the rear passenger-side door and jumped in. Teese asked the cops what they were doing in the area, and they responded, "What do you think we're doing around here?" Then she asked them what they wanted to do and said a blow job would cost them $20 each. They agreed. Teese wanted to take them back to her house, but they declined that offer and settled on the driveway of her house instead. When they arrived at her house on East School Street, the detectives called Woonsocket police, who responded and arrested Teese.

And even what happened to Audrey, Christine and Stacie hasn't stopped other women in Woonsocket from taking to the streets to support their drug habits. Maybe they thought they were safe because Mailhot was behind bars. Unfortunately, for thirty-three-year-old Vicki Connolly, at least, that wasn't the case. In November 2007, Vicki's body was found by hunters in the woods of Burrillville, a small town not too far from Woonsocket.

According to a story in the *Woonsocket Call,* Vicki's mother, Allison, last saw her daughter when she picked her up at the Price Rite store on Diamond Hill Road and drove her to her apartment on Libbus Street, just about a day before Vicki disappeared on September 6.

The last words Vicki said to her mother were "Bye, Mum, I love you."

Police believe Vicki disappeared sometime after speaking with her roommate and heading out late at night to see some friends. People reported seeing her in the area the day after she saw her mother. While police were investigating Vicki's disappearance, someone found her purse in the Social Street area of Woonsocket a few weeks after she was reported missing. It looked like it had spots of blood on it. Her Social Security card and license were still in her purse, but not her cell phone. Her family tried calling her cell phone, but it wasn't working.

Then two hunters chasing a deer in the Burrillville woods discovered Vicki's body. After her body was identified, Burrillville police, working with Woonsocket detectives on the case, said she had been murdered, although at the time they weren't sure exactly where she had been killed or who had killed her.

In an eerie coincidence Vicki's aunt was Dianne Goulet, who had been murdered by Marc Dumas seventeen years earlier. And Vicki's body was found on November 9, the same date Dianne's body was found behind Shaw's Meats on Social Street.

Like the other women who met violent deaths, Vicki, too, had problems with drugs. After her divorce she took up with a crack user. It was another bad relationship. During the eighteen months before she disappeared, Vicki continued to struggle with drugs. She tried to get off the streets, but she just couldn't make a complete break. She really wasn't a bad person—none of them were. In fact, she had only had one prostitution arrest.

Before she got hooked on drugs, Vicki had been a good wife, and a good mother to her son Marc, who was eleven when her body was found. She was a teacher's aide in Marc's school in Woonsocket.

But everything went downhill after her divorce. Her new boyfriend got her into drugs. He even sold her car to finance his drug habit. Knowing she couldn't take care of her son, she gave her ex-husband custody of the boy.

But all through the bad times, Vicki tried to turn her life around. She got a job and was seeing a counselor. She even entered a substance abuse program, but maybe the lure of the drugs was just too much. Or maybe her life on the street finally caught up with her.

Despite the ever-present dangers, these women are so desperate for the money they need to feed their habits that not even the risk of death will keep them from the gritty streets of Woonsocket trolled by johns looking for sex.

Chapter 22

Nearly four years after Christine Dumont was murdered by Jeffrey Mailhot, her family put up a permanent memorial at River Island Park in memory of her and the other women Mailhot murdered—Audrey Harris and Stacie Goulet.

"This is something we've wanted to do for a long time," Christine's brother, Robert, told the *Woonsocket Call* in November 2007.

Robert and his sister, Madeline, had the simple memorial erected after receiving the go ahead from Woonsocket mayor Susan Menard, who also donated a tree that was planted at the memorial.

Robert told the newspaper his family had never recovered from losing his sister, as well as both his parents, over a five-month stretch beginning in November 2003.

"It's been tough on the entire family because the pain is still there," he told the *Woonsocket Call*.

Tragically, on January 14, 2008, Robert hanged himself in a cell at the Woonsocket police station, just forty-five minutes after he had been arrested and jailed for breaking and entering his landlord's apartment. His family said he was still depressed over his sister's murder.

Madeline said she hoped the memorial to her sister and the other murdered women would bring closure to their families.

"It's something that will never go away," she told the *Woonsocket Call.* "You would never think something like this can happen in a small town, but it did. It's something that not only my family, but the entire city, will remember."

The plaque on the simple pink stone memorial reads: *With love and fond memories we dedicate this tree to Christine Dumont, Audrey Harris and Stacie Goulet.*

Epilogue

Ed Lee and Steve Nowak did what they set out to do—help bring the person who murdered Audrey Harris, Christine Dumont and Stacie Goulet to justice and restore the citizens' faith in the Woonsocket Police Department.

But their efforts just weren't enough. In fact, the Woonsocket police are under even more scrutiny than they were in the months and years leading up to the Mailhot case.

For one thing, prostitutes still walk up and down Arnold Street and the surrounding area, hoping to get the money for their next fix. And johns still drive up and down the streets, looking to get lucky. Despite the best efforts of police to curb prostitution in their city, it's two steps forward, one step back.

And as for the department itself—not much good has happened since the Jeffrey Mailhot case.

In November 2007, five Woonsocket police officers were disciplined for not properly searching a woman they had arrested. That woman was able to smuggle a loaded gun into a jail cell, where she was held overnight until her arraignment on drug possession charges the following day. The police found the gun the next day as the woman was getting on a van headed to district court in Providence for her arraignment.

The gun, a Colt .380 automatic, apparently fell out of her pants.

After an internal investigation Police Chief Michael L. A. Houle reprimanded the officers who processed the woman. Two officers, who faced charges of unsatisfactory performance and lack of knowledge of police directives, each received a two-month suspension without pay. One officer received a four-day suspension without pay, and another received a two-day suspension with-out pay for unsatisfactory performance and lack of knowledge of police directives. An additional officer received a letter of reprimand for unsatisfactory performance.

The police department then ordered all its officers to be retrained in search and seizure procedures, as well as procedures for custody and control of prisoners.

That incident was just the latest in a series of incidents that resulted in investigations and suspensions in the police department. All of the incidents caused people to question the department's leadership.

In May 2007, Police Chief Michael Houle was suspended for two days without pay after he admitted destroying drug evidence that he said was tainted with broken blood vials and uncapped hypodermic needles.

The city's public safety director, Michael Annarummo, issued a report on the incident saying Houle's decision to dispose of the evidence was not well-thought-out and that his actions were "unbecoming of the chief of police."

The investigation was launched after Houle admitted

incinerating eight large cardboard boxes filled with bags of drugs because he wanted to clean out the evidence room.

In the report Annarummo said that an internal audit revealed that evidence concerning ten out of 110 pending drug cases was missing. He said instead of destroying the evidence, the chief should have contacted the public works department and the fire department after he found what he considered to be a biohazard.

Annarummo recommended that the chief develop written policies for destroying controlled substances, as well as for handling contaminated or hazardous evidence. He also said the department had to hire an expert to look at the way the evidence room was run, as well as establish a computerized system for tracking evidence. The public safety director said the department also had to employ a full-time evidence officer.

Houle said he was going to remedy the situation.

Then in July, Houle suspended two officers, Captain Walter Warot and Lieutenant Timothy Paul, who was involved in the Mailhot case, on charges of violation of department operational policies and insubordination for their part in an investigation of another officer.

The two officers were investigating Patrolman Steven Fairley, who was the officer who actually found Stacie Goulet's remains in the landfill, for allegedly tampering with a police department computer to embarrass another officer. Those charges were later dismissed in superior court.

Then, of course, on January 14, 2008, Christine Dumont's fifty-two-year-old brother hanged himself with his shirt in a jail cell at the Woonsocket police station forty-five minutes after he was arrested and incarcerated for breaking and entering his landlord's apartment. Robert Dumont lived across the hall from his landlord, who was on vacation at the time. After his arrest police brought Dumont back to the police station and put him in a holding cell.

Dumont's sister Madeline Desrochers, who has had her problems with the Woonsocket police in the past because of the way they initially handled Christine's disappearance, said her brother would still be alive if the officers on duty had been doing their jobs and watching him.

Deputy Police Chief Richard Dubois defended his officers, saying they followed departmental procedures regarding prisoners. According to Dubois, police use surveillance cameras to monitor prisoners in holding cells. In addition, he said, an officer is required to check on prisoners every hour.

In this case, at around 10:45 P.M., about forty-five minutes after Dumont was placed in the cell, the dispatcher who was monitoring his cell noticed that he seemed to be pressed up against the bars of the cell door—something that happens regularly, Dubois said, because prisoners grab hold of the bars, then yell or spit.

But several minutes later the dispatcher observed that Dumont's body was still in the same position, so an officer went to check on him and discovered that he had used his shirt to hang himself. Efforts to revive Dumont failed.

The RISP and the internal affairs department of the WPD are investigating Dumont's death.

"I just can't believe this," Madeline Desrochers told the local paper. "What is going on with this police department? He would still be alive if they were doing their jobs."

Dumont was the third person to die in the custody of Woonsocket police since 2003.

In 2006, forty-one-year-old Timothy Picard died after a Woonsocket police officer trying to subdue him during a struggle in the booking area shot him twice with a Taser. Police had arrested Picard on domestic assault charges. Emergency personnel took Picard to the Landmark Medical Center, where he was pronounced dead.

In September 2003, forty-six-year-old Janet Barr, of Woonsocket, choked on a concealed object she tried to swallow while she was being held at the Woonsocket police station on drug charges.

According to the attorney general's office, she choked while she was involved in a "brief but violent confrontation" with Woonsocket officers. She lapsed into a coma, was taken to Landmark Medical Center and died five days later. After the medical examiner ruled that Barr died of "cardio respiratory collapse due to acute cocaine intoxication," the attorney general's office cleared the Woonsocket Police Department of any wrongdoing in her death.

After Robert Dumont's death in January, things just seemed to get worse for the beleaguered department. Later that month Woonsocket police officer Marsha Bish, the ex-wife of the chief Michael Houle, resigned from the force. She had been under suspension for a number of issues. Bish was one of the officers who received a two-month suspension without pay stemming from the incident involving the prisoner who smuggled the gun into a jail cell.

And the police union alleged that Houle violated departmental procedures by helping Bish get onto the force in 2004. According to news reports at the time,

Houle once investigated Bish, then a police dispatcher in Franklin, Massachusetts, for using her position there to have the Woonsocket police serve papers on an ex-boyfriend. Houle, who was a lieutenant at the time, said the Woonsocket police should not have been involved. Then, in 2004, Houle and Bish were married and she was hired by Woonsocket police.

At the end of December 2007, Local 404 of the police union had given Houle a vote of no confidence. The union president explained that police officers were concerned that Houle was not communicating with his command staff, made rash decisions and showed favoritism to certain officers.

At the beginning of February 2008, approximately twenty-five Woonsocket police officers and the head of their union attended a meeting of the Woonsocket City Council to express their frustration at the way the department was being run and to ask when a review of the department would take place. The union wanted the city to bring in outside experts to review the way the department was being managed.

The union head told council members that after Robert Dumont hanged himself in his jail cell, the chief did not sit down with department heads to talk about what had happened and to review the videotape of the incident.

Susan Menard, the city's mayor, said union members were airing their complaints because they had not yet been able to reach an agreement on a new contract. She said the union didn't like the chief because he wouldn't let them run the department.

At the end of February 2008, the union head notified the mayor that in the summer of 2004, Chief Houle and Deputy Chief Richard Dubois changed test results in

order to change the rankings of police recruits. He said
the tests were normally sent out to the exam company to
be corrected. According to the allegations, the chief and
deputy chief helped change test scores so that Marsha
Bish, then Houle's wife, could get hired by the Woonsocket Police Department.

An internal investigation was launched into the allegations of wrongdoing by Houle and Dubois. Then just
four days after the allegations were made public, Houle
announced his retirement.

In a letter sent to the mayor, he wrote:

> *My credibility as Chief and attempts to make posi-
> tive changes in the Police Department continue to
> be stonewalled and challenged. This is due to mis-
> leading and false information being provided to the
> media and lack of support by various people who
> have chosen to become involved and interfere in the
> day to day operations of the Woonsocket Police De-
> partment. I can no longer assume the position of
> Chief of Police without considering the affects [sic]
> this negative publicity has made on my family.*

The mayor had promoted Houle to chief in 2005. Initially Menard said that Deputy Chief Dubois, who still
faced the allegations he helped changed the recruits'
test scores, would run the day-to-day operations until
further notice.

Although the union head said he felt bad the chief
was leaving under a cloud of suspicion, he believed it
was the best thing for the department.

"Since he came in, we have had nothing but
controversy—the evidence room, the exam scam. . . .

Morale has been down for a while. We look forward to somebody with a fresh new face," Sergeant John Scully of the Woonsocket police union told the local paper.

But then Dubois also submitted his letter of resignation, writing, *[T]he last two years have proven to be one struggle after another. Whether it was dealing with certain members of the City Council trying to have me removed from my position, or the constant interference from union officials in almost everything the Chief and I tried to do, the job I once loved became a constant strain.* Dubois added that the job had affected his health.

So in the beginning of March 2008, the mayor handed the reigns of the Woonsocket Police Department to state police lieutenant Eric Croce until the city hired a new chief. After the announcement, rank and file Woonsocket police officers said they were relieved the chief and deputy chief were gone, because their mismanagement had negatively affected the department.

Two days after making that announcement, Mayor Menard said she was retiring from public service, as of June 15, 2008, so she could spend time with her family in Utah. However, she also acknowledged that the turmoil in the city contributed to her decision. She said one of her priorities before she left office would be to hire a new police chief.